patti smith

an unauthorized biography

Victor Bockris and Roberta Bayley

simon & schuster

Simon & Schuster
Rockefeller Center
1230 Avenue of the Americas
New York, NY 10020

Designed by Jeanette Olender
Manufactured in the United States of America

10 9 8 7 6 5 4 3 2 1

Library of Congress Cataloging-in-Publication Data
Bockris, Victor, 1949–
Patti Smith: an unauthorized biography / Victor Bockris
and Roberta Bayley.
p. cm.
Includes discography (p.   ), bibliographical references
(p.   ), and index.   1. Smith, Patti.
2. Rock musicians—United States Biography.
I. Title.
ML420.S672B63   1999
782.42166'092—dc21   99-29435   [B]   CIP
ISBN 0-684-82363-2

This book is dedicated to
Cindy Bullens
and to the memory of
her beautiful daughter,
Jessie

c o n t e n t s

patti smith

"A biography is written because its subject
has a calling as an artist, which is a very
rare thing. That, to me, in itself is worthy
of examination: What does it mean to be
called? What does it feel like to be called?
What kind of life does one have being
called?"

patti smith

Patti Smith's transformation into a rock icon began on February
10, 1971, at St. Mark's Church on the Lower East Side in New
York. She stepped up to the podium that night as the opening act
of a reading staged by the prestigious St. Mark's Poetry Project,
and after her performance there was no looking back: Patti Smith
had arrived. Though it would be another four years before the
transformation was complete, it was on this night that the blue-
print was laid down.

I attended the reading with Andrew Wylie. We were poets and ran a small poetry press called Telegraph Books. We had just acquired a book from Gerard Malanga, for whom Patti was opening that night, and had come to see our acquisition in action. As we took our seats, we were astonished by the large, stylish crowd that filled the church and the hubbub of its excited conversation. St. Mark's had readings every Wednesday night, and the standard audience ranged from twenty to fifty people, the majority of whom wore jeans and T-shirts and were as poor as they looked. For this evening, however, both Patti and Gerard had called upon their prominent friends and acquaintances to attend: Bob Dylan's old sidekick, the musician and songwriter Bobby Neuwirth, had brought the rock contingent, which included impresario Steve Paul and his two stars, the blues guitarists Edgar and Johnny Winter. Jim Carroll was there with some fashion models, and Robert Mapplethorpe, who had been instrumental in persuading Gerard to have Patti open for him, had gone out of his way to lean on some of his new high-society patrons to attend. The influential rock journalist Lisa Robinson, an early Patti Smith supporter, was there, along with the ebullient talent scout Danny Fields. There were a number of people from Andy Warhol's Factory and the Theater of the Ridiculous, as well as residents of the hip Chelsea Hotel and regulars from Max's Kansas City. New York's leading poets, including Allen Ginsberg and John Giorno, rounded out the full house.

This crowd was a good example of the mixing together of people from different fields—poets, actors, writers, musicians, composers—and different generations—great, fabulous old people and fabulously trashy young people—that so characterized the New York hipster scene in the seventies. It was classless, and, above all, everyone appreciated everyone else. No one was looked down on; no one was snubbed. And Patti was entering an extremely positive environment in the perfect role and at the perfect time, for being a poet had never been cooler than it was at that moment.

The Poetry Project's director, Anne Waldman, a major poet herself, introduced Patti as "a terrific poet, a great songwriter, and a really good friend." As Patti stepped to the podium a feeling of electric excitement and undiluted joy enveloped her—it was the first really great night of her life, the beginning of all things to come.

The audience greeted her with raucous applause, but despite such encouragement, Patti approached the reading as a confrontation. Her take on the New York poetry scene was so negative that to overcome her paranoia, she fixed in her mind the image of the nineteenth-century French poet Arthur Rimbaud, who, when he was displeased by another poet's reading, would climb on the table from which the offender was reading and urinate on his manuscript!

Seizing the podium as if it were her anchor, Patti started seducing the crowd with the voice of a needy ten-year-old girl, coyly asking them to let her know if she could not be heard, "Because I don't want to beat off alone up here, it's really dumb." Then, pulling back sharply from this image, she plunged into an homage to Bertolt Brecht, whose birthday it was. Backed by Lenny Kaye on electric guitar, she whipped off a short rendition of "Mack the Knife," a Brecht song made famous by the great German cabaret artist Lotte Lenya, whose latest album Patti had just reviewed in *Rolling Stone*. In this setting, Lenny's raw chords coming out of a tiny amplifier were as poignant as Patti's voice. With that number under her belt, Patti switched back to the first person and announced that she dedicated her reading to crime. Employing a broad rhythmic tone, she chanted: "To all that is criminal, the great pit of Babel. Everybody tells about the great tower that they rose up to face God, but no one talks about the pit that was being dug at the time, so that men could stick their tongues in the mouth of Hell. To that Hell—"

It became obvious that Patti was not doing a poetry reading but rather delivering a performance. As she steamed on, she pulled the audience into her vortex, listing the names of famous people, such as Genet, who had been in jail, and famous escapes from notorious jails like Devil's Island. From there she segued into different types of criminals and contests, naming among others, the singer Johnny Ace, who blew his brains out playing Russian roulette just before he was scheduled to perform, Jackson Pollock, James Dean, Mayakofsky, and the legendary jazz drummer Gene Krupa. She wrapped up her rocking introduction by making the leap that was at the center of her work, from crime to religion, dedicating her reading also to Mary Magdalene "the only woman who could make our savior weep," and of course Christ, whom she chose to characterize as being a greater escape artist than Houdini, and, inexplicably, the greatest homosexual on historical record, because he was capable of instructing twelve men to lick his feet.

"We climaxed the reading with Lenny's sonic interpretation of a stock-car race on electric guitar while I read 'Ballad of a Bad Boy,'" Patti recalled. "It seemed to have a negative effect. I took that as a positive sign."

Photographer Leee Black Childers went to the reading "because St. Mark's was where you went. It meant you were part of the scene." Like many of the spectators, he had come to see Malanga read, but seeing Patti open proved a happy surprise. "In the beginning, she looked like a poet, with big, dark, sunken eyes in a pale, gaunt face, with that pageboy hairdo. She looked like a Rossetti," he said later. "Already her show wasn't like a poetry reading, even that early on. It had a cadence to it. The only thing you could compare it to today would be rap music. She repeated words, repeated phrases over and over and over. It bounced off itself and caught the audience up in the rhythm, which most poetry readings didn't do. Most poets would just read the poetry and you had to try desperately to figure out what you were listening to and then it was over. Patti didn't give you that grace; she hit you with it. And then, she hit you again and she hit you again and she hit you over and over and over, sometimes with the same phrases, and so it was like music."

"It was full blown and amazing," said scenemaker Terry Ork. "Her performance was like a surrealistic incantation, the creation of a whole mood. I don't think that that incantatory power ever really made it onto record—it never does, but especially in her case. She would virtually be possessed and transported."

The poet Aram Saroyan thought similarly, writing, "Patti Smith dominated the setting with a pro dynamism that was as unmistakable as it was charming. There she was, perhaps a hundred pounds in all. She was clearly already a star; it was just a question of getting the message out to the world."

"The whole evening was a very good success," remembered Malanga. "There was a good feeling in the audience, a lot of friendly faces. I thought Patti had something exciting about her, and there was such a spiritual commitment in her feelings about poetry. I felt that I had discovered in her a magic which was very exciting—Patti was a breath of fresh air. There was something so liberating about her, in terms of her cocky attitude about life and poetry and who her heroes were. Her role models were Arthur Rimbaud and Frank O'Hara, and with her fusion of rock 'n' roll and poetry—which I think in her mind was the kind of thing Rimbaud would have been into had he lived in the twentieth century—she was identifying Rimbaud as the first punk poet."

After the reading, Gerard and his entourage went to Max's Kansas City for an evening of drinks and conversation, after which he'd go home with the girl of his choice. Yet while Malanga and his Factory acolytes were still at the top of their game, Lenny Kaye contends that the changing of the cultural guard—the demise of the sixties and emergence of the seventies—started that night. Now, the rockers would replace the actresses, writers, and artists on the banquettes of Max's notorious back room.

Instead of going to Max's that night, though, Patti returned to the Chelsea Hotel with Sam Shepard to drink tequila and listen to Hank Williams. She later spoke about that night at St. Mark's and what it meant to her: "People felt that I was stepping on hallowed ground, being irreverent. But I didn't care because the people who were supportive were cool. I didn't really expect it to go anywhere. I didn't think I was all of a sudden going to start doing poetry readings, or make a record and have a rock 'n' roll band. Sam and I wrote this little play together called *Cowboy Mouth*, in which my character is talking about the hope that someone would come and make sure that rock 'n' roll wouldn't die." *

V. B.

"Patti Smith is like Christmas on earth."
Richard Hell

* Patti Smith's quotes throughout this book are culled from the many interviews she has given throughout her career, as indicated in the source notes at the end of the book. Patti Smith was not interviewed by the author in connection with this book, nor did she authorize this book's publication.

g o a t   g i r l

> "Even as a child, I always used to imagine
> that I was being secretly filmed. I'd pretend
> Bergman was shooting a movie. Or one of
> the saints, in shooting the whole earth, was
> doing a zoom on me."
>
> *patti smith*

From an early age, Patti Smith exhibited many of the characteristics that would be the hallmarks of her artistic persona: a wild and unpredictable imagination, a contentious relationship with religion, and a rebelliousness against conformity and traditional gender roles.

Patricia Lee Smith was born in Chicago on December 30, 1946, the first child of Beverly and Grant Smith. Grant, whom Patti later described as a onetime track star and former tap-dancer, was a factory worker, and Beverly, called by her daughter a jazz singer with a "cigarette tenor," was a housewife. They lived on the South Side of Chicago. One of Patti's earliest memories places her on a Chicago stoop singing "Jesus Loves Me" while waiting for the local organ grinder and his pet monkey.

In 1950, the Smiths moved to the East Coast, to Philadelphia, where they lived in what Patti described as GI housing in the largely black neighborhood of North Philadelphia. By this time, there were more children for Beverly to care for and Patti to play with; brother Todd was born shortly before the move and sister Linda followed shortly after it. To support the family, Grant worked the night shift as a machinist for the Honeywell Corporation.

"We lived in Philly till I was about eight years old," Patti remembered. "My grandparents lived in Upper Darby, but I lived in North Philadelphia on Newhall Street. My mother used to take me to Leary's bookstore and would buy me a bag of books for a dollar, stuff like Uncle Wiggly and *The Wizard of Oz*, then we'd go to Bookbinder's or get steak hoagies at Pat's."

If her childhood was not idyllic, it was happy nevertheless, for even then, Patti found comfort in her own counsel. "When I was a little girl," she said, "I was very gawky and homely—real nervous and sickly and all that. But I was always happy. Really sort of brooding, but happy. Always optimistic, because I had this vision that I was going to do something. I always knew that I was more than what I seemed. Kids would make fun of me because I was skinny and all that shit, but I would just laugh; I made jokes. I was the class clown—I didn't care, because I knew that time would do right by me."

When Patti was seven, she came down with scarlet fever. The illness gave her severe, feverish hallucinations, which provided fuel for her already vivid imagination. And while the hallucinations would much later serve as valuable sources of creative juice, at the time they served only to make her feel "different." As a result of the scarlet fever, too, her hair started to fall out. "I was a very sick little girl and skinny, they didn't even know if I would live," Patti said later in a somewhat dramatic statement to a journalist, going on to reveal that scarlet fever was not the only malady to afflict the Smith household. "We had no money, and my brother and sister were in the hospital with malnutrition." This description makes Patti's family situation sound more like life in a Third World country than in fifties Philadelphia. In addition, Patti's left eye always wandered, and her parents could not afford the operation to fix it. "I had this cast eye that used to go up in my head. I had a creepy-looking eye patch and glasses. Kids used to be scared of me because they thought I had an evil eye."

Despite it all, though, Patti told herself from an early age that she was special, destined for better things, bigger things, and that kept her going. "When I was a little kid, I always knew that I had some special kind of thing inside me. I mean, I wasn't very attractive, I wasn't very verbal, I wasn't very smart in school. I wasn't anything that showed the world that I was something special, but I had this tremendous hope all the time. I had this tremendous spirit that kept me going no matter how fucked up I was. I just had this light inside me that kept spurring me on. I was a happy child, because I had this feeling that I was going to go beyond my body physical, even when I was in Philly. I just knew it."

The way Patti recounts it, her childhood was really just a waiting period before she hit the big time. "I had my whole life planned out since I was a little kid. I had an absolute swagger about the future. I wasn't born to be a spectator. The tragedy about the ugly duckling was that no one ever took him aside and said, 'Look—you're ugly now, but it's going to pay off later.' That was my view of myself: I figured I'd just bide my time. I'm a real optimistic person. I was the kind of girl you would never find in *Mademoiselle*, but I used to tell my friends, 'I'm going to get into all those magazines when I grow up.' " Her path there would be strongly influenced—albeit unwittingly—by both of her parents.

As a girl, Patti deified Grant, though he was distant and aloof. "My father was very spiritual and intellectual but he was disinterested," Patti recalled. "Not in a bad way, but he worked hard at Honeywell and had his own intellectual pursuits. He worked all the time. My father was always into developing the country of his mind. He hungered to read about everything."

When Mr. Smith was not at work, he lost himself in some epic Bible tale or one of the loony UFO books that flooded the market in the early years of the Cold War. When he became bored with that, he might spend his energies searching for the perfect system to beat the ponies—anything rather than dealing with his family. Looking back, Patti described him as "part God, part Hagar the Spaceman from Mega City," which has a decidedly satiric stab to it when you see that Hagar looks like a crazed Viking as drawn by R. Crumb. Never at a loss to praise her poor Dad, Patti insisted that he had planted in her a permanent hunger for reading, not realizing that reading itself was probably at first just an attempt to gain his attention by emulating him.

Whatever the case, Patti read everything from traditional fairy tales to the Bible and comic books. From Robert Louis Stevenson's *A Child's Garden of Verses* she moved to Louisa May Alcott's classic *Little Women*, and there found a lasting role model. The Smith family, like the March family in the novel, lived under constant financial pressure, and, like Jo March, Patti wanted to resolve the family's predicament by becoming a writer. "I really loved Jo, the unconventional one who struck out on her own. The writer. After I was seven, when I read *Little Women*, I wanted to be like Louisa May Alcott. I started to write. Jo was so great. I really related to her. She was a tomboy, yet guys liked her and she had a lot of boyfriends. I thought of myself as Jo in *Little Women*, raising a family. She was a real big influence on me, as much an influence as Bob Dylan was later. She was so strong, and yet she was feminine. She loved guys; she wasn't a bull [dyke] or nothing. So I wanted to write."

Yet Jo March was not only a writer, and Patti took that to heart, too. "Jo in *Little Women*, with all those fairy tales and plays, introduced me to the writer as performer," Patti pointed out. "She would write those plays and perform them and get her sisters laughing even in the face of death. So I wanted to be like her, a chick who wrote and performed what I wrote and so used to write these dumb little plays and then I wrote these banal little short stories but I wasn't good. I showed no promise." In fact, prose would be Patti's weakest link to literature. As a poet and a lyricist she was able to find a space for herself that worked. As a prose writer she never got a voice she could call her own.

Meanwhile, Patti was developing a religious consciousness as well. Although he studied the Bible, Grant Smith was an atheist and admonished his children not to be pawns in "God's game." ("He used to blaspheme and swear against God, putting him down," Patti remembered.) But on the other hand, Beverly Smith was, in Patti's words, a "religious fanatic" who taught her children the doctrines of the Jehovah's Witnesses. Patti often had to accompany her mother when she distributed copies of the Witnesses' publication *Awake* to the neighbors, and the experience could be humiliating, especially when the neighbors yelled at or threatened them. But not everything about her mother's religion was so difficult. "My mother taught me to pray, and when she explained to me that there was this higher order and we could talk to Him when we liked, I couldn't wait to get to bed."

Beverly Smith also introduced Patti to music. "My mother sang, and first I was crazy about forties and fifties white jazz singers like Chris Connor and June Christy. When I was a child, I loved opera, loved Puccini. I loved Maria Callas. I'd sit there and cry. I didn't understand what it was about—I didn't understand Italian, obviously—but the sound, the concentration and perfection of that sound, would just take me soaring. I actually did opera when I was young: I played a young tenor Gypsy boy in Verdi's *Aïda*. As a matter of fact, had I lived at a different time and in a different place, had I lived in Italy, I'd probably have wanted to be in opera. But being an American in the fifties, trying to pursue opera in Philly, forget it. Nobody was going to buy that.

"I dreamed of being a jazz singer like June Christy and Chris Connor, of approaching songs with the lethargic charge of Billie Holiday, of championing the downtrodden like Lotte Lenya's 'Pirate Jenny.' I never dreamed of singing in a rock 'n' roll band—they had yet to exist in my world. But my world was rapidly changing.

"One day, this boy who had an RCA Victrola said, 'Wait till you hear this,' and he played 'The Girl Can't Help It' by Little Richard. My mouth just dropped—it was an instant recognition; it really got me below the belt. Little Richard got my mind at nine, and I felt the desire to live."

When Little Richard entered Patti's life, the Smiths were living in the southern New Jersey suburb of Woodbury Gardens, where they moved into a single-story ranch house in 1955. Patti's youngest sister, Kimberly, would be born there in 1958, and Patti would look appreciatively on the period and what it meant to her: "I really loved that I was from South Jersey because it was a real spade area. I learned to dance real good . . . there was a lot of colloquial stuff I picked up; that's where I get my bad speech from. Even though my father was an intellectual, I wanted to be like the kids I went to school with, so I intentionally never learned to speak good. I thought, I couldn't use it on the dance floor, so what good was it? And I never really liked white stuff. It embarrassed me."

It was not an easy transition initially, though. After four years in the city of Philadelphia, Patti had a hard time adjusting to suburban life. She imagined that the neighbors called her family witches, and also remembers a "weird racial attitude" that she did not understand "because I wasn't brought up with prejudices." But "we didn't care," she wrote. "We were laughing and dancing and damned." She spent most of her time at home with Todd and

Linda, and in her poem "Autobiography" describes the family drawing closer: Mrs. Smith affectionately called Patti her "goat girl." Patti felt as if she had telepathic connections with her brother Todd and sister Linda, claiming that they were "double blood brothers" because, "we drank each other's blood." "Our minds were one," the poem concludes. The Patti Smith we know is very influenced by her family's dynamic. Many rock stars turn their backs on their parents. When she became famous, Patti would draw her parents and siblings closer to her.

As the oldest, Patti assumed the role of leader, and Beverly remembered her getting her brother and sister to clean by announcing, "OK, we're going to play war, and I'm the sergeant. Todd, you do the bathroom; Linda, you do this; and I'll go out. When you hear my footsteps, if you're not done, you'll be court-martialed!" Alternately she would bark the order, "Let's play mean father! You be the kids, and I'll beat you to death if you don't have the house clean."

Eventually, the Smith children's sphere widened to include, of all things, clashes with other groups of "Irish Kids." Patti's brother Todd later detailed his role in one of Patti's finest gang-related triumphs in a magazine article. "I became part of a gang at that time called the Buddy Gang Cool Cats," he wrote. "It was headed by our most capable warrior and leader, Patti, my sister. I was the last and youngest member, a loyal, never-say-die commando with little confidence that I would perform up to the leader's standards in our war against evil Jackie Riley's gang. Remarkably, there were no deaths associated with this warfare. Even the bloodshed was limited to an incredible piece of marksmanship by Patti, in which she threw a small piece of slate stone at an advancing enemy. The slate whistled through the air with impending doom written all over it. The aim proved nothing less than perfection as it made contact, separating the enemy from his vaccination scab. We were now a true force to be reckoned with and now the enemy knew it."

Perhaps unsurprisingly, Patti hated the overtly feminine images prescribed for girls by 1950s society. They affected her deeply. She saw herself as the classic tomboy who abhorred being female. In all the adventure shows on TV or in comic books she always identified with the male lead, never with his female counterpart. In fact, she never identified with any female images in the culture that she was aware of. The 1950s were a particularly difficult time to be a girl if you did not want to be a girl, because girls' clothes accented the feminine. Dragging herself through school dances in female flounces of pink taffeta, she felt as obvious as "a boil on a bare back." Consequently, through her early teens Patti was the perennial wallflower. She loved her family but felt detached from the human race. And she latched onto the popular notion that she was an alien from another planet.

Patti was very naive in how she regarded herself as a female. "I was so involved with boy-rhythms that I never came to grips with the fact that I was a girl," she said. "I was twelve years old when my mother took me inside and said, 'You can't be wrestling outside without a T-shirt on.' It was a trauma. In fact, I got so fucked up over it when my mother gave me the big word—that I was absolutely a girl and there was no changing it—that I walked out dazed on a highway with my dog, Bambi, and let her get hit by a fire engine."

Patti's difficulty in coming to terms with her gender was eased somewhat by her discovery of art. Her father took her to one of the many Philadelphia museums when she was twelve, and what she found there made her put aside her commitment to writing, at least for the time being. "I had never seen art up close before," she said. "I was totally taken by that expression of oneself. From then on, I wanted to be an artist." Her interest increased when a high school teacher showed her a mirror of her own features in the paintings of Amedeo Modigliani and Chaim Soutine. "I was real self-conscious about being skinny, and I had one teacher who said I shouldn't be. She took me to the school library and she showed me art books and said I looked like an El Greco or a Modigliani.

That was the first time I could relate to something physical. I really was tormented because I was so skinny. When we got weighed in gym class I used to put locks in my pockets. With a lower-class upbringing, it was real desirable to have big tits and a big ass, and I wanted boys to like me. But they didn't—they liked me as a pal. Art totally freed me. I found Modigliani, I discovered Picasso's blue period, and I thought, Look at this, these are great masters, and the women are all built like I am. I started ripping pictures out of the books and taking them home to pose in front of the mirror."

Pursuing her interest in art, however, posed a serious dilemma, for Beverly Smith's Jehovah's Witness faith strictly forbade any form of artistic expression—to actually practice art made damnation inevitable. To Patti, though, the choice was clear. "By the time I was about twelve or thirteen I just figured, well, if that was the trip, and the only way you could get to God was through religion, then I didn't want him anymore." She remembered the moment of her decision dramatically. "I was just outside and there was this huge storm brewing. I was standing outside and I was sick . . . sick of being a Jehovah's Witness, because they said there was no place for art in Jesus' world. I said, 'Well, what's going to happen with the museums, the Modiglianis, the blue period?' They said it would fall into the molten sea of hell. I certainly didn't want to go to heaven if there was no art in heaven."

Patti finally found some solace in religion when in school her teacher gave the class an assignment: each student was to pick a country that he or she would monitor and report on throughout the year. While her classmates chose England or Paris [sic], Patti chose Tibet! Tibet? In those days the cold war was still raging and places like Tibet did not exist in American classrooms. "No," her teacher told her, "You can't choose Tibet. Pick another country, Patti." "No, no," Patti responded. "I want it to be Tibet and that's it!" Faced with such determination in one so skinny and frail, the teacher backed down.

Now Patti launched herself into a big, abstract investigation of

Tibet. First of all, where was it? Then, she didn't have much to work with since the Chinese had instituted a news blackout in terms of the outside world knowing anything about what was happening in Tibet. Consequently, when she said her prayers at night, she now added to her list of requests some news in the papers regarding Tibet.

The first time Patti got an inkling of being on the right track in her life came about two months later, in March, 1959, when there was an uprising in Tibet, which was ferociously quashed by the occupying Chinese army, and the Dalai Lama was forced into exile. On the one hand this was good news for Patti, since it gave her something she could sink her teeth into. On the other hand, it signaled the arrogance it takes to be a rock star when Patti presumed that her prayers were the cause of the uprising. Regardless of reality, Patti now started praying for the safety of the Dalai Lama. Claiming that the peaceful prayers of the Tibetan Buddhists especially affected her in the imminent nuclear war scare-scam the Eisenhower government was laying on the populace, she fell in love with Tibet. The Tibetan Buddhists' essential mission, she believed, to keep up a continuous position of prayer was what kept the globe from spinning out of control. Admitting that she did not really understand the situation, Patti stuck to her guns on her assignment. Now, the very notion that Tibet existed made Patti feel protected.

Patti's battle with religion would become a major source of inspiration and creative energy for her as an artist. Through writing, visual art, and music, she would find her own spiritual path. "Religion is always to the exclusion of other people," she explained, "and that's why on my records, or in everything I do, I try not to exclude anybody. The imagery of religion is fantastic, but I can't get into the dogma . . . the one cool thing about music, or the one cool thing about art, is that it's not to the exclusion of anybody. That's why I think art and music are the new answers for religion. People desperately want to believe in something, but because every time they try to believe in something they're given a bunch of rules, it doesn't happen."

Reconciling her art and religion presented Patti with one type of challenge, and she ran into another when she entered Deptford High School in 1960. By that time, the civil rights movement had been gaining momentum for the better part of five years, and was regularly in the headlines. And while Deptford High was integrated, that only brought the conflict into the classroom. Patti's reaction was to date someone black, insisting all the while that she was not on a liberal crusade but was just following her instincts. When her parents backed her up, their house became something of a sanctuary for like-minded students, which did not increase the Smiths' general popularity around town. Things came to an ugly climax one Friday night when the police called Patti's parents at 1 A.M., asking them to come pick up their daughter, who was being held for breaking curfew. When Beverly arrived at the station, she found that Patti's date, a black friend from school, was being held in a separate cell without even being allowed to call his parents.

Meanwhile, as her adolescence bloomed, Patti began to discover her own sexuality, complete with sexual fantasies that sometimes tended toward the offbeat. At first, she didn't quite know what to make of it all. "I was horny," she told an interviewer later, "but . . . nobody told me that girls got horny. It was tragic, 'cause I had all these feelings inside me. I was like one of the boys in school who flap their legs frantically under the desk. I always had this weird feeling between my legs and I had no idea what it was. I didn't know girls masturbated. I never touched myself or anything . . . I did it all in my mind. I was so horny in school it felt like my body was filled with electricity. I felt like I had neon bones or something. All my report cards said, 'Patti Lee daydreams too much.' I didn't know what it was, but I couldn't wait to get home each day. And when I got home, I'd just lay down and let my mind spill out.

"When Anne Frank was real big and *Life* was doing all that stuff on Nazi atrocities, I'd read that stuff and I'd get really crackin' down there. Anytime I'd read about a dog getting beaten or any weird thing, it would trigger me off, and the only way I could relieve myself was by lying in bed and putting a flashlight on inside of my brain. There'd be this flood of light and then these movies would start up in my mind. Nothing specifically dirty or anything, just a lot of abstract action. It was like being horny in a really vague way. My one regret in life is that I didn't know about masturbating. That's really sad. Think of all the fun I could've had!

"Most girls, I guess nobody has to tell them how to do it—they just figure it out. I had to be told. Some girl actually had to show me with a hairbrush, demonstrate exactly what to do. I just never figured that stuff out naturally. When I was younger, I couldn't come. I figured there was something wrong with me. I went to all these doctors, and I kept saying, 'There's something wrong with me.' Most broads don't come, but nobody told me that. I used to beg girls in the bathroom at school, 'Please tell me, is something wrong with me?' It was like, 'Would you look at my pussy and see if it's made right? I'll look at yours.' And all of a sudden they'd think I was a queer. The doctors would say, 'Oh-ho-ho. You're a normal young girl.' They'd say stuff like 'Tell your partner to engage in more petting.' *Petting.* Let me be your dog."

The opposite sex, however, posed its own problems for Patti. "I never had any dates. I never really had any boyfriends. I was the girl who did the guy's homework. I was really crazy about guys, but I was always like one of the boys. The guys I fell in love with were always completely inaccessible. I didn't want any middle-of-the-road creep—I always wanted the toughest guy in school, the guy who carried the umbrella and wore white shirts with real thin black ties. I was really nuts over this guy named Butchie Magic, 'cause he let me carry his switchblade. But I couldn't make it with guys.

"I was always trying to pick guys up. I'd ask guys out and stuff like that. I had no pride. I was the biggest lurch at dances, waiting for the ladies' choice. I'd lunge at my prey like a baby wolf. I was really skinny, and guys would tell me I wasn't their type. But I was ready. I got along better with the niggers, but they didn't wanna fuck me either. They kept saying, 'You gotta stay a virgin, 'cause if we find the right colored guy, he'll pay five hundred bucks for a virgin white girl.' I believed in love, so it never worked out."

Like many an adolescent, at the same time that she was dealing with her raging hormones, Patti was also casting about for an identity. Like an urchin in a Charles Dickens novel who is about to turn into a rare beauty, when she was fifteen Patti came upon a mirror in some ancient game warden's hut and lugged it up to her room. Thus commenced a series of exercises. First, she would sit down opposite the large oval mirror and press her hands against its hard surface, trying to discover herself. This détente with the mirror is common among creative teenagers. To remind her of what she was trying to be, Patti taped a picture of Audrey Hepburn in the hipster's black clothes with white socks of 1959 onto it. Next to it she stuck a "blue period" Picasso. She identified with his alien, angular, melancholic harlequin.

"The only time I ever tried to cultivate being sexy was when I read *Peyton Place*. I was about sixteen and I read that this guy's watching this woman walk and he can tell she's a good fuck by the way she walks. It's a whole passage. He's telling Allison McKenzie, 'I know you're a virgin.' And she says, 'Well, how?' and he says, 'I can tell by the way you walk.' And I though, Uh-oh, everybody knows! I was ashamed to be a virgin, so I tried to cultivate a fucked walk. I tried to figure out what it looked like. I figured I'd watch any hot woman I could. I mean, look at Jeanne Moreau—you watch her walk across the street on the screen and you know she's had at least a hundred men."

Throughout her teens, music was an important consolation to Patti. In school, while the straitlaced white kids organized their lives around football games and cheerleading, Patti joined a jazz club where she could tune in to the cool sounds of Miles Davis,

John Coltrane, and Thelonious Monk. "My mother always got me great records when I was sick," she remembered. "In 1963, I got Coltrane's *My Favorite Things*. I tried to hang at jazz clubs like the Showboat, just to see the musicians, but I was way too young, though I once made it into Pep's to see Coltrane for a few minutes before I got thrown out. You had to be eighteen, so these people helped me get dressed up, trying to look older. I was basically a pigtails-and-sweatshirt kind of kid. So I got in for fifteen minutes and saw him, and then they carded me and kicked me out. He did 'Nature Boy.' I was in such heaven seeing them, [Coltrane and band members] Elvin Jones and McCoy Tyner, that I wasn't even disturbed that I got thrown out."

Patti was so enamored of jazz musicians that for a time she tried out the identity of a jazz poet. "As a teenager, I also imagined myself as a jazz poet . . . I'd just listen to Coltrane and then write poetry." The poetry did not last long, though, and she turned to another outlet for her creativity. "I realized I was a lousy writer, so I started to paint." Painting wasn't easy, either, but for different reasons: "I was a lower-class person with upper-class aesthetics. I was like a girl with no money living in a farm area reading *Vogue* magazine."

Meanwhile, her growing list of heroes came to include Jean-Paul Sartre and Jean Genet, Jeanne Moreau and Joan of Arc.

Despite her various travails, though, Patti found a lot to enjoy in high school, particularly during her last two years. She hung out with a small group of socially aware students, and among them found her first steady boyfriend. According to Patti's high school yearbook, by her senior year she was quite involved in a number of activities. Besides acting in the school play and singing in the school chorus, she was on the prom committee, the football committee, and the prestigious bulletin-board committee. The yearbook gave Patti the nickname "Natasha," after the character in the popular Rocky and Bullwinkle cartoon show, because of her long black hair and the deep Russian accent that she often affected.

The yearbook, though, says nothing of Patti's romantic dreams, which she revealed later to writer Scott Cohen. "When I was in high school, to me being a model was the heaviest. It was the logical extension of being an artist's mistress. Like in Modigliani's time, it was always the mistress that held the great artists together. Fuck art—it was obvious the chicks were where it was at. Besides wanting to be an artist's mistress, I wanted to be a movie star, like Jeanne Moreau, or Anouk Aimée in *La Dolce Vita*—I couldn't believe her in those dark glasses and that black dress and that sports car. I thought that was the heaviest thing I ever saw: Anouk Aimée with that black eye. It made me want to have a black eye forever. It made me want to get a guy to knock me around. I'd always look great."

As she moved away from high school and out into the world, Patti was still focused on hero worship and the cultivation of a perfect image. Before long, though, a deep need for self-expression would begin to emerge as she faced problems that she never could have anticipated.

piss factory

1964-1967

"Maybe some people loved their teenage
years; I found them really difficult."

patti smith

Patti graduated from Deptford High in June 1964. She spent the
summer between high school and college working in a toy factory,
which made children's products ranging from prams to play-
things. Her experience here was a grim one that would inspire
what is arguably the first punk record—"Piss Factory"—which
arose in part from an incident in which Patti had her head pushed
into a toilet bowl full of piss by her fellow workers. "I used to get
carsick when I did piecework at the factory in South Jersey," she

explained. "I'd have to inspect baby buggy–bumper beepers, and I'd wind up puking in the bathroom. I'd have to take little yellow pills. I inspected beepers, steel sheets. It depended, it changed every week. I cut leather straps for baby carriages, made big cardboard boxes for baby mattresses. Toys, strollers, all that stuff. The stuff those women did to me at that factory was horrible. They'd gang up on me and stick my head in a toilet full of piss."

In a perverse way, though, Patti's time at the toy factory helped reinforce her interest in poetry and art, and intensified her first exposure to a poet who would be one of her strongest influences. "One day, it was my lunch break. There was this genius sausage sandwich that the guy in the little cart would bring, and I really wanted one, but the thing is the guy only brings two a day and the two ladies who ruled the factory, named Stella Dragon and Dotty Hook, took these sausage sandwiches. There was nothing else I wanted—you get obsessed with certain tastes. My mouth was really dying for this hot sausage sandwich, so I was real depressed. I went across the railroad tracks to this little bookstore, I was roaming around there and I was looking for something to read and I saw *Illuminations*, by Rimbaud—you know, the cheap New Directions paperback of *Illuminations*. I mean, every kid has had it. Rimbaud looks so genius. There's that grainy picture of Rimbaud, and I thought he was so neat looking I instantly snatched it up. I didn't even know what it was about; I just thought Rimbaud was a neat name. I probably called him Rimbald and I thought he was so cool. So I went back to the factory and I was reading it. It was in French on one side and English on the other, and this almost cost me my job, 'cause Dotty Hook saw that I was reading something that had foreign language and she said, 'What are you reading that foreign language stuff for?' and I said, 'It's not foreign,' and she said, 'It's foreign, it's communist, anything foreign is communist.' Then she said it so loud that everybody thought I was reading *The Communist Manifesto* or something, and they all ran up and, of course, complete chaos, and I just left the factory in a big huff and

I went home. So I attached a lot of importance to that book before I had even read it, and I just really fell in love with it."

Rimbaud, who was born in the north of France near Belgium on October 20, 1854, and died of syphilis in Marseilles on November 10, 1891, would emerge in Patti's imagination as the first punk poet. Although he stopped writing at the age of nineteen, the body of work he created to that point was so powerful and so revolutionary that it has been an enduring influence on writers ever since. Rimbaud's extraordinary life and work took on the quality of a myth for many, and echoes of his thinking may be found in the work of rockers ranging from Brian Jones to Kurt Cobain. Patti, who would call him her "brainiac amour," was affected deeply too. "When I discovered the poetry of Rimbaud, I actually stopped writing for a while because I felt that I'd found the ultimate language," she said. "Somehow I knew this was the perfect language. It looked like it glittered. I knew some day that I would decipher it." One thing Patti did decipher and seize on was his dictum that to receive vision one must derange the senses, and his insight that women would soon come into their own as artists, unleashing powerful, magic abilities. With such ideas, Rimbaud was the perfect guide for the path that Patti would explore in her own art.

Around the same time that she discovered Rimbaud, Patti found another of her strongest influences in Bob Dylan. As in the case of jazz, Beverly Smith was responsible for introducing Patti to this music. "My mother was a counter waitress in a drugstore where they had a bargain bin of used records. One day she brought this record home and said, 'I never heard of the fellow, but he looks like somebody you'd like,' and it was *Another Side of Bob Dylan*. I loved him. I've always loved singing, but I never knew how to approach singing out of my poems. Dylan released that in me."

By the autumn of 1964, Patti had to decide whether to get a job or to go to college. Her hellish experience at the factory made college the more attractive choice, but the Smiths were unable to afford the tuition costs of the private art schools in Philadelphia that Patti had her eye on. So, instead, Patti accepted a place at Glassboro State Teachers College under the pretense of wanting to become an art teacher.

For the adventurous Patti, Glassboro, as opposed to the Museum School, was a real letdown, as she found its students unexpectedly conformist and middle class. As she searched for artistic inspiration, Patti slunk around the school corridors like a spy, wearing a trenchcoat and dark glasses, making cryptic comments and trying to give the impression that she was a sophisticated, even decadent, libertine who had been to bed with lots of men. She presented such a strange and—for the early sixties—spacey persona that she believed the other students thought she was on drugs, some kind of "commie pinko," or just a weird beatnik who didn't wash.

The two years that Patti ultimately spent at Glassboro were disappointing and led to her disillusionment with college altogether. One problem was Patti's inability to adapt to Glassboro's standard teaching methods, which became clear the day that she was assigned to a class of children at a nearby grammar school. Her assignment was to oversee the construction of paper-chain Christmas-tree decorations. According to Dusty Roach's *Patti Smith: Rock 'n' Roll Madonna*, Patti, left to her own devices, took the project and ran with it, leading the students in a completely unrelated activity.

Not content to teach the kids how to make their decorations, Patti improvised a story about a kingdom called Alaria where, among the foggy ice-capped Himalayan peaks, there lived a snow prince who would appear with clouds upon clouds of colorful balloons. The cold mountain winds would toss the balloons up and down, to and fro, and all around Alaria. Then, having described this magical setting, Patti instructed the students to pretend that they were the wind by jumping up and down and blowing with all their might. After some kids started gasping for air, she told them to sit down and immediately draw the wind. Meanwhile, as Patti was grooving along, her horrified instructor went to the school library, and tried to look up Alaria. Discovering no such place, she rushed back to the classroom to pop Patti's bubble. The upshot of the incident was that Miss Smith was henceforth forbidden to use her own teaching methods at the college.

Patti and Glassboro may not have been a good combination from an educational-theory perspective, but Patti seized on her college years as an opportunity to learn as much as she could on her own about all the magnificent artists and writers whose images kept exploding in her brain and to explore them in her own art and writing. "I read a lot of Spanish poetry by Lorca, and I wrote these long, stupid romances about men in love with their dead wives," she remembered. "Very Spanish: orange trees and glowing moons and incestuous brothers and sisters, and fathers kneeling in the dirt trying to get their dead wives to show them some warmth—or killing their wives! It was always the same long story; archaic language, terrible, terrible stuff. My big line was 'Ach! You are as cold in death as you were in life!' I thought it was really great. I used to make up these long, dramatic poems about getting arrested by a beautiful blond Nazi guy and having pleasurable torture, but that didn't mean I wanted Hitler back or I was a racist. It's just . . . you're in the adolescent terrain, which is very violent."

Glassboro wasn't entirely a washout for Patti, either, for just as she had made a connection with a teacher at Deptford, she encountered another sympathetic mentor among her professors at Glassboro. Dr. Flick fueled her romantic imaginings of the artistic life; as Patti put it, he "really got it through to me that often criminals were failed artists, like Hitler wanting to be a painter. I learned all the stuff you have to do like have TB, eat hashish, sleep in gutters."

In addition, Patti made a contact at Glassboro that would last for the rest of her life. Janet Hamill, a fellow student, was part of a group of New Jersey writers toward whom Patti gravitated. Working with the group, Patti found the kind of communal working situation that she would thereafter always find most comfortable. She learned much about the craft of writing. "I was secretly ashamed of my writing," she reminisced, "because all my best friends were great writers. I didn't have any confidence in myself. I was so romantic, and I thought all you had to do [to become a great writer] is expel the romance. I had no idea the romance of language was a whole thing in itself. I had no idea of what to do with language. I mean, I used to record my dreams. I had no conception of style of words."

According to one of her friends, Patti gave the impression of having had "a very difficult childhood," and was always seeking a way out. As it had in her early life, music provided solace. Patti remembered the release of Bob Dylan's single "Like a Rolling Stone" vividly: she was a freshman in college and she and a group of her friends cut school and spent the day talking about the song. "It helped me get through all those difficult adolescent times when you feel like a jerk and isolated," she recalled.

Yet while she found inspiration in Dylan and "Like a Rolling Stone," Patti's real epiphany came with another band. One night when Patti was home from college, she heard her father shouting "Jesus Christ! Jesus Christ!" from the TV room. "I ran in panting," she later wrote in an essay called "The Rise of the Sacred Monsters" marking this milestone.

What she saw was the Rolling Stones on *The Ed Sullivan Show*. It's hard to really see a group on TV because you never get the impact of an overview of five young guys rocking out. You never get to see how all five are dressed in drop-dead elegance, wearing combinations of negro-pimp and Edwardian-gentleman styles sieved through the imaginations of such British fashion designers as Mary Quant, who were taking over the world in parallel with the Stones, the Beatles, and Dylan. The clothes you wore in those days were absolutely as important as the music in getting the message out to millions of teenagers: "Buy our record!" On top of which the Stones played the tough R&B of the Chicago ghettos with insolent grace, broadcasting it to millions of impressionable young girls who saw what Patti saw: The bulge in Mick Jagger's tight white jeans, the greasy hair and spotty face of the irrepressible Keith Richards, and the blond bouffant of the band's Mr. Shampoo—Brian Jones. The bass player and the drummer who hung out behind the other three had faces that looked as if they had been carved from stone. The band's fifth U.S. single, "Heart of Stone," was climbing the charts as their first top ten hit in the United States.

The Rolling Stones hit Patti where they hit millions of teenage girls: "my pussy dripped. my pants were wet and the Rolling Stones redeemed the white man forever. No wonder the Christian God barred the image.

"That was my introduction to the Rolling Stones. they did time is on my side. my brain froze."

Grant Smith's reaction to the Stones notwithstanding, however, rock 'n' roll was nothing new to the Smiths. Philadelphia, a short distance from Woodbury Gardens, was a great city for rock 'n' roll, and in the fifties and sixties, all the big acts played there. It also had its own "Philly sound," and was home to one of the great DJs of the day, the personable and exciting Jerry Blavat, the "Geater with the Heater," who was Patti's favorite. Well aware of such circumstances, Grant and Beverly Smith knew that they could not ban rock 'n' roll in the house, though Grant did forbid the children to play it when he was at home. Consequently, as soon as he left for work, Patti, Linda, and Todd would race to the radio or record player and put on the forbidden music. They sang the choruses together, pretending they were on stage.

The influence of rock on Patti was profound, as it was on most kids her age: they were a generation who saw rock 'n' roll invented in their lifetime. As children they connected to Elvis and Little

Richard and the first generation of rockers, then in their teens they experienced firsthand the British invasion led by the Beatles and the Rolling Stones. The music was a unifying force. "I guess I still feel that rock 'n' roll is the closest we've come to a universal language," Patti said later. "When I listened to Dylan, the Stones, [Jimi] Hendrix, and Jim Morrison, I felt part of something."

Patti first saw the Rolling Stones in the flesh during their 1966 tour, at Philadelphia's prime arena, Convention Hall, which stood on the edge of the University of Pennsylvania campus. A local boy drove her to the gig in his pickup truck, entering the city via South Philly. The Stones were in their "19th Nervous Breakdown" phase, reaching the end of their first wind. Mitch Ryder and the Detroit Wheels opened for them, and though Ryder, who ripped off his shirt to expose a marvelous torso, was much more blatantly sexual than Jagger, when the Stones came on to deliver their third twenty-five-minute set of the day (they had already played two matinees in Chicago), they were simply magic. In a conversation with Sonic Youth's Thurston Moore thirty years later, Patti remembered that night: "I was sitting in this auditorium, with mostly other white girls. And then the Rolling Stones came on and all of a sudden girls started screaming and ran toward the stage. I had a front-row seat. And I had no choice, they just pushed me into the edge of the stage. I had never seen anything like this, ever. I was so embarrassed. They acted like such freaks, screaming. One girl broke her ankle. It was some kind of collective hysteria they had learned reading about people going to see the Beatles.

"Mick Jagger looked very nervous. The funniest one was Keith because he was really young and nervous and his ears were big and he had pimples and his teeth were kind of bucked and cute. But I loved Brian Jones. He was sitting on the floor playing one of those Ventures electric sitars, and these girls kept pushing me and pushing me. They pushed me right onto the stage and then I felt myself going under and I was gonna be trampled and out of total desperation I reached up and grabbed the first thing I saw: Brian

Jones's ankle. I was grabbing him to save myself. And he just looked at me. And I looked at him. And he smiled. He just smiled at me."

Patti's enthusiasm for the Rolling Stones was so extreme that it became a more powerful influence on her poetry than the Bible. And, for a while, its front line—Brian Jones, Mick Jagger, and Keith Richards—took the place of poets and painters as her foremost heroes and role models.

Despite her infatuation with the Stones—not to mention the revolutionary, electric work of Bob Dylan—however, it is notable that Patti continued to see herself primarily as an artist, and she went on visiting Philadelphia museums, absorbing everything she could from the Renaissance to the twentieth century.

She processed what she saw and learned from a unique perspective, for fixated as she was on celebrity, Patti often took more interest in the artists' lives than in their work. "I got seduced by people's lifestyles, [people] like Modigliani, Soutine, Rimbaud," she explained.

American artists, she thought, held nothing for her, for she could find no "genius American lifestyles" that could match the likes of their European counterparts. That all changed, though, when an inspirational example of American art as celebrity (and vice versa) came to Philadelphia in the autumn of 1965. Pop artist and filmmaker Andy Warhol, then at the zenith of his career, attended the opening of his first retrospective, at the Institute of Contemporary Art on the University of Pennsylvania campus. He was accompanied by his stunning entourage, led by Edie Sedgwick. Their presence caused a near riot, the sort previously associated only with rock 'n' roll stars. Patti was transfixed. "It was like seeing a black-and-white movie in person," she recalled. "Edie Sedgwick with the blonde hair and the dark eyebrows—she didn't mess around. Platinum hair and black brows. She was really something. I saw her and Andy Warhol at the ICA. She really got me. It was something weird. Like, I really think you know your future if

you want to. There I was—I had really bad skin, I was really skinny and really fucked up—but I knew I was goin' to do work for *Vogue*. I didn't know how, but I just knew it."

In 1966, Patti got the chance to pursue an art education, when she won a scholarship to the prestigious Philadelphia Museum of Art's Saturday morning classes, which gave her the opportunity to get some feedback on her own work. If nothing else, the classes inspired her sartorially. Immensely impressed by the way the Jewish girls in her art class dressed, Patti completely adopted their black-tights-and-turtleneck style when she returned to college in the fall. The costume led her classmates to peg her as an antiwar activist, but they were mistaken. Patti, in fact, was so caught up in rock 'n' roll and art that she was unaware even that the country was involved in a war. She was busy imagining herself as the mistress of Bob Dylan, Jackson Pollock, or Harry Houdini. Such fantasies distracted her from her studies at Glassboro, where her academic record, already poor, further deteriorated. "I failed everything—I was so undisciplined," she later boasted.

Her fashion also affected how the rest of the world treated her. "Everyone in New Jersey thought I was weird," said Patti. "Sometimes in South Jersey I wouldn't get served in a restaurant because of the way I looked, and I never understood it—because I wasn't that conscious of image. I would wear black turtlenecks because I liked it. I never tried to look any way for shock value or anything like that, but I always would affect people in a certain way. All I was was romantic."

In 1966, during the summer between her sophomore and junior years, Patti discovered that she was pregnant. The father, some ne'er-do-well, conveniently disappeared, leaving her to face the problem alone. So, the pregnancy made Patti acutely aware of her strong calling to be an artist, and she knew that having a child would make that life impossible. With abortion both illegal and dangerous, she made up her mind to carry the baby to term then immediately give it up for adoption. To do so, she would need her parents' support, and she was lucky in that she felt comfortable enough to share her problem with them.

At first, Beverly Smith was overwhelmed by her daughter's news, but in the end both she and Grant agreed to support Patti. Dr. Flick, her mentor at Glassboro, helped cover up the situation by arranging for Patti to take some phantom courses in New York, and found her a place to stay with a couple who would keep her out of sight. The period of isolation provided Patti with time for introspection and study undertaken against a backdrop of the Beatles' *Revolver* and the Stones' *Aftermath*, with its signature song, "Stupid Girl." She was forced to recognize her female body, which was in itself a burden, on top of being overwhelmed by all the physical discomforts pregnancy visits upon the female (which Patti spelled as *feel male*). All she could see was a pregnant, bloated creature crawling along "like a lame dog or like a crab." She saw herself ripping the hair out of her skull and clawing her way through the desperate days of loneliness and depression. She could think of only one word to describe herself, and she repeated it over and over again like a mantra: "bitch . . . bitch . . . bitch."

In February 1967, the Rolling Stones released one of the signal singles of the decade, "Ruby Tuesday"/"Let's Spend the Night Together," and Patti had a baby. The two events helped propel her out of what might otherwise have become a quagmire of depression. "Let's Spend the Night Together" became the anthem of the sexual revolution. The Stones' music helped propel Patti past postpartum depression and the aftermath of giving up her baby as soon as it was born. The Stones, she wrote, did not play drug music; they were the drug. Their music stripped away any feelings of guilt.

Despite Patti's later claim that she had a cesarean birth (and a big scar to prove it), she told at least one close friend that she had a

regular vaginal birth. Regardless of the delivery method, Patti stuck to her plan and immediately gave the baby, a girl, up for adoption, the only caveat being that she not be raised a Catholic. Years later, Patti would give a simple explanation for giving up the child: "I gave it up . . . because I wanted to be an artist—simple as that. I wanted to create and re-create in my own way. I didn't want to create through another person—at that point in my life."

new york city

1 9 6 7 - 1 9 6 9

"There's no place that seduces you
and perverts you and inspires you like
New York."

patti smith

In the spring of 1967, with sixteen dollars in savings, Patti bought
some art supplies, got on a train, and headed for New York, the
city of Big Dreams. While she would later claim that her first two
weeks were spent sleeping on the subway or on building stoops, in
reality she moved in with friends. Within days, Patti found a job at
Brentano's bookstore on Fifth Avenue, smack in midtown Manhattan.

The city provided a pleasant anonymity. "New York was like a huge cathedral," said Patti. "No one stared at me. I could hide . . . When I came to New York, people immediately accepted me in the sense that I was anonymous." New York also proved eye-opening. "I was a very naive person," Patti recalled. "Even with getting 'in trouble,' I was sort of virginal, and there were so many weird things in New York. A lot of sexual stuff—not just happening to me, just happening—that I had to realize was a part of life. I had lived such a sheltered childhood, so family-oriented, and all of a sudden I was on my own. And that's when I learned that anything is possible. People don't realize we have these built-in seven-league boots. The body can go anywhere. It is physically capable of sustaining almost any kind of abuse, or any dream."

With a job and a place to live, Patti was free to pursue her mission—which, as she told Scott Cohen, was "not to be an artist but an artist's mistress." Adhering to what she called "a completely French view of art," Patti found her inspiration in "biographies of great people like Edith Piaf, who really dug their men and worked for them." Her first step, then, was to find an artist. There were many places where she might have looked for one in the New York of 1967: Andy Warhol's Factory was in full swing, and anybody could walk right in, presuming they had the confidence, and meet any number of artists. Cooper Union, the tuition-free art school in the East Village, or the booming St. Mark's Poetry Project, then at the height of its fame under the wing of poet Anne Waldman, were both enclaves for artists. And perhaps the most obvious place she could have looked was Max's Kansas City, the downtown watering hole that catered to artists, the underground elite, and slumming celebrities. Patti, however, ventured into none of these places, choosing instead to investigate the Pratt Institute of Art in Brooklyn, where she fantasized discovering the man of her dreams.

Venturing into the environs of Pratt, looking for a friend, Patti stumbled into the wrong apartment and came upon the man who would forever change her life. A sleeping elfin sprite not unlike herself in appearance, he was a nineteen-year-old art student named Robert Mapplethorpe. He, coincidentally, worked at another Brentano's.

Their meeting seemed precordained; Patti always had a knack for encountering the right people at just the right moments to help her focus her vision of herself, thereby facilitating her development as an artist. At Deptford High, a teacher introduced her to Modigliani and El Greco. At Glassboro, there was Dr. Flick. Now, in Robert she recognized someone who would nurture and inspire her, a recognition that was immediate and mutual. They needed each other, for as Patti recalled, "I was nineteen years old, really shattered. I'd been through a lot of hard times. I had all this powerful energy, and I did not know how to direct it. Robert really disciplined me to direct all my mania—all my telepathic energy—into art. Concentrating on the god within, or at least a creative demon. I was really emotionally fucked up."

Shortly after their meeting, Patti moved into the apartment that Robert was sharing with students Pat and Margaret Kennedy on Waverly Avenue in Brooklyn. Margaret immediately pinned Patti as manipulative and controlling, according to Patricia Morrisroe in her biography of Mapplethorpe. And though she could be sweet, Patti could likewise be cruel, and seemed to hate other women, especially attractive ones. Margaret experienced this latter side of Patti, who would criticize Margaret's cooking and do everything she could to intimidate her. In one notable incident, when Margaret's in-laws visited from Wisconsin, a completely nude Patti walked casually into the living room and said hello, shocking the conservative midwesterners. Conflict between the two women made it obvious that the foursome of Patti, Robert, and the Kennedys would not work.

Robert was so enamored of Patti that instead of staying with the Kennedys, he elected to find another place with his new friend. Soon he and Patti were sharing a floor-through apartment in a brownstone on Hall Street in Brooklyn. Theirs was a bleak little apartment that Robert brightened with Indian tapestries, beaded curtains, and religious objects, as well as his own work, while they both adapted the space to their respective needs: Patti went about creating a writer's workshop by hanging the famous photograph of Rimbaud from the cover of the New Directions edition of *Illuminations* over her desk and laying down an appropriately hip soundtrack that alternated tracks by French beat chanteuse Juliette Greco with cool jazz or the Rolling Stones; Robert spent his energies creating his own art nest, replete with sketch pads and objects to add to his sculptures. Unlike Patti's eclectic musical tastes, Robert's soundtrack was spare, often consisting of a lone Vanilla Fudge album, played over and over relentlessly for up to twelve hours at a stretch.

Still, Patti found inspiration both inside and out. The streets around Pratt catered to and for the art students, poets, mathematicians, and priests who occupied the university. The combination of being broke and of not having television sets led to a lot of creative conversations. "Everybody had a vision," Patti wrote.

In their own apartment, instead of watching TV, Patti and Robert watched each other. Robert recognized how equally disturbed and creative Patti was, and knew that if she could be grounded long enough, she would make something of her demons. For her part, Patti felt confident that Robert might be somehow able to complete her, and under his direction, she slowly began to bloom.

Meanwhile, to support themselves, Patti and Robert left Brentano's to work at F.A.O. Schwarz, the famous toy store, Patti as a cashier and Robert as a window trimmer. Patti did not last long, though, soon leaving for a job at Scribner's bookstore. The switch worked well, for when Robert complained that his job was really cutting into his time to "make art," Patti jumped in with an offer to support him—which she could afford because she was working full-time at Scribner's. Gerard Malanga remembered her technique: "Patti was working at Scribner's and she told me to come by, I could get any book. She implied she'd be giving me any book I chose, for free—at least I *thought* I was going up there to get a free book. I picked out a book I wanted—it was David Bailey's book of photographs, *Good-bye Baby and Amen*, a big coffee-table book which cost forty dollars, which was pretty expensive at the time. We went to the wrapping table and she personally wrapped up the book for me, tied it up with a string, then looked at me and said, 'Why don't you give me twenty bucks?' I realized it was not going to be a freebie. I gave her the money and she put it in her pocket, escorted me to the door, and handed me the package. I said, 'Thanks a lot.' I was happy: I'd spent less than I would've spent." This was the single instance in which Patti ever gave Gerard Malanga any kind of thanks or recognition for the considerable amount he did to ease her way into the poetry world. Malanga opened at least three doors for Patti. This was her thanks.

By day, as Patti toiled away at Scribner's, Robert stayed home and pursued his art. At night, with rock 'n' roll blaring from the hi-fi, he would smoke pot, take speed, or drop acid, while Patti, who eschewed drugs at the time, made a simple dinner, then joined him with her sketchbook. They saw themselves as the brother and sister in Jean Cocteau's *Les Enfants Terribles*. "We were twenty years old, we lived in Brooklyn, totally isolated," Patti recalled years later. "I worked in a bookstore, I came to the apartment and we spent most of our time drawing, looking at books, and spending all of our time together, hardly ever seeing other people."

One person they did occasionally see was Patti's friend from Glassboro, Janet Hamill, who provides another perspective on Patti and Robert's arrangement. As she indicates, Patti's hunger for celebrity was alive and well, and shared by Robert. "They were both totally enraptured by the idea of being artists and living outside of society, but they wanted to be rich and famous, too. Fame was particularly important to Patti, because after losing the baby she needed a way to reaffirm herself. Robert and Patti were always telling each other, 'We're going to make it, and we'll do it together!' "

On Hall Street, Patti moved from drawing to painting, and then to writing. Through writing, Patti found that she could turn herself into a composite of her cultural heroes. "I felt the people I could learn from were the rock-and-roll stars. In the sixties it was Jim Morrison, Smokey Robinson, Bob Dylan, the Rolling Stones. In the fifties, I can still get excited about Humphrey Bogart. I like people who're bigger than me. I'm not interested in meeting a bunch of writers who I don't think are bigger than life. I'm a hero worshipper."

At the same time, as she gained confidence, Patti began to explore and draw sustenance from the wonderland of New York, taking the subway out to Coney Island with Robert, or running and dancing through the streets of Manhattan by herself, dreaming of the heroes who had lived and worked there, from Billie Holiday and Frank O'Hara to Jackson Pollock, whom Patti described in her writing as "the great dancing abstract expressionist," whose "Jazzy dance steps burst into some of the most exciting paint splashes in history." In "The King Curtis Death Kit," a piece Patti wrote about her early days in the city, she paid homage to such New York icons as Pollock and Franz Kline, the Women's House of Detention on Greenwich and Seventh Avenues, Marcel Duchamp, Dylan Thomas, Cassius Clay and Houdini, George Raft, Janis Joplin, and Jim Morrison. Through the essay, she skips and skids from Second Avenue and Tenth Street, up past Madison Square Garden to Forty-second Street, where she plays pinball at Playland, then cuts west to Twelfth Avenue to the empty helicopter yard, dark and forbidding. The piece ends with Patti gazing rapturously at the Empire State Building, seeing in its immensity and style the imagination of the city.

Back at Hall Street, Patti and Robert were soul mates in every sense, but in their sex life there was something missing. Robert did not arouse in Patti the feelings of grand passion that she found essential in a romantic relationship, and she soon began aggressively pursuing another artist, a handsome young painter named Howie Michaels, who she showered with gifts and flattery. When she finally told Robert of her decision to move in with her new lover, he collapsed, crying out dramatically that if Patti left him, he would become gay!

"It was more than a fight," Robert recalled with some understatement. "We split up for a little while."

After she left, Mapplethorpe flew out to San Francisco, capital of the gay world, to fully explore his sexuality. "The first fight I had with Patti, I went to California," Robert remembered. "I left school and just went out there for about four weeks. I flew out not knowing anyone and met some boy on the plane who was sort of a hippie, and he was going to stay in a commune, so I just went with him. It was amazing." Robert returned to Brooklyn and, having come to terms with his homosexuality in San Francisco, soon fell in love with a young man with whom he began having an affair.

Robert's coming out was a severe shock to Patti. She stopped by Hall Street one day shortly after his return from California to collect some of her things and found Robert surrounded by photographs of naked men and various accoutrements of his new gay lifestyle. To her, this just didn't make any sense: if Robert was gay, it negated everything that they had shared. According to several friends, Patti went berserk, and her hysteria apparently so unnerved Howie Michaels that they broke up. Patti fled to the sanctuary of Janet Hamill's apartment on West Twelfth Street in Greenwich Village. For a time, Janet felt that Patti was really suicidal.

To distract herself from it all, in May 1969 Patti took a leave of absence from Scribner's and flew to Paris with her sister Linda to search, she said, for Rimbaud's ghost. "We stayed at the Hotel of Strangers, in the attic room where Charles Cros and Rimbaud lived together," Patti said, going on to claim, "In fact, I'm sure I

slept in the same bed because the proprietor said nobody rented this room because it's the attic room. It was like in the movies when they go into the haunted house and they hit everything and there's tons of dust and spiders and the bed is shaped like bodies. It was a tiny bed on a metal ramp. You could see the outline of bodies where the people had slept. It was so dirty. I said, 'I will pay anything, just let me stay up there.' "

Patti and Linda stayed in Paris for nearly three months. While there, they joined a troupe of street performers, accompanying the musicians and fire-eaters. Patti's instrument was a toy piano. Working the cafés between the Dom and Coupole on weekends like a character out of Dickens, she also became an expert pickpocket.

Although Paris struck Patti most deeply in a visual way ("Paris to me is completely a city of images. I always felt that I was in a black and white 16 millimeter film"), while there she continued her metamorphosis from painter to writer. "I wanted to be an artist, I worked to be an artist for maybe six years," she explained. "As soon as I became a good artist, all of a sudden I couldn't draw . . . in 1969 . . . I put my piece of paper and my canvas in front of me, and I could see the finished product before I even touched the paper. It was frightening to me: I'm not interested in the finished product; I'm interested in creating the moment. The finished product is for the people who buy the stuff, and I'm not interested in doing stuff so other people can get their rocks off. [In Paris] I was still painting, but my paintings were becoming more and more like cartoons, and the words were standing out more than the images. I had gone to Paris to find myself as an artist, but I came back to New York filled with words and rhythms. After putting seven years into it, I gave up art just like that in one day."

Writing allowed Patti to celebrate the people she admired most. In a significant switch, however, although she still wrote poems about Bob Dylan and Brian Jones, the majority of her new subjects were female. This was a vital step in her development because, while the subjects certainly qualified as heroines, the poems were in fact all about herself. Through writing, Patti started to re-make herself out of a combination of all her heroines, and took her first steps toward becoming an autobiographical songwriter. "I did not know hardly any of the girls I wrote about," she pointed out. "I could only write about my best friend Judy when she was away from me for a year. Then all of a sudden she became a muse. I met Edie Sedgwick a few times but she had nothing to say to me. Who was I? But I thought she was swell; she was one of my first heroines. I don't like women who are attainable."

After three months, Patti did not leave Paris so much as she fled it, spooked by separate yet equally weird hallucinations about her father and the Rolling Stones, especially Brian Jones. Upon land-ing in New York, Patti sent Linda back home to find out how Grant was; she went straight to Robert, who took her in and kicked his boyfriend out. It turned out that her father had suffered a heart attack, but would be OK. Robert, on the other hand, hav-ing long neglected his dental hygiene, had ulcerated sores on his gums and had developed a serious infection. Patti decided to move him to the Chelsea Hotel, a renowned Manhattan artists' haven, on West Twenty-third Street. Stanley Bard ran the legendary ho-tel and had long had the habit of taking in poverty-stricken artists in whom he believed, often taking their art as collateral for their rent. Despite his never having heard of Patti Smith or Robert Mapplethorpe, Patti had soon talked Bard into giving them the key to the smallest room in the hotel, on the tenth floor. Flashing him one of her more charming grins, Patti dashed out into the lobby to drag the sick and shivering Robert into the elevator. And so they ascended into what would become the true launching pad for both of their careers. As she remembered the time at the Chelsea, "William Burroughs was there, and Gregory Corso, and the Jefferson Airplane and Janis Joplin and Matthew Reich [a mu-sician tipped for stardom in the sixties who would marry actress Genevieve Waite and later have a breakdown from which he would never fully recover]—who was also an early influence on me—and it was really a good time. It was time for us to strike out on our own . . . Robert as an artist, and I had been writing some of my poetry."

In July 1969, the same month that Patti and Robert moved into the Chelsea, Brian Jones of the Rolling Stones drowned in his swimming pool. His untimely death had a profound impact on her. "I was with her the night that Brian Jones died," recalled a friend. "She was just crying hysterically. I was upset too, but she just kept talking about 'Baby Brian Jones' and 'Baby Brian Jones's bones.' " Patti began writing a "black rock 'n' roll mass, based on numerology and spells—like in medieval language, but with rock 'n' roll rhythms."

"At this time I was writing my Brian Jones poems," said Patti. "Of course they were rock 'n' roll oriented because they were about Brian, and I would write them in the rhythm of the Stones' music. I wasn't trying to be 'innovative'—I was just doing what I thought was right, and being true to Brian."

Jones was the sort of star around whom his followers wove inspired legends: Patti had a vision in which Brian was still, but only barely alive, and she wanted to talk to him but got sidetracked in observing the delicate embroidery of lace on his cuff. Within hours of his death the whole world would know about it, she reflected. She saw the Rolling Stones "moving toward a mortal mergence of the unspoken moment and that hot dance of life," which could be taken as a statement on Brian Jones's death, or as a vision of the rapidly approaching mayhem of Altamont.

Through it all, Patti's quest for fame remained unabated. To satisfy it, she and Robert made a series of visits to New York's hippest locale at the time, Max's Kansas City, on Seventeenth Street and Park Avenue South, a short walk from the Chelsea. Art was never far from their minds, though, and an incident from one night's walk to Max's vividly reveals how Robert saw the world—and the perspective that he helped Patti develop. One night, Patti and Robert came across an abandoned pair of shoes. "We had no money to get anything to eat, no money for art supplies—we were considerably down," remembered Patti. "Then, in the streetlight, there was a perfect pair of pointy-toed alligator-skin shoes, really high-end and expensive, just sitting there. They had to be worth three or four hundred dollars. I looked at the shoes and said, 'Clothes or art?' Robert replied, 'Both.' He took off his huaraches, put on the shoes with no socks, and stuffed in newspaper to make them fit. All of a sudden he was a new man. He couldn't buy anything to eat, but he had new shoes. Later, he came home and put them into an installation. . . . Everything was always Life or Art. It was magical when something could cross over and be both."

Max's was the only club that catered to the denizens of the underground art world. The club was divided into two main areas: the front room was the domain of the painters and artists who were friends of the owner, Mickey Ruskin, while the back room was the province of the downtown elite, and entry had to be earned. Andy Warhol and his entourage made the back room their nightly hangout.

When they first started going to Max's, Patti and Robert couldn't get in at all. "Mickey didn't want Patti Smith in at first because she looked too grungy," said Philip Locascio, who worked at the club. "There was still that very affluent clientele that ate in front and along the side, like Visconti, Antonioni, and that very sophisticated movie crowd. They enjoyed the costumes that everybody wore, they liked to look at it, but they didn't want to be terrorized by it."

"Andy felt that both Robert and Patti were just too hungry," recalled Terry Ork. "Robert had tried many times to be accepted at the Factory. I don't think Andy was too taken with either of them. I think part of it had to do with Patti's sexual thing. I think homosexuality was a threat to her."

Leee Black Childers, a photographer and downtown bon vivant who haunted the back room at Max's with drag queen Jackie Curtis, offers a contrasting memory. "I couldn't understand why they couldn't get in," he said. "I thought Robert was quite cute. Patti'd be in ugly, dirty ripped clothes. I guess Mickey Ruskin thought they didn't have the right look. The doorman was the one who was saying no. Patti and Robert would sit on the curb out in front of Max's and talk to everyone as they came and went. Everyone would take them glasses of wine and things and so it didn't take long until they were getting in."

Still, they weren't *really* "in." Once past the door, Patti and Robert would sit alone at a table, nursing a Coke and maybe splitting a salad, waiting for someone to talk to them. "We hung out at Max's every single night until like three in the morning trying to get a big break," Patti remembered. "I don't even know what we were trying to get a break for. We hung out there every night for about six months and nobody even said hello to us."

A breakthrough occurred when Danny Fields invited them to join his table. Fields, who had managed Iggy Pop and Detroit's MC5, among others, was a popular figure at Max's, and being invited to his table immediately conferred on them considerable status. "She and Robert used to come to Max's every night, stand in the doorway, and stare at all the chic people and wish that they would be invited to sit down and hang out with them," Danny recalled. "Finally I said, 'Well, come sit down, you two, who are you?' " No one knew quite what to make of them at first. Were they lovers, siblings or best friends? Straight, bisexual or gay? Artists, writers, or groupies? Luckily, no one really cared: Max's housed a scene where such ambiguity was itself a form of cachet.

"1969 to 1972 was my peak period, when I made the transition from psychotic to serious art student," said Patti. "I like to work. I like that anguish you go through when you're writing something. I like to battle with language." Patti would spend the first three years of the seventies turning herself into a successful poet. Though the possibility of being in a band or doing rock 'n' roll was hinted at in conversations with her friend Penny Arcade, she put distance between herself and the concept for the time being. Patti was eerily prescient about what the times required. The early seventies would be a confused transitional period for the rock musicians who had thrived in the sixties. A plethora of ambitious and talented artists would destroy themselves in their attempts to make themselves the stars of the early seventies. Patti had always been ambitious, but now she watched and waited for the perfect moment she knew would come.

the outrageous lie

1969-1971

> "Everyone began to think of themselves in
> mythological proportions."
>
> ***leee black childers***

Patti Smith made her first appearance in front of a New York audience in 1969, in the Theater of the Ridiculous play *Femme Fatale*. The cast included the Warhol stars Mary Woronov, Jackie Curtis, Penny Arcade, and Jayne (then Wayne) County. *Femme Fatale* was written by Jackie Curtis, who would later star alongside Candy Darling in Warhol's *Women in Revolt* (1973). Unlike Candy, who was drop-dead gorgeous in drag, Jackie was clearly a man in a dress, and played it that way, with frizzy hair and glitter make-up over unshaved stubble. The play was based on Jackie's experiences with the underground actress Penny Arcade and John Christian, an actor who had starred in *Cockstrong*, written by John Vaccaro. Christian was to star in *Femme Fatale* too, but by the time the play went into production, he was suffering from agoraphobia and refused to leave his apartment. Jackie decided then that John's part would be played by a woman, and cast Patti Smith. A star was born.

Patti had become involved with the Warhol set when she and Robert Mapplethorpe were hanging out at Max's Kansas City. From day one, Jackie Curtis mistrusted her, telling Penny Arcade that she thought Patti a "social climber." "Jackie never liked her," said Leee Black Childers, who was Curtis's friend and roommate at the time. "She didn't want to be around her at all."

Patti, though, had a look that was completely her own and that was something to be valued. "Some people thought Patti was this ugly girl," explained Penny Arcade. "You know, when ugly was a sin. But she wasn't ugly—it was just that nobody looked like that then. She was really skinny and weird, a precursor of the whole punk thing."

Around the time that Patti was insinuating herself into Max's back room, the Warhol drag-queen crowd began playing a game that they called the Outrageous Lie. According to Leee Childers, the concept was first invented by Jackie Curtis, who became its biggest proponent. The thinking was that while if you simply lied, you would surely be caught, if you created an absolutely Outrageous Lie, you would be believed. So, Cyrinda Foxe (who in the 1970s would marry David Johansen of the New York Dolls and then Aerosmith's Steven Tyler, and in 1977 star in *Andy Warhol's Bad*) began telling people that she was shot off the back of a motorcycle in Texas by Hell's Angels and had the scars to prove it; Wayne County had a fabulous brown silk jacket and told everyone that it was given to her by Joan Crawford—never mind that she had found it at a flea market. The lies grew and grew, gaining momentum, Childers said, as "Everyone began to think of themselves in mythological proportions."

Childers remembers Patti joining the game, too, and through it winning her part in *Femme Fatale* and taking her first steps toward fame. "At the rehearsals for *Femme Fatale*, Patti confessed to us that she had become pregnant at nineteen, and as the baby grew, it became impatient and it kicked until *wham!*—this leg came right through her stomach and was hangin' out! We were all kids, including Patti, and we all went, 'Ooohh, ooohh, my God, it kicked its way straight out of your stomach?' Now, I don't think that could ever happen, but we all believed it at the time. I think she believed it, because that's the other thing about Outrageous Lies: you gotta believe it or they don't work.

"Jackie studied what'd gone before, in the way of who got away with what. Jackie's particular case was hopeless, because she was a man in a dress who would never, ever look like a woman. Still, she studied it and she worked it and she passed it on, and what she passed on, among many things, was the concept of the Outrageous Lie. If the lie is so outrageous, not only can you get away with it, but it creates a center of glamour around you.

"And that [the baby] was Patti's Outrageous Lie, and it existed for years and years and years with me, until I finally told it to someone one day at a party, and the person said, 'A baby can't kick a leg through someone's stomach and both of them live,' and then I went 'Oh!'

"So it was the era of the Outrageous Lie. And the relevance of that was, we lived it: each of us told our individual one or two or three or four, depending on our energy and the amount of speed we took—we told our Outrageous Lie. But we also basically lived the Outrageous Lie; we lived the completely Outrageous Lie— Jackie Curtis, Candy Darling, Holly Woodlawn, Jayne County, and Patti Smith. There was no possible reason that that girl [Patti] should have been a great star, on the face of it. If you analyzed what she had going for her—nothing. Don't ever analyze! Because she had everything going for her—it was in her brain. And she used the Outrageous Lie like we all did—to bridge the gap; to get in Max's Kansas City, to get into St. Mark's Church. Once she was there, there was no doubt in anybody's mind that there was some amazing something happening, and she didn't need the Lie any longer."

Femme Fatale's director, Tony Ingrassia, had hired Patti essentially for the way she looked, since nobody had seen her act. Patti surprised everyone. "She had great instincts as an actress," said Leee Childers. "She could have been a great actress; she was fabulous, the audience loved her, you could feel it.

"She played every scene so perfectly," Childers continued. "The Theater of the Ridiculous is based on improvisation, and so even if you're given the lines, you've got to be able to do something with them, because the lines generally don't mean much. And Patti astounded everyone with her stage presence and with her confidence. Audiences adored her. She could have gone on to become a great actress. She still may do that. She has the magic that audiences immediately see. Jackie was way over the top, and Penny is very much of a burlesque woman, but Patti played it very still, very stiff, very intense, very mean, very threatening, and it worked like crazy. Patti always got raving applause at the end of the show."

After her success in *Femme Fatale*, Patti went on to appear with Wayne County and Penny Arcade in Ingrassia's production of *Island*, which the director rewrote and restructured especially for her. According to Childers, Ingrassia loved working with Patti— she was easy to work with and took direction well. Childers said of her, "You told her what to do and she did it. She didn't try to do it, she just did it."

"I think she was very serious about her acting, and very proud of it too," concluded Bebe Buell, someone who would soon become another friend.

Although these improvisational plays were as off-Broadway as a production could get, within a certain group of people they were important and got Patti noticed. In fact, it would have been difficult *not* to be noticed: *Island* was set on the deck of a Fire Island beach house, and Patti occupied the stage's "beach," closest to the audience. "She was two feet from the audience," said Childers. "Very much a focal point, almost like the fool in Shakespeare, commenting on all the fools—the real fools up there on the deck. She was onstage most of the play talking about the idiots on stage!"

Among others impressed by her performances was Andy Warhol, who came to almost every performance of *Island*. "He was there so much it was embarrassing, because we had to keep [the performance] up," said Childers. "The first time, it's a thrill, but the eighth time? 'Oh, my God, Andy is still here!' He was coming all the time, he was entranced with it. He was entranced with Cherry [Vanilla] and Wayne and the whole production, but very much part of the entrancement was Patti."

Thus, after so recently being on the fringe looking in at the party, Patti had made her grand entrance. Her persistence would pay off in more ways than one, too, for it was while acting that Patti got the first inklings of her real calling. She found acting too confining—she realized that she longed "to spar with people, to make contact."

Indeed, she began to do so in her personal life. While keeping their room at the Chelsea, Patti and Robert were now doing well enough to also rent a loft together just down the block at 206 West Twenty-third Street. (Interestingly, given Mapplethorpe's later subject matter, 206 West Twenty-third would in the nineties be the site of an S&M-themed restaurant called La Nouvelle Justine, where patrons eat out of dog bowls served by drag queens dressed as dominatrixes.) Robert spent most of his time working in the loft on his art projects, and this left Patti free to network. She was looking to stretch out, to take her success in the Ingrassia plays and scare up some action. Not having found the support she needed among the drag queens, Patti soon hooked up with the eminently heterosexual Bobby Neuwirth, who once was one of Edie Sedgwick's lovers. Neuwirth was supposedly the coolest of the cool, a musician and village raconteur who had been virtually inseparable from Bob Dylan until the two had a falling out in the late sixties. Gerard Malanga remembers the Neuwirth of that time as someone with "a really nasty attitude": "He just had no manners, he was a very crude person, just an unbearable person to be with in the seventies," said Malanga. "I could never see what Bob Dylan saw in Bobby Neuwirth."

Maybe it was his knack for effectively stroking the egos of people he liked. He looked at one of Patti's notebooks and, Patti said, "immediately recognized something in me that I didn't even recognize in myself." Neuwirth was the first person to take Patti seriously as a poet and encourage her. "He really loved my poetry. He built up my confidence and kept inspiring me to keep the music in my poetry. He said we needed a poet."

Neuwirth also introduced Patti to the rock 'n' roll crowd—Kris Kristofferson, Janis Joplin, Johnny and Edgar Winter. Joplin would have the most influence on Patti, perhaps because she treated her as an equal. The two of them would get together in the bar of the El Quixote and dish, Patti trying to match Janis drink for drink, often ending up lying on her bed while the ceiling spun in circles. "We used to talk about how she couldn't reveal herself as fragile," Patti told Scott Cohen. "I didn't care how I revealed myself. I was acting real unimpressed then because I thought I was gonna make it in the art world," Patti remembered. However, it was writing, not art, that was coming to dominate her existence. Slowly Patti began to get articles and record reviews published in the rock magazines. "I wanted so much to be a rock writer," Patti would say, "I used to devour those magazines."

The Chelsea Hotel, in fact, was a heady place to be in the late sixties and early seventies. Barry Miles, a British writer who was in New York for a time then working on a William Blake record with

Allen Ginsberg, remembered that "there was a whole gang of people then, a sort of moving party at the Chelsea, of which Patti was a part. Almost any night, you could call down to Josie on the switchboard and say, 'Where's the party?' and she'd say, 'It's in Dr. Johnson's apartment'—Dr. Johnson, the black professor, she often had parties—or else it would be in Harry Smith's room."

Harry Smith was a filmmaker and a collector of folk music, artifacts, and books who influenced many artists including Bob Dylan and Allen Ginsberg. He had an impact on Patti as well. "Harry really encouraged me," she said. "I used to sit in his room at the Chelsea and sing for him." (When Harry Smith died in 1991, his archives were donated to the Anthology Film Archives in New York, where Patti Smith now heads the fund-raising committee.)

William Burroughs too spent time at the Chelsea and was another influence on Patti. "Burroughs showed me a whole series of new tunnels to fall through," she said. "He was so neat. He would walk around in this big black cashmere overcoat and this old hat. So of course Patti gets an old black hat and coat, and we would walk around the Chelsea looking like that. Of course, he was never too crazy about women, but I guess he liked me 'cause I looked like a boy."

Patti also met Jim Carroll at the Chelsea. Though he would later fuse music with his poetry, at this time Carroll was mainly a nineteen-year-old heroin addict, albeit one with a literary reputation: part of his novel *The Basketball Diaries* had been published in the *Paris Review* three years earlier. His book of poems about life at the Chelsea, *Living at the Movies*, would be nominated for a Pulitzer Prize.

Jim Carroll played a vital role as the midwife of Patti Smith the poet by being Jim Carroll, by example. He was the kind of figure she had imagined a poet should be. Once, when he was sick or otherwise detained, Patti railed against St. Mark's Poetry Project for not giving him another reading because, they said, he was unreliable. Jim Carroll, who might just as likely have been found passed out in the gutter in front of Max's as surrounded by a retinue of admirers at a table inside, reminded her of Rimbaud.

Before long, Robert Mapplethorpe, Patti Smith, and Jim Carroll were going everywhere together. With their androgynous look—soon the height of 1970s chic—the trio caused quite a stir wherever they went, whether it was to the seedy Times Square area or a trendy downtown art or club opening. With Patti and Robert, the sharp-witted and perceptive Carroll got a front-row seat from which to view the rise of two stars. He agreed with Patti's assessment of her own potential—that success was just a matter of time as long as she made the right moves. She had a sense of humor and inventiveness that Carroll found charming.

Jim moved into Patti and Robert's loft. Because he was so similar to them in every way he became the third enfant terrible. The three of them were the advance guard of the seventies. They *were* the seventies that had not happened yet. They were living in a future they would individually and equally make out of their own visions, lifestyles, and work. Their support of each other was a natural reflex, like supporting yourself. But, on a more formal front, Jim Carroll's enthusiasm for Patti's poetry took her one step further on her course. Even when Patti and Jim were lovers it did not upset the delicate balance of relations with Mapplethorpe, and the three were able to continue growing together, until all three had become like an octopus, its tentacles seeking in every direction for contacts, sustenance, and checks. Somebody should write a treatise on the collaboration between Jim Carroll, Robert Mapplethorpe, and Patti Smith. It's a subject that would be well worth the effort.

Jim was also able to learn from Patti. He was as impressed by her visions, ambitions, and energy as she was by his, and she inspired him to work just as much as he inspired her. In fact, just as Kerouac had told Burroughs over and over again that Burroughs was a writer and would write a book called *Naked Lunch*, Patti repeatedly told Jim that he would be a singer-songwriter in a rock 'n' roll band. (From 1978 to 1980 Carroll did have a rock band, releasing his first album, *Catholic Boy*, on Rolling Stone records and achieving cult status.) Like Mapplethorpe, Carroll would remain close to Patti over the years.

Patti's relationship with Carroll ended when he refused to stop seeing a fashion model on the side. He later admitted to regretting his choice, and through the years the two would remain friends.

In the autumn of 1970, Patti met the next man who would play a role in her artistic growth. Sam Shepard was an underground playwright whose already considerable body of work—twenty plays—had notched six Obie awards from the *Village Voice*. He was only twenty-six when he met Patti and, like Jim Carroll, something of a sensation. He played drums with a rock band called the Holy Modal Rounders and possessed the charisma of a rock star. Physically he fit the mold of Patti's previous lovers: he was slim, rangy, and tall, with deep blue eyes and a winning smile. And though he was married at the time to a beautiful woman named O-Lan and had a young son, he and Patti nevertheless began a passionate love affair.

As in the past, Patti's sexual relationship provided fuel for her art. "I learned from Sam," said Patti, "because Sam is one of the most magic people I have ever met. Sam is really the most true American man I've ever met, in as far as he's also hero-oriented. He has a completely western-romance mind. He loves gangsters, he loves cowboys. He's totally physical. He loves bigness—you know Americans love bigness. In his plays, there's always a huge Cadillac or a huge breast or a huge monster. His whole life moves on rhythms. He's a drummer. I mean, everything about Sam is so beautiful and has to do with rhythm. That's why Sam and I so successfully collaborated. Intuitively he worked with rhythm in his blood. I do it intellectually. He does it from his heart. We were able to establish a deep communion."

With Sam Shepard, Patti was for the first time involved with someone whom her soulmate, Robert Mapplethorpe, felt threatened by. But Patti was deeply in love, and nothing could dissuade her. In an act that had greater significance for Patti than Sam, they each had a tattoo engraved by the Italian beatnik artist Vali, who lived in the Chelsea and had been a heroine of Patti's since she was a teenager. She gave Patti a prophetic lightning bolt. Sam got an appropriate hawk moon. "Patti said Sam was beautiful and special and talented and that he was going to go somewhere," said Bebe Buell, who met Patti after the affair with Shepard was over.

Shepard "was an important force in my life," said Patti. "We wrote the play and took it right to the stage. We wrote *Cowboy Mouth* on the same typewriter—like a battle. And we were having this affair—he was a married man, and it was a passionate kind of thing. [In the play] we were talking about two people—two big dreamers—that came together but were destined for a sad end. It was the true story of Sam and me. We knew we couldn't stay together. He was going back to his wife, and I was going on my way. But even though it was an unhappy love affair, it was a very happy union. He inspired me to be stronger and make my move."

Patti's last time onstage acting was on April 29, 1971, playing Cavale to Shepard's Slim in *Cowboy Mouth*, the title of which was taken from a line in Bob Dylan's song "Sad-Eyed Lady of the Lowlands."

In the most telling passage in the play, Cavale (Patti) speaks about rock 'n' roll as the new religion destined to replace the High Church in pomp, ceremony, and revelations. She starts out saying that *she* cannot be the angel or saint people imagine they want— "Somebody to get off on when they can't get off on themselves." That's what Mick Jagger and Bob Dylan had been doing in 1966 and 1969. It had given her hope, she recalled, for the future of rock 'n' roll, but both stars had become too conscious of their role. The thrust of her rap is that while Jesus and the disciples and, beyond them, "The Lord" had worked for a long time, life was too hard now. God doesn't understand our pain. We need a new saint: "Any great motherfucker rock and roll song can raise me higher than all of Revelations. We created rock and roll from our image, it's our child."

Terry Ork had always supported the work Patti was doing, but now he felt that her possessiveness was getting way out of hand. "I had known Sam Shepard long before Patti. One day I was lounging on his bed talking about art and writing. I had been bringing Nick Ray [director of *Rebel Without a Cause*] around to rehearsals of *Cowboy Mouth*, and Nick was enchanted, and we wanted to film it. Patti walked into Sam's room, looked and me and said, 'Get the fuck out of here, this is my man!' "

Sam Shepard's feelings were likewise battered by Patti's possessiveness. After just one performance of *Cowboy Mouth*, he quietly left town: he couldn't face reenacting his adulterous relationship in public; it was too much like having a love affair on stage. He headed for Vermont, later to move with his wife to London, leaving Patti waiting at the theater to go on. She had never been so humiliated. Moreover, Sam's change of heart and abrupt departure was devastating, and Patti would express her pain for everyone to see: on more than one occasion she was carried out of Max's by friends, crying and drunkenly screaming Sam's name.

In episodes such as these, Patti was beginning to live out her personal dramas on the public stage, and in so doing she began to create her own legend. Despite the blow of Sam's departure, her triumph at the February reading at St. Mark's Church was still resonating, and Patti was nothing if not a survivor. There were poems to write, identities to forge, and new lovers to discover. Patti Smith was on the rise.

seventh heaven

1971 - 1973

> "To escape from horror bury yourself
> in it."
>
> *genet*

After the St. Mark's poetry reading, Patti was swamped with offers
and advice about what direction her "career" should take, for, despite any protestations to the contrary, it was indeed beginning to
look like a career. Former club owner Steve Paul, who managed
the careers of Edgar and Johnny Winter, thought Patti had enormous potential as a rock 'n' roll singer and suggested that she put
aside her writing for music. He had an act in mind for Patti, pair-
ing her with guitarist Rick Derringer, whom Paul also managed.

Things went so far as to have photos of the duo taken. "They were gonna be Ricky and Patti, or Ricky D and Patti Lee, something like that," Bebe Buell recalled. There was also talk of Patti becoming the singer for Blue Oyster Cult, but nothing came of that either. "Steve Paul thought perhaps she could be the Barbra Streisand of the seventies," said rock writer Lisa Robinson. "But Patti knew she didn't want to be a pop leather queen." Patti didn't want to do music unless she could do exactly what she wanted, and nobody was offering to let her do that—yet.

In the watershed summer of 1971, Patti concentrated on her writing like she'd never done before. She felt the time had come to write a book. Rather than dwell on Sam and write a lachrymose account of her loss, she penned a series of poems that on the surface appeared to be raw and sexy celebrations of her heroes and heroines, but, as she pointed out, were really autobiographical— "all about me." Through this poetry, she set out to construct the new Patti Smith from the composite characteristics of her idols. This Patti would no longer place herself under anybody's thumb, unless it fit her mood of the moment. She would now be the interviewee, not the interviewer.

"I really didn't fall in love with writing as writing," Patti explained. "I fell in love with writers' lifestyles. Rimbaud's lifestyle— I was in love with Rimbaud for being a mad angel and all that shit. Right before I met Telegraph Books, two things happened that really liberated me. The major thing was reading Mickey Spillane. I started reading Mickey Spillane and Mike Hammer, his 'Hammer language,' like 'I ran. I ran fast down the alley. And back again.' I mean, he wrote like that. Three-word sentences, and they're like a chill. They're real effective, and I got seduced by his speed. At the same time I started reading Céline. I've never been able to get through a whole book by Céline, 'cause it's just too intellectual, but the idea that he could freeze one word and put a period—he dared put one word—*yellow* [for example]—and follow it by forty other words like forty movements, also like some kind of concerto or something. He's not as seducing to me as Mickey Spillane, but I juggled the two. And then the third thing, I was reading Michaux. He's so funny.

"I think I'm a good writer," she continued. "I'm a good writer in the same way Mickey Spillane or Raymond Chandler or James M. Cain is a good writer. There's a lot of American rhythms. I mean, I can seduce people. I got good punch lines, I got all the stuff that Americans like. Some of it's dirty. There's a lot of good jokes. I mean, I write to entertain. I write to make people laugh. I write to give a double take. I write to seduce a chick. I wrote 'Girl Trouble' about Anita Pallenberg. Anita Pallenberg would read it and think twice and maybe she'd invite me over to the South of France and have a little nookie or something. Everything I write has a motive behind it. I write to have somebody. I write in the same way I perform. I mean, you only perform because you want people to fall in love with you. You want them to react to you.

"I don't consider writing a quiet, closet act: I consider it a real physical act. When I'm home writing on a typewriter, I go crazy. I move like a monkey. I've wet myself, I've come in my pants writing . . . Instead of shooting smack, I masturbate—fourteen times in a row . . . I start seeing all these strange spaceships landing in the Aztec mountains . . . I see weird things. I see temples, underground temples, with the doors opening, sliding door after sliding door, Pharaoh revealed—this bound-up Pharaoh with ropes of gold. That's how I write a lot of my poetry."

Patti was again living with Robert Mapplethorpe, who proved his true friendship by taking her back and devoting himself to her care after the dramatic breakup with Sam Shepard. She could always turn to Robert—he was the only man in Patti's life who did not in any way feel threatened by her. Even as strong a man as Sam had destroyed some of Patti's drawings during an argument, an act friends thought stemmed from his jealousy of Patti's own prodigious talent. More than any of her other lovers, Mapplethorpe gave her total, unequivocal support, at times when she might otherwise have lost her mind. His care was selfless and in the true spirit of artistic collaboration.

Rebounding from Sam, over the summer of 1971, Patti had a brief though deeply felt affair with musician Todd Rundgren. Rundgren had started in Philadelphia with a band called the Nazz, and by 1971 was a successful pop musician in his own right, as well as a producer and engineer. Patti appreciated him musically, too. In August she reviewed his solo album, *Runt*, in *Rolling Stone*. Rundgren was another figure in line with Mapplethorpe and Carroll, a real original who was still a little bit ahead of his time. Patti pointed out that a lot of critics had branded Rundgren "too esoteric," but, in her opinion, he was one of the few musicians on the scene still writing and singing his songs "like Smokey Robinson and Ronnie Spector." She also praised the range of his voice, from "a Las Vegas choir boy" to a "backstreet a capella."

According to Bebe Buell, who would be Todd's next girlfriend, Patti had strong feelings about Rundgren. "She really loved him with all her heart," said Buell. "She told me how she felt about him; she told me how the 'Room of Burning Fire' was about a bad visit with Todd . . . after [which] she went home and started a fire with a pile of paper . . . They were very dear connected souls." Bebe actually would visit Patti for advice about her relationship with Todd. "What we'd do is put on records and sing along to them, using hairbrushes for microphones, and stand in front of the mirror and sing," said Buell.

"Patti loved the power that being a woman brought her, but she wanted to be a boy, too," said Bebe. "She told me one time, 'I'm not Todd's type, I'm not beautiful and blonde, and I look like a boy.' I said, 'For a boy you have the biggest breasts I've ever seen!' A lot of people didn't know how big her boobs were because of the way she wore them. She would wear a nice baggy T-shirt or a man's shirt with a good flattening bra or no bra, which brought them down even flatter. She was very well endowed. My God, I almost fainted when she showed them to me!"

Turning down Steve Paul's offer of stardom took guts, but Patti had lots to spare. The blood of a writer was pumping through her veins, giving her an adrenaline-like rush. The torrent of words that ran through her mind constantly grew stronger; she was writing new poems every day, and everything in her life turned into poetry. Often, it emerged fully formed, as it did in this particular incident: One night Patti was in her room at the Chelsea with Robert and her sister Linda. It was hot and they were broke, and Patti snapped at Linda, igniting a fight. Angry, Linda stormed out of the room. When it got dark and she still had not returned, Patti started to freak. In a reflex action, she took the F train to Coney Island, where she and Robert had often gone for solace, and stayed there until dawn, watching the stars and listening to the sea. Returning to Manhattan, again by subway, Patti ran back to the Chelsea to find Linda still missing. In a shaky emotional state exacerbated by lack of sleep, Patti dashed down the verses to a poem called "Redondo Beach." Then, exhausted, she fell asleep. When she awoke, Patti discovered that Linda had returned and that her lyrics needed no revision.

In the autumn of 1971, Patti retreated into a relationship with yet another new lover. Allen Lanier played keyboards in Blue Oyster Cult, a successful heavy-metal band, and he proved to be as successful as Robert Mapplethorpe was at focusing Patti's energy. Becoming involved with Lanier was a good example of Patti's survivor instinct, too, for he was quite different from her other lovers but exactly what she needed now: a place to hide out, slow down, cool out, and take stock. Frantically busy for three years, writing, performing, and bouncing from one passionate affair to another, she had spread herself too thin, let her heart get broken too often. She needed to reconnect with that part of herself that required letting the subconscious take over.

"Everybody was asking me to do stuff," Patti commented. "So I went into hiding. I'd been through so many shattering experiences, especially with men . . . Bobby [Neuwirth] broke my heart, he really did, and I was dispersing myself all over New York. So it was the right time for me to just sit down and find out what was going on inside me—I had been working on the surface for so long. I was never phony; it's just that I was moving more on an image basis than on a heart or soul basis."

Patti recognized that Allen Lanier suited her need to get in touch with her feminine side and stop being the aggressive, outgoing tomboy. She viewed this relationship as highly successful, for it provided her with the rest she needed. Patti felt that the next time she went out she was going to have to really make it, so her relationship with Allen was like a pit stop to check out and repair her inner workings. Part of it had to do with getting in touch with the woman inside. For a while she tried to lead the life of a housewife—for artistic reasons.

"Allen wasn't dangerous, he was a nice guy" said Deerfrance, a sometime singer who lived with musician Fred Smith, later of Television, and knew Patti fairly well. "I think that's as close as she ever came to finding a guy like her father. Patti's father was a very religious man. I think Patti had the little girl thing of being in love with your father. That was a strong thing with her. Everybody had issues with their parents, but nobody talked about it. Everybody else got stoned and mutilated themselves instead. She was looking for the love, always looking for the boyfriend. Her father was supposedly a good man, which is rare. None of us had good fathers, and she did. So she went from boy to boy, thinking that she could re-create that, that she could find a good man. Then she'd hook up with someone who was obviously not good. When she finally did find a good guy, she didn't stay with him. That's what girls always do: go with the dangerous one."

As the least flamboyant of Patti's extraordinary gallery of lovers, Allen Lanier might have seemed at first an unlikely candidate to be Patti's prime collaborator as she metamorphosed from a poet into a rock 'n' roll singer. But Allen had a lot to offer. Unlike Shepard, Carroll, Neuwirth, and Mapplethorpe, Lanier was not a tortured artist, but, rather, a stable, dependable man who treated rock 'n' roll as more of a job than a calling. Through him, Patti was able to learn a lot of the nuts and bolts of the music business. Withdrawing from the limelight for a time, she absorbed everything around her like a sponge. This was clearly the period in which she put together the pieces of the puzzle that would form the act that would take her right to the rock 'n' roll stage.

Before the end of 1971, Allen had moved into the Twenty-third Street loft with Patti and Robert. Mapplethorpe was not at all threatened by Allen, who easily fitted into their daily life. Eventually, however, Patti wanted more privacy to nurture her relationship with Allen, and, besides, she no longer found it amusing to witness the constant, all-hours parade of Robert's downtown tricks and uptown patrons flowing through the loft. Allen and Patti began looking for an affordable apartment in Greenwich Village, and Robert's patron Sam Wagstaff would soon buy him a loft downtown.

Nineteen seventy-one was a peak year for rock writers, an almost exclusively male group whose lives were so dramatically affected by rock 'n' roll that they wrote about it with an intensity that matched the Beats writing about sex, drugs, and Zen. Patti distinguished herself as a rock writer that September when a large portfolio of her poems was published in *Creem,* the Detroit-based rock monthly that was a rawer, harder, irreverent sister to *Rolling Stone.* Patti was well on her way to becoming what she claimed she had always wanted to be: "one of those rock writers."

Now that she had the gig, though, she realized that it was not going to work. "I stopped doing rock writing because I couldn't wait to meet Rod Stewart, but then when I met him I didn't want to ask him about his work; I wanted to show him mine," she said. "Because of my ego and my faith in my own work, I don't like meeting people on unequal terms. So I figured I'd stop doing that and would wait until they discovered me, and we could meet on equal grounds."

Before she actually left, however, the conflict reached its peak in an interview she did with Eric Clapton. After asking him what his favorite color was, she turned off the tape recorder and ran away, leaving a bemused Clapton alone, stroking his beard.

Gerard Malanga was shocked to read Patti's comment in *Creem* about the St. Mark's show: "It was Gerard's night . . . I was supposed to be the dumb little group supporting the big star," Patti wrote, obviously not willing to give anyone else credit or even acknowledgment for her success. Yet despite the comment, Malanga persuaded Telegraph Press to publish a book of Patti's poetry. It was the only book that the press ever published on which we agreed without any hesitation, it was so obviously right for its time. Patti took no small amount of persuading, however, because, for a short time in the spring and summer of 1971, she was high on the list of New York's "Hot 100" who were going to Make It, and was turning down offers right, left, and center.

So, why did she give her first book to a small, unknown publisher that offered her no contract, no advance, and no royalties? Telegraph Books had offered to print one thousand copies of her book in its uniform format and do its best to sell them at one dollar each, cheap even in 1971. What Patti seemed to like about Andrew and me was our energy. We came on like the City Lights of the seventies, calling ourselves the "electric generation" and talking big. Like Patti, we believed in poetry passionately and were dead serious about what we were doing. Patti responded to our intensity.

It was Andrew who clinched the deal. A short essay he'd published in February 1971, the month of the St. Mark's reading, may have convinced Patti that she had found someone on the same intellectual wavelength as herself. The essay, which appeared in a special Andrew Wylie issue of the Philadelphia magazine *Telegrams*, was direct and forceful in summing up where he stood on the topic of poetry at the beginning of the decade: He could no longer relate to long works like Ginsberg's "Howl" or Pound's

Cantos. Living as we were in an extremely violent, fragile time, he was drawn to short, almost amputated works. The essay went on to express an intellectual's interpretations of the vibrations he felt surrounded by, concluding that just to be alive in such times was an act of violence. The essay was a response to the social and cultural confusion that marked the beginning of the seventies, after the sixties had exploded in our faces at Altamont, in the eyes of Charles Manson, and with the increasingly dangerous drug scene that had changed from something peaceful and friendly to something violent, dangerous, and criminal. Patti received a copy of the essay and was most likely impressed by its sense of urgency regarding making it now, about doing something now.

What the culture clearly needed was some kind of leader, or at least a voice it could call its own. Whether Patti Smith was aware of it or not, she had provided that voice for the first time at St. Mark's Church on the now-historic occasion of her first reading there. And while she did not yet have the confidence that she would need to answer this call, she would soon acquire it through a series of highly successful poetry readings. It didn't come immediately, though, for she did not follow the St. Mark's success with any further performances in 1971. Her next triumph would not be until she read in London, almost a year after St. Mark's.

In January 1972, Patti flew to London to read at the publisher John Calder's Better Books series with Gerard Malanga, Andrew Wylie, and myself. The event, held in a small, luxurious porn theater hired for the occasion by Calder, was a tentative step onto the international stage, and Patti used it to make a considerable impact on the small, though influential, London poetry scene. One hundred twenty-five people, including Michael Horowitz and Eric Motram, showed up—an unusually high number for a poetry reading, which might normally attract fifteen or twenty. This turnout was due in part to Malanga's reputation, and in part to that of Lou Reed. Reed, a founding member of the Velvet Underground, was in town recording his first solo LP. A summit meeting between the Velvet Underground's great interpretational dancer and the composer of "Heroin" made the weekly music papers, and drew attention to the reading. Malanga's reading did not disappoint; he was outstanding, holding the attention of the entire audience throughout. Patti, meanwhile, was unknown in London (although a nude still of her from Sandy Daley's film *Robert Having His Nipple Pierced* had recently appeared on the cover of weekly listings magazine *Time Out*), but she really mesmerized the crowd as she opened the second half of the evening.

Part of Patti's talent was sizing up an audience, and she showed this in London. Hitting the spotlight in her signature skin-tight black pants and an extra large T-shirt, in her little girl voice she coyly explained to the crowd how she had forgotten to bring along the piece she had planned to read, that she'd left it in the hotel. She told them that she was nevertheless going to try to remember the poem as she went along and would appreciate it if "you guys would just like, you know, give me a break and stuff." Then she bent into the microphone and spit out a dark, convoluted story. After about six minutes, she had the audience completely mesmerized, at which point she dramatically stopped. A look of pain came crossed her face and she shook herself, muttering, "Gee, uh, I forgot it!" She arched her back, scratched around her crotch, and then, laughing conspiratorially, begged the audience to stay with her. She forged ahead, smiling through the second half of her recitation as if it was all part of the show. By the time the set finished, Patti had completely won over the audience. This was no small feat, either: as an American, a woman, and a poet with a predilection for rock imagery, she faced a steep uphill battle going in. But Patti's innate charisma evoked an undeniable, positive response from even skeptical audiences. Thanks to Patti's reading coupled with Gerard's success, some of the awed poets who stayed afterward told Bockris and Wylie that the Telegraph Poets, as we were billing ourselves, had changed the London poetry scene overnight.

The visit to London also gave Patti a chance to see Sam Shepard, who was living there with his family. The always-accommodating Gerard Malanga, who had done more than anyone to encourage Patti as a poet, gave the couple the key to his room in the chic Portobello Hotel, where they spent an afternoon. The following day, Patti turned up at a Telegraph Books photo session outside Ezra Pound's house in Kensington—with Shepard. After making us swear that we wouldn't tell a soul that she was seeing Sam, Patti proceeded to make out with him wildly, right there in the street, while Gerard snapped photographs. She had gotten so into the confrontational mode that everything she did became a confrontation.

Back in New York in the spring of 1972, *Seventh Heaven* was published. Usually, such an event is, or should be, among the most positive experiences of a poet's career, but Patti also turned this into a confrontation. When Andrew and I had taken delivery of the manuscript from her, she made us feel like the most important people in her life, and went on about how much she admired our uniform-format books and the other writers whose work we had published. When I returned to her Twenty-third Street loft a few months later with forty copies of her book, however, she was surprisingly cold and withdrawn, as if my visit was a burden. As I followed her across the room to a desk where she had been sitting, looking for somewhere to put down the box of books, she started complaining about how she had been tricked into signing a contract that gave her no royalties, that we were only out to rip her off. Angered and hurt by such a silly charge and one that seemed to lessen the value of the moment, I attempted to explain that it would be impossible for us to cover our costs even if we sold out the entire edition. But try as I might, I could see that this was making little impact on her, and that the idea that we had robbed her was fixed in her mind.

The truth was that in 1972, month by month, week by week, success was coming closer and closer for Patti, and with it the paranoia that can destroy all of its pleasure. That day, I finally managed to persuade her to do a major interview to celebrate the book's release. Agreeing, she paused and looked at the book closely, for the first time. Like all our books, *Seventh Heaven* was designed as a five-by-seven-inch paperback. On the cover it had a black-and-white photograph of Patti, with the book's title above the photo and her name below it. We had accepted Patti's manuscript as it was and made no editing suggestions, even down to the photograph she wanted for the cover. Opening the book was a dedication to Mickey Spillane and Anita Pallenberg, followed by a saying: "and god created seventh heaven, saying let them/ all in. and caused it to be watched over by the/ bitch and the aeroplane."

This was followed by a contents page, which flashed to the reader, like an advertisement, the names of Joan of Arc, Edie Sedgwick, Marianne Faithfull, Amelia Earhart, and Céline, as well as the words "cocaine" and "crystal," and titles like "Death by Water," "Girl Trouble," and "A Fire of Unknown Origin," which almost rumbled with the promise of a short, sharp, fiery set of lyrics rather than poems. Indeed, in flipping through the book's forty-eight pages, one noticed that most of the poems were, if not always short, certainly quick reading, since the lines were often only three or four words long. The whole book could be read in twenty minutes, and probably was by those fans who snapped it up, eager to get to know more about this new figure who had suddenly arrived on the scene—for the first time there was something of Patti's that they could take home and treasure. Due to poor distribution, however, the book's first edition sold only about seven hundred copies, but it received more reviews than the majority of poetry books because of a carefully orchestrated campaign among Patti's rock writer contacts in *Creem*, *Crawdaddy*, and *Rolling Stone*. The reviews were good; as a set, the poems are tight, and they work. Moreover, they are the seeds out of which "Piss Factory" and *Horses* would grow.

Patti ended up carrying a copy of the book around with her for two weeks, remembering that she "liked to carry it on buses and hoped people would recognize it was me on the cover." Today, she is still proud of it: "I'll stand behind that book. I think it's a damn good book." Musician and poet Richard Hell (later a member of Television), who had met Patti through Andrew Wylie in 1972, thought *Seventh Heaven* a breakthrough. "Patti's book was really cool," said Hell. "It sort of flaunted its street, its real-life world. It was full of references to Bob Dylan and Anita Pallenberg, and all about sex and drugs and violence. It was about the true environment, but at the same time it was very sophisticated writing. Patti had tapped into a level of pure-blood intensity, but she also had a great ear for the music of the words. The writing had a timeless quality in terms of its construction and its music and was very pretty, but at the same time unpretentious and street-aggressive. It was dazzling."

One person less than happy about the book's release was Gerard Malanga, who had been largely responsible for getting it published in the first place. "When the book came out, I felt the way I felt about her remark in *Creem* [about the St. Mark's reaching]. She was thanking Bobby Neuwirth and this guy and that guy, but she never mentioned me. Also, I thought that dedicating the book to Anita Pallenberg was brownnosing. Anita remarked that she didn't even know who Patti Smith was and thought it was a bit presumptuous."

Seventh Heaven was the first complete work written by Patti Smith on her own, and it remains her finest, most complete achievement in the poetic field and her best book. Deborah Frost, in her 1997 essay in *Rock Women*, sees *Seventh Heaven* forming the base of Patti's oeuvre, and representing the first work in a trilogy that would be filled out by "Piss Factory" and *Horses*. By itself, *Seventh Heaven* defined Patti's public persona, and helped pave the way for the work that would make Patti world famous as a rock 'n' roll singer-songwriter.

Patti made a second pilgrimage to Paris in the early summer of

1972, accompanied again by her sister Linda. This time, rather than searching for Rimbaud, her visit focused on Doors singer Jim Morrison, who had died there one year earlier and was buried in Père Lachaise, the famous cemetery. At Morrison's grave she had a vision, which she wrote about in "Jukebox Crucifix," a final essay for *Creem* magazine.

This was one of her better prose pieces and has since its initial publication been anthologized. It commences with Patti admitting that she was going to Paris to rid herself of the demons who were holding her back, injecting her with fear of moving on. She hoped Jim Morrison might rise out of his tomb and duet with her in an a capella version of "What's Wrong with Me!" Instead, she discovered herself standing by his grave in a torrential rainstorm "trying to conjure up some kind of grief or madness."

Two hours later, covered with mud and paralyzed by fear, she suddenly realized that she had to let go of all her old role models. No sooner had she come to this conclusion than, like a great vision accompanied by choirs of angels, brand-new, exciting plans, and visions of dramatic new journeys stormed through her brain. Suddenly, she couldn't think of anything except of getting back to New York and back to work. On her way out of the cemetery she made a pit stop at Rimbaud's grave, but he didn't say a word either and it just got colder. Finally, with one great effort, she tossed off the incubus of her dead role models. The living ones continued to have a hold on her.

Returning to New York, in July 1972 Patti saw the Rolling Stones at Madison Square Garden on the final night of their U.S. tour. It gave her hope for the future of poetry: "Jagger had done two concerts and was on the brink of collapse—but the kind of collapse that transcends into magic. He was so tired he could hardly sing. What was foremost was not the music but the performance. It was his presence and his power to hold the audience in his palm. He could've spoken some of his best lyrics and had the audience just as magnetized. I saw the complete future of poetry. I got so excited I could hardly stand being in my skin, and that gave me faith to keep on going."

On August 15, in the front room of her loft and in the presence of her sister Linda, Patti and I finally conducted the interview we'd discussed to hype *Seventh Heaven*'s release. It was published in October in a three-hundred-copy underground magazine in Philadelphia created by the poet Jeff Goldberg primarily for that purpose. Read today, in light of the plethora of mythmaking interviews that Patti has given since, it appears to be remarkably honest.

Patti spoke of her self-image and her ambitions, giving a more revealing account of herself than she would ever give again into a tape recorder:

I'm not a fame fucker, but I am a hero worshipper. I've always been in love with heroes; that's what seduced me into art. . . . But poets have become simps. There's this new thing: the poet is a simp, the sensitive young man always in the attic, but it wasn't always like that. It used to be that the poet was a performer and I think the energy of Frank O'Hara started to reinspire that. In the sixties there was all that happening stuff. Then Frank O'Hara died and it sort of petered out and then Dylan and Allen Ginsberg revitalized it, but then it got all fucked up again because instead of people learning from Dylan and Allen Ginsberg and realizing that a poet was a performer they thought a poet was a social protester. So it got fucked up. I ain't into social protesting.

I've found [presenting poetry as public art] has more to do with the physical presence. Physical presentation in performing is more important than what you're saying. Quality comes through, of course, but if your quality of intellect is high and your love of the audience is evident and you have a strong physical presence, you can get away with anything. . . . Billy Graham is a great performer even though he is a hunk of shit. Adolf Hitler was a fantastic performer. He was a black magician. And

I learned from that. You can seduce people into mass consciousness.

Asked if she was bisexual, Patti claimed that she was "completely heterosexual": "I tried to make it with a chick once and I thought it was a drag. She was too soft. I like hardness. . . . I like bone. I like muscle. I don't like all that soft breast." She also explained the feminine influence on her work: "Most of my poems are written to women because women are most inspiring. Who are most artists? Men. Who do they get inspired by? Women. The masculinity in me gets inspired by female. . . . I fall in love with men and they can take me over. I ain't no women's-lib chick. So I can't write about a man because I'm under his thumb."

Patti felt that her primary function as a poet was to "entertain," but also important to her was to "give people breathing room." Her meaning, she explained, was that

I don't mean any of the stuff I say. When I say that bad stuff about God or Christ, I don't mean that stuff. I don't know what I mean; it's just it gives somebody a new view, a new way to look at something. I like to look at things from ten or fifteen different angles. . . . [So] it gives people a chance to be blasphemous through me. The other thing is that through performance I reach such states in which my brain feels so open, so full of light, it feels huge. It feels as big as the Empire State Building, and if I can develop a communication with an audience, a bunch of people, when my brain is that big and very receptive, imagine the energy and the intelligence and all the things I can steal from them.

She named her three favorite living American poets as Jim Carroll, Bernadette Mayer, and Muhammad Ali, "because they're all good performers. Ali's . . . got great rhythms. He's a good writer in a certain frame of reference. He's entertaining. Bernadette Mayer because I like what she does conceptually. She's a real speed-driven poet."

"I get a kick out of myself. . . . I act like a bitch, a motherfucker. It's like when I'm doing this interview—I act real tough, and then my boyfriend comes in and I apologize to him and say, 'I'll be finished quick, baby.' I'm like a chameleon. . . . I can fall into the rhythm of almost any situation as it calls for me. . . . I'll be a sexpot, I'll be a waif. . . . I'm flexible. I can marry the moment."

The writing methods Patti applied to the book were described in detail, using "Judy" as an example:

Most of my poems I write two ways. I write them from first writing a letter to someone who will never receive the letter or I write recording a dream. "Skunk Dog" was a complete dream.

Judy was a girl I was in love with in the brain. I'm in love with her because we have similar brain energy. We can travel through time. We have this fantastic way of communicating. But she doesn't let me touch her. She's one girl that maybe I would like to have done something to. At one point, I was really obsessed with her and she wouldn't let me. . . . She went away to Nepal and right before she left she grabbed me and kissed me and I was so shocked I pushed her away and she said, "You blew it," just 'cause I was too chickenshit. . . . [A]s soon as she reached out for me I got scared. I'm a phony.

So anyway, Judy was away, and I loved her so much I couldn't stand it. I started dreaming of her. So I was trying to write her a letter, but when you really love someone it's almost impossible to write them. It's people you love the most who you can't communicate with verbally. I had such a strong mental contact with this girl that I couldn't talk to her. So I was at the typewriter. It's made writing a much more physical thing. I write with the same fervor as Jackson Pollock used to paint. . . . I started writing down in a line, just words but, you know, words that were perfect, words like "kodak," "radiant," "jellybitch," and I just tried writing these words. . . .

I was trying to write her a letter but I had no idea where she was, so obviously it was a piece of narcissism. . . . I was trying to project with words and language a photograph of Judy.

With the help of the interview as well as publicity from Patti's rock-journalist friends, *Seventh Heaven* caused more of a stir than most poetry books by new authors. In turn, Patti started thinking of herself as a successful writer. The book definitely furthered her reputation in the ranks of the underground and the avant garde, where being published by anyone other than oneself was considered a success. To capitalize on the attention surrounding the book's publication, Patti returned to the stage and gave as many readings as possible. "I sell 'cause I got a good personality and people really like me," she said excitedly in our interview. "When people buy my book, they're really buying a piece of Patti Smith. That book is autobiographical. It sheds the light of my heroes on it."

Seventh Heaven presents a self-portrait of Patti in the images of her male and female heroes. Having straddled the gender barrier all her life, she comes down on both sides of it. Her female models—Marianne Faithfull, Anita Pallenberg, Joan of Arc, Amelia Earhart, and Edie Sedgwick—have in common that they gambled with their lives to achieve distinction, and, for the most part, lost. The same can be said of their male counterparts: Brian Jones, Jimi Hendrix, Jim Morrison, Keith Richards, and Bob Dylan. In both galleries, however, there are one or two who fell but rose again, like Marianne Faithfull and Bob Dylan, and it is these characters whom Patti praises or wants above all to be. "Most women writers don't interest me because they're hung up with being a woman, they're hung up with being Jewish, they're hung up with being somebody or other," she said. "I mean, to me, Erica Jong ain't a woman, she's just some spoiled rich girl who'd rather whine than go out of her brain."

Despite such tough talk, Patti was in reality wrestling with what it meant to be a woman. Of the time, on another occasion, she said, "When I was writing my *Seventh Heaven* book, I was in my early twenties and going through this crisis that I had to learn to become a girl. I started buying dresses and gold bracelets and trying to walk in high heels, buying silk stockings, garter belts, sitting around completely self-conscious with all this stuff, trying to figure out what all this stuff meant."

"Patti was so girlie," recalled Bebe Buell. "She liked to put on a dress. She liked to make dinner and do laundry. She could be downright subservient to a man. It wasn't a contradiction to her. She felt you could embody all the things that men embody, but you could still be a woman."

Adopting yet another mask, Patti took a page from the Tennessee Williams play *A Streetcar Named Desire* and cast herself as a Stella Kowalski–like figure, and pontificated on the pleasures of being punched around by a lover. "It was the first time I considered that a woman's true position was on her back, the first time I assumed a completely passive role . . . I'm different now, I don't mind getting knocked around a little."

"The French poet Rimbaud predicted that the next great crop of writers would be women," Patti reminded another rock writer, Nick Tosches. "He was the first guy who ever made a big women's-liberation statement, saying that when women release themselves from the long servitude of men they're really gonna gush. New rhythms, new poetries, new horrors, new beauties. And I believe in that completely. Everytime I say the word 'pussy' at a poetry reading, some idiot broad rises and has a fit. 'What's your definition of pussy, sister?' I dunno; it's a slang term. If I wanna say 'pussy,' I'll say 'pussy.' But all these tight-assed movements are fucking up our slang, and that eats it."

Nick Tosches had met Patti in the early seventies, right around the time he got married. "I remember that because Patti gave me a really nice painting as a wedding gift," Tosches recalled. "Richard Meltzer and I went to see her do a poetry reading at St. Mark's Church. She was playing with our friend Lenny Kaye for the first time. It was the only time I ever sniffed lighter fluid in a church."

Before the end of the year, Middle Earth Books in Philadelphia published Patti's second volume of poetry, a slim pamphlet entitled *Kodak*. Around this time, too, Patti began to hang out at the Gotham Book Mart, whose owner, Andreas Brown, was much like the Chelsea's Stanley Bard in making a point of recognizing and supporting young artists who showed promise. He gave Patti a show of her drawings in the gallery above his shop, bringing her one step closer to being an established New York artist. ("Patti always looked bizarre and emaciated," he recalled. "I felt sorry for her.") And throughout, she was writing. Returning to the loft every night, Patti would "sit at the typewriter and type until I feel sexy," she confided. "Then I'd go and masturbate to get high, and then I'd come back in that higher place and write some more." From this vantage point she fought to extricate herself from the influence of the St. Mark's and New York–school poets, and in doing so rapidly penned the poems that would become her third book, *Witt*, published by the Gotham Book Mart in September 1973.

In early 1973, Patti acquired a manager, Jane Friedman. Friedman ran the Wartoke Concern, a publicity firm, and had a good head for business. She was a natural manager, who liked to take care of people and used her imaginative ideas to produce the results they wanted in their careers. Her original and creative approach to her work had garnered her clients including Stevie Wonder, and Patti hoped Jane's guidance would allow her to focus on her music and grow as an artist. Jane, however, was not eager to manage Patti Smith, who looked like she lived on five dollars a day. Not one to give up easily, though, Patti, whose ability to find people's Achilles' heels got her over a number of hurdles, pretended to be suffering from terminal tuberculosis—and Jane agreed to see her. Instantly charmed by Patti's happy ugly-duckling routine, she took her into the Wartoke family.

At the time, Jane was regularly furnishing acts for the Mercer Arts Center. The Mercer, a three-story building that housed a video room, various workshops, and a club called the Oscar Wilde Room, was the coolest place on the downtown scene that season. New York's premier group of the day, the New York Dolls, was the house band. The Dolls were very influential as far as the downtown (and later the world) music scene was concerned; they were the first New York City rock 'n' roll band to really make a splash nationally. In the sixties, there were Long Island groups like the Vagrants and the Rascals, and after that came the Greenwich Village folk-rock scene with bands like the Magicians and the Lovin' Spoonful, and the influential Velvet Underground from Andy Warhol's Factory. All of them gained some notoriety and were important in the city, but in 1973, the Dolls ruled the downtown New York scene. And while their costumes were arresting—they wore sequined pants with off-the-shoulder tops, ladies' pumps or platform boots, and hair sprayed and teased out to there—the original music they played was based on American rhythm and blues and straighforward rock. By their very existence, the Dolls gave a certain inspiration and focus to the New York rock scene, which in turn spawned groups like the Forty-second Street Harlots, the Miamis, and Teenage Lust. They also inspired Jane: in the up-for-grabs atmosphere of the ever-changing New York underground, 1973 was a good year for poetry, and Jane dreamed up a slot for Patti to do ten minutes of material opening for the Dolls. It quickly became a regular gig.

When Patti met Jane, she was in the midst of putting together a poetry act, soon to be dubbed Rock n Rimbaud. Using props like a megaphone and a toy piano like the one she'd used in Paris, and borrowing a little courage from Lenny Bruce, she dived onstage only to find herself facing a tidal wave of vicious catcalls and jarring japes. But rather than caving in and running off crying, "They don't like me!" Patti shot back better than she got, putting away the hecklers with tougher, funnier lines. The word Jane used to describe her at the time perfectly sums up the soul of Patti Smith circa 1973: "valiant."

Until she joined forces with Friedman, though, Patti had not known how to capitalize on the momentum that her work and her appearances generated. Friedman, on the other hand, *did* know, and the relationship between the two women is one of the legends of punk rock. Friedman began to book Patti in various venues on a regular basis so that she could hone her performance skills. She performed at the Mercer Arts Center throughout that spring, reading her poetry and learning to deal with feisty audiences. Developing her act through these appearances, Patti turned her defensiveness into her shtick, modeling herself as much on the talk-show host Johnny Carson as on Rimbaud. The result was a surreal combination of literary pop-culture references, delivered in a bebop style.

She drew much material from her early years. "There's a lot of New Jersey in my stuff," she told Nick Tosches. "South Jersey. It's all railroad tracks, hanging out by the tracks. I guess it all goes back to that. Most of the cool people I knew in South Jersey are dead now, or in jail, or disappeared. A couple are pimps in Philly. I haven't seen them in about twelve years, but a week doesn't go by that I don't think of 'em. The coolest things I have, the coolest rhythms, all come from my life in South Jersey and Philly. All my dance steps, all my sensibilities. I think about all that old stuff a lot when I'm onstage. Those people, they haunt me in a real sweet way."

Patti's act was benefiting from the regular gigs, and getting attention, too. Ed Friedman, who worked at the St. Mark's Poetry Project, witnessed an outstanding performance by Patti that summer: "It was amazing. There could've been easily fifty, sixty, seventy people on this rooftop of a big industrial loft. It was the biggest audience that we'd had."

That same month, Allen Ginsberg described and dissected Patti's style for a Philadelphia journalist. "What Patti Smith seems to be doing may be a composite—a hybrid—of the Russian style of declaimed poetry, which is memorized, and the American development of oral poetry that was from the coffee houses, now raised to pop-spotlight circumstances and so declaimed from memory again with all the artform—or artsong—glamour that goes along with Liddy Lane . . . maybe. Then there's an element that goes along with borrowing from the pop stars and that spotlight, too, and that glitter. But it would be interesting if that did develop into a national style. IF the national style could organically integrate that sort of arty personality—the arty Rimbaud—in its spotlight with makeup and T-shirt."

The latter half of 1973 also brought the first intellectual assessment of Patti's poetry. Kate Bullen published a piece in the *Oxford Literary Review* called "Sexual Bruising," in which she wrote

Patti Smith first received her telepathic wisdom rhythms in the petrol scented plains of America's "Garden State," New Jersey. She soon jumped her small-town compass, slipping into her sexy black pants, balanced out by her schoolboy jacket. In the early seventies Patti Smith was a member of Warhol's androgynous beauties living under the florescent lights of New York City's Chelsea Hotel . . . Her performances were sexual bruisings with spasms of Jagger and the off-key of Dylan. Her musical poems often came from her poetical fantasies of Rimbaud.

This was heady stuff for a guttersnipe from New Jersey, but somehow oddly fitting: Patti was that rare bird who can relate and appeal equally to the salons of the establishment and the dungeons of the underground. And now that she was emerging from the underground, Patti was beginning to feel a sense of urgency—suddenly she was in a hurry to make it. In May, she moved up to play Kenny's Castaways, opening for singer Cathy Chamberlain's Rock

and Rag Revue. There, Patti did some of her more risqué material, including her poem "Rape," which shocked the critic for the
Village Voice who was there that night. He wrote that Patti was "in
the vanguard of cultural mutation; a cryptic androgynous Keith
Richards look-alike poetess-appliqué."

Patti saw the review and responded. "When I wrote that poem
'Rape,' I thought there were great jokes in it, like 'I'm a wolf man
in a lamb skin trojan.' I think of myself not as male or female or
rapist but as a comedian. When I'm writing, I'm just like a novelist. Novelists have to slip into the skins of all kinds of people, and
so do I. I'd like to taste everything in life and I probably won't get
a chance to rape or murder anybody, so sometimes I just psych
myself up to feel like a rapist or a murderer. To write that rape
poem, I read all these articles about Richard Speck [a notorious
mass murderer who killed seven student nurses in the sixties]. He
was a really disgusting guy—he wore ski sweaters and had short
hair. And I just lurked about the room for a while, letting the saliva
come out of my mouth, till I felt like Speck."

In September 1973, the Gotham Book Mart published Patti's
third book of poems, *Witt*, aligning her with such renowned poets
as W. H. Auden and Edith Sitwell, only solidifying her reputation.
"By the time the Gotham Book Mart published *Witt*, Patti had become a legend on the New York poetry circuit," wrote Nick
Tosches. "She was feared, revered, and her public readings elicited
the sort of gut response that had been alien to poetry for more
than a few decades. Word spread, and people who avoided poetry
as the stuff of four-eyed pedants found themselves oohing and
howling at what came out of Patti's mouth. Established poets
feared for their credence. Many well-known poets refused to go
on after Patti at a reading, she was that awesome."

learning to stand naked
1973-1975

> "The occupation of rock 'n' roll is so
> appealing now—it's an outlet for passions
> and ideas too radical for any other form."
> *richard hell*

Now that Patti had hit her stride as a poet she immediately began
to broaden her act. The first thing she did was hook up with
Lenny Kaye again. He had come to her rooftop reading and said
hello afterwards, and Patti started visiting the record store where
he worked. Soon they were a duo.

Patti and Lenny were not thinking of themselves as a rock band
just yet, but rather as an act: a poet who used rock 'n' roll imagery
and rhythms, accented by an electric guitar. Chris Stein, then

playing in the Stilettoes with Debbie Harry, didn't think that Patti was really serious about her act at that point. "The first time I saw Patti, she was speaking at some Notre Dame show," Chris recalled. "She did a poetry reading and then brought Lenny out to play with her. He was playing real lousy, just bashing these chords out and drowning her out and she'd abuse him. It was almost a comedy routine that they did. She was just poking fun at the whole rock 'n' roll syndrome."

That December, between Christmas and New Year's, Patti did a four-night stand opening up for folk/protest singer Phil Ochs at Max's. At these shows, for the first time, Lenny Kaye stayed on stage throughout. Patti was moving closer to music and further from spoken poetry with each show.

What she was doing then might be called performance art today, but at the time it was impossible to categorize. John Rockwell attempted to define it in the *New York Times* when he described Patti as "a chanting poet who lifted her words beyond language with the power of music. From the first, she used the idiom of rock, but she wasn't so much a rocker as a poet-shaman who used rock to make a statement. The art was raw, bizarrely theatrical, populist. But it was art, nonetheless."

At the beginning of 1974, Patti and Lenny decided to add keyboards to their act. Coincidentally, Danny Fields was having an affair with a beautiful young guy named Richard Sohl, who happened to be a piano player. So, when Patti and Lenny told Danny of their ideas, he introduced them to Sohl. "We advertised for a piano player," Patti remembered. "And all these guys came in saying, 'Hey, wanna boogie?' Me and Lenny were stoned, trying to talk all this cosmic bullshit to them, like, 'Well, what we want to do is go over the edge.' Finally, Richard Sohl came in wearing a sailor suit, totally stoned and pompous. We said, 'This guy's fucked up.' Lenny gave him the big cosmic spiel, and Sohl said, 'Look, buddy, just play.' We felt like we were the ones getting auditioned! So Sohl said, 'Whadaya want? Ya want some classical?'

He played a bunch of Mozart. 'Ya want some blues?' He played a bunch of blues. I mean, the fuckin' guy could play anything! So we started talkin', and it turned out that he'd been raised as a Jehovah's Witness, which I had been, too. We'd both rebelled against the same shit, and that helped. So we just brought him in."

With his introduction into their "band," Patti and Lenny christened Sohl DNV, which stood for "Death in Venice," because of his resemblance to the character Tadzio in the Luchino Visconti film of the Thomas Mann novella.

They valued him for his musicianship as much as his attitude. "He had this one element, which was totally important for us: he could space out," Lenny emphasized. "He could get a space and just go, and not worry that the song ended, and he had the technique. I mean, as a guitarist I was pretty rock 'n' roll, I was very rhythmic, I didn't have a lot of solo strings. I certainly was untrained, but he was classically trained, so he could move everything harmonically, and he was so atmospheric in his playing that wherever we went, he could go, and we went any place."

The band rehearsed for hours and hours, perfecting their repertoire, in an office owned by Jane Friedman's company, Wartoke, situated behind a billboard on Times Square. Over time, Patti developed a close friendship with Sohl, and soon depended on him as much as she did on Lenny. In a lot of ways, the group was at its purest when it was a trio, a perfect balance of communication and trust.

Early in 1974, Patti appeared at Reno Sweeney, a trendy downtown cabaret. Lisa Robinson, the doyenne of the New York rock press and Patti's first champion, reviewed the show. "What Patti was doing right was very interesting and important as well. Although she was tired, she looked fabulous in a black satin pantsuit and white satin blouse. She moved comfortably through a variety of musical changes; seemed at ease with herself, even in a black feather boa, and not at all self-conscious. Mixed in with some of her poems were 'Speak Low,' the tribute to Ava Gardner, and

'One Touch of Venus' that went with it; Cole Porter's 'I Get a Kick Out of You,' dedicated to Frank Sinatra, whom Patti described as the 'Picasso of America.' "

As Patti herself had earlier, the group gained momentum and reputation, attracting an array of the curious. Andy Warhol, whose *Interview* magazine had featured Patti in 1973, attended one performance; Joey Ramone, whose band—the Ramones— would soon explode in the vanguard of punk, attended another. Nobody could pin down just what Patti Smith was doing, but they wanted to find out, and that, in turn, inspired the band. "We knew we were having an effect on the audience. That's what gave us the strength to keep going," said Lenny. "Patti was always possessed with a great deal of charisma, she always could reach out and grab an audience, and was always riveting. I never got tired of watching her. She'd be funny and then she'd read these poems and it wasn't like you had to think about what they meant—the images were really strong, they were totally street."

Even with more and more people turning up for Patti's shows, as far as she and Lenny knew, they were the only ones in New York with a mission to wake up a complacent scene.

They were almost right. Patti was friendly with the poet and bass player Richard Hell, but neither she nor Lenny had ever seen his band. Often credited with being the man who invented punk, Hell had formed a band with Tom Verlaine called the Neon Boys, which in 1974 evolved into Television, and they began playing regularly at a Lower East Side club called CBGB.

CBGB's, as it was known—for Country Bluegrass and Blues— was a bar on the Bowery at Bleecker Street that had existed in some form or another, under various names and ownerships, as far back as the turn of the century, when the area was home to vaudeville houses and bawdy theaters. Later, the Bowery became a kind of derelict row, lined with cheap hotels and cheaper bars, though many of the theaters, such as the Bouwerie Lane and the Amato Opera House, remained. When Hilly Kristal moved in and opened the place that would be CB's, in the early seventies, he conceived of it as a place for country and jazz, maybe with some poetry readings, and he built a small stage in the back next to the pool table. Originally called Hilly's on the Bowery, the bar catered to a motley group of Bowery denizens including the biker crowd, most notably Sandy Alexander, head of the New York chapter of the Hell's Angels. CBGB's initial clientele was composed of professional, full-time drinkers who often waited in line outside the place as early as eight in the morning to get a choice seat at the bar. Music didn't much interest them. And though there was a popular jazz place called Tin Pan Alley only a block away, as far as attracting a music crowd, Hilly's remained firmly on the wrong side of the tracks. Max's and the Mercer Arts Center were essentially the only places downtown for rock bands to play, and Max's tended to book bands with record-company support. When the Mercer collapsed (literally), a void was created. But while Wayne County had appeared at Hilly's once in 1973, until that March day in 1974 when Tom Verlaine and Richard Lloyd, the third of Television's four founding members, wandered by and asked Hilly for a chance to play, the Bowery bar was an unlikely candidate to step up for the Mercer, and far from being a cultural flashpoint.

All that changed when Television took over. Along with other local groups, they began playing regularly at the club. As more bands played, more musicians began coming down and hanging out, checking out the competition and socializing with friends. Soon, there was a crowd of downtown music regulars who came for the cheap drinks and the low-key atmosphere. With glitter rock on the wane, this was the inauspicious beginning of a new scene—one that everyone had been waiting for, whether they knew it or not. There was no velvet rope at CBGB's: the cover was two bucks and all of it went to the bands. Most regulars got in for free, though, so nobody was exactly getting rich—but something was definitely happening. Blondie, Chris Stein and Debbie Harry's band, lived across the street, Joey Ramone around the corner, and Patti's old friend from the Chelsea William Burroughs would soon take up residence just six blocks away.

On April 14, Patti and Lenny attended a press screening of the movie *Ladies and Gentlemen, the Rolling Stones*, a documentary of the Stones' 1972 tour. Patti dressed for the occasion in what she called her Charles Baudelaire look—a boy's black suit, with a crisp white shirt and skinny black tie. After the movie they took the subway downtown to CBGB's.

If Patti's career can be seen as a series of epiphanies, the one that followed meeting DNV was seeing Television live at CBGB's that evening. It was nothing short of a revelation. First, there was the magnificent front line of Tom Verlaine, Richard Lloyd, and Richard Hell; then there was the music—jagged, awkward, and spiky, but still mesmerizingly beautiful. A thrill like a series of electroshocks ran through Patti that night, the same feeling she'd had the first time that she'd heard Little Richard when she was a child, or the Rolling Stones when she was a teenager. It was so moving, so raw, so exposed and alive that she could hardly stop herself from bursting into tears.

CBGB's was a place that nurtured a group of artists who might never have found a home for their work elsewhere. Like the Beat generation or the pop art movement, punk rock began as a small but intense group, not more than one hundred strong. "The feeling of CBGB's was that it was like a basement or a recreation room that you took over," said journalist Roy Traykin, who wrote about the club many times for the *Soho Weekly News*. "Every night you would meet someone else who was involved, a lot of artists and students in this great melting pot. There was a real feeling that here were new ideas, something happening, like Paris in the twenties or London in the early sixties. It was a scene you could really call your own." Film director Mary Harron, an early CBGB's regular, concurred. "When I'd walk to CBGB's, I'd get so excited—everything was new. It was so exciting because I knew I was walking into the future. It was too good to be true."

Patti Smith shared with Richard Hell and Tom Verlaine a poetry background. In fact, when Hell met Patti, he was still publishing books himself, and had just started a new series called Dot.
The first Dot book had been *Yellow Flowers* by Andrew Wylie; the
most recent was entitled *Wanna Go Out?* by Theresa Stern—a
pseudonym for a collaboration between Hell and Verlaine. (It was
in this book that the term "Blank Generation" first appeared in
print.) Hell had plans to do another with Tom Verlaine, and he
had approached Patti about publishing a book of her poetry. She
had agreed, but just about the time that Hell had finished manu-
scripts from both Tom and Patti—Tom's was all typeset and ready
to go to the printer—he ceased publishing altogether. Rock 'n'
roll had become too time consuming for the young musician. Before long, the same would be true for Patti.

"Richard Hell was hanging out with Patti, and they were all
doing poetry," remembered Deerfrance. "Then Tom met Patti
through Richard. Patti liked Tom, and Tom's a hard guy to like.
Richard's much more accessible, so of course she went for the
hard one. Patti was always so supportive of her boyfriends. She
really helped Television in a large way. One time Television was
playing, and Patti showed up with a bouquet of flowers and
walked down the aisle to the foot of the stage and handed them to
Tom."

Upon seeing the band, Patti had immediately told Television's
manager, Terry Ork, "I want Tom Verlaine. He has such an Egon
Schiele look. You gotta get that boy for me." To Ork, it was a cut-
and-dried affair: "Tom was enamored of Patti as a poet and scenemaker. He believed that she was gonna make it. Plus, I guess he
liked her physically; they had the same kind of body structure."
Patti, meanwhile, saw Tom as a creature of opposites. "The way
he comes on like a dirt farmer and a prince. A languid boy with the
confused grace of a child in paradise. A guy worth losing your virginity to," is how she described him in a piece in *Rock Scene*.

"Everybody knew that Patti was nuts for Tom," said Television's rhythm guitarist, Richard Lloyd. "But I think Tom was am-bivalent. He did not want to get swallowed up by anybody."

Despite still living with Allen Lanier, Patti, like most of her contemporaries, had a casual attitude toward monogamy and didn't feel guilty about pursuing Tom. Besides, she figured, Allen was having his own affairs on the road. The only person who was wary about the romance was Richard Hell, though his concerns had nothing to do with Patti. "When they became an item, it re-ally gave Tom leverage," he explained. "Patti'd become a real star locally and brought with her all of her crowd, Lisa Robinson and all the media people. From the start, there was friction in Televi-sion, but when Patti and Tom started going out, it really hurt the balance of power. I was furious at the time; I really resented it. But it wasn't Patti's fault."

Patti's neighbor, painter Duncan Hannah, would run into her occasionally at the laundromat where she would be, in her words, "washing my old man's clothes," meaning Allen Lanier's. Patti talked to Hannah about the triangular relationship between Allen, Tom, and herself, which she wrote about in the song "We Three," and she told Bebe Buell that Tom was "the most beautiful guy in the world." Once, Debbie Harry accidentally came upon Tom and Patti kissing out behind CBGB's. "Tom blushed and Patti went, 'Fuck off!' " said Debbie. "But then, Patti didn't really ever talk to me much."

Fueled by the excitement of her gigs with Television at CBGBs, Patti decided to make a record. Robert Mapplethorpe, who was beginning to have some success with his photography, gave Patti a thousand dollars to cut a single at Electric Ladyland on West Eighth Street in Greenwich Village, the studio built by Jimi Hen-drix shortly before his death. Though it had been modernized in the few years since Hendrix had used it, the studio still held a lot of mystique. There, while Robert paced around the studio chain-smoking like a nervous executive, Patti, Lenny, and DNV laid down some history.

Patti's strongest suit had always been her ability to improvise; she had made a study of improvisation and could spontaneously invent lyrics in front of an audience or in the recording studio. One of her models was talk-show host Johnny Carson, whom she called "the master of the monologue, the human parachute." "I like the task of drawing on oneself," she later wrote. "From one's ancestors, one's God, to be a human saxophone."

Patti would take one of her poems, chant over a one- or two-chord guitar background, then segue out of the poem into a classic rock song. By applying this method with different combinations of poems and songs, she would eventually produce something as original as an Andy Warhol painting. "All our things start out initially as improvisations," she said, explaining the technique. "Lenny and I work out tunes as they go along. I have words and know how I think they should go, so we just pull it out and pull it out further until we get somewhere."

The A-side of their first record, "Hey Joe," written by Dino Valenti and previously recorded by several artists including Jimi Hendrix, is a fine example of Patti's improvisational technique. For inspiration, she drew on current headlines. In 1974, Patty Hearst, a young woman from one of America's wealthiest families, had been kidnapped by a radical group calling itself the Symbionese Liberation Army. The SLA had then staged a bank robbery and brought Hearst along, dressed in army fatigues and carrying a machine gun. The image of the young heiress captured by the bank's video monitors was flashed around the world, turning the unfortunate girl into a symbol of extremist revolution.

Patti latched on to the Patty Hearst story, telling a friend that every time she heard Patty's name on the radio or TV, she wasn't sure if they were talking about Patty Hearst or Patti Smith. It was a little bit like what Andy Warhol had experienced with the revelation of the Watergate tapes: For years, Warhol had been promoting the idea of taping everybody, all the time, then suddenly his idea was in the headlines every day. Patti immediately pinned similarities between herself and the image of a fatigue-clad, machine-gun-toting Patty Hearst posing in front of a Symbionese Liberation Army flag; this guerilla-girl image echoed her own pose as a revolutionary rock 'n' roller. The story contained the classic themes of rock 'n' roll—danger, rebellion, and sex. Rock's mostly male practitioners' credo was, in essence, "We've come to take your daughters, rape them, and they'll like it." In Patti's hard, scrappy corollary, she wondered out loud whether Hearst "had been getting it every night from a black revolutionary?" implying that she was lucky if that were the case.

"Piss Factory," the B-side, was based on Patti's experiences while working in the toy factory in Pitman, New Jersey. Although, as she said later, "the truth was stronger than the poem," "Piss Factory" was perhaps the most truthful thing she ever wrote, direct autobiography. The song ends with her vow to leave that squalid life behind: Improvising the kind of classic "I'm getting out of here" riff that many singers end songs with, she prophesied how she was going to go to New York City and become a big star.

The single was recorded in mono, and its label read "Produced by Lenny Kaye for Robert Mapplethorpe," and most of the record sleeves were signed by Patti. It was released on the independent Mer label and distributed somewhat casually. Wartoke took a tiny ad in the *Village Voice* announcing both its release and some upcoming Max's shows. The record could be ordered by mail or bought in specialty record shops like Village Oldies or Greenwich Village Disc, or in small bookstores like the Gotham Book Mart and East Side Books. Despite such low-key, inauspicious beginnings, the single would come to be recognized as a classic and was rereleased in 1977 on Sire Records. Described by one writer as "perhaps the most important record [Patti] ever made," "Hey Joe"/"Piss Factory" is thought of by many as the first punk record.

Meanwhile, Patti continued using the stage as a rehearsal room, developing her persona and songs alike, and producing works such as her great rendition of "Gloria." Onstage, Patti became her songs, dissolving into the brilliant shower of words. One Philadelphia critic wrote,

> As a performer, Smith owed much to the incantatory chants of Allen Ginsberg and the jazz recitations of Jack Kerouac, but her real antecedent was the ancient tradition of the shaman—the tribal sorcerer who acted as a medium for extrasensory worlds. With her hypnotic torrent of images, Smith could truly transport an audience outside itself. While Jim Morrison might have defined the other side, it was Smith who actually broke on through.

From August 28 to September 2, 1974, Patti (with Lenny and DNV) and Television shared a bill at Max's Kansas City, honing their skills and cementing their places in the downtown–New York hierarchy. The "Hey Joe"/"Piss Factory" single had just been released; everyone was feeling the momentum beginning to build. Patti reveled in the enthusiasm of the Max's audience—though many were there to see Television, they certainly stayed to see Patti, a good portion of them for the first time.

"The first time I saw Patti perform was in 1974," said Deerfrance. "I used to work the door at Max's, and Patti played upstairs. I would go up there, and it was just her and Lenny and DNV upstairs, and it would be a special thing. She would get up on that tiny stage and really tear it up. She was just spectacular."

For anyone who saw these shows at Max's, there was no doubt that something brand new was happening. As Television careened through songs like "Hard on Love," "Fuck Rock and Roll," and "Love Comes in Spurts," Patti was creating a surreal montage with her images of Brian Jones, Patty Hearst, Jimi Hendrix, and the Velvet Underground. Also, playing at Max's—on the bill with a rock band—and with the electric backing of Lenny and DNV,

Patti had begun to change her whole approach to performance. She was doing a lot more singing rather than her usual scatting Kerouac bebop. "Patti was always trying to get a moment to happen," said Deerfrance. But whereas someone like "Bruce Springsteen made you get into it, he was right in your face, . . . [Patti] did it so differently. She didn't have a prop, she didn't have an extension of herself, it was just her. She was doing it like she was trying to get her guts out."

The Max's shows were revelatory for another reason, as well. While Patti describes it as being "like a bird flew out of my mouth," Bebe Buell is more succinct, recalling, "I noticed for the first time that she could sing. And I saw the difference. Her voice went from her throat to her chest. Patti actually had power and control. And she got real good."

She was a smart performer, too, noted two reporters from the *New York Times* who were working on a profile of her. "Using techniques similar to those recommended by Antonin Artaud, who created the 'Theater of Cruelty,' she sets up a powerful dramatic tension by alternately scaring and eliciting protective feelings from an audience. She aims for the groin and the spine, and as soon as people realize she wants them to like her, they usually do, and things start to cook."

"I don't think we really started taking it seriously as anything until we played Max's," recalled Lenny, but, suddenly, they began to feel that they might be at the beginning of a rock renaissance. Patti, for one, saw it in their counterparts, if not her own band. As a fan of Television, Patti penned a remarkable piece on the band for the October issue of Lisa Robinson's *Rock Scene* magazine. Called "Learning to Stand Naked" (a title adapted from a line in Bob Dylan's "It's Alright, Ma [I'm Only Bleeding]). The article declared that it was one of rock 'n' roll's rules that at any given time there would always be at least one band that would stand naked, which meant being the best by being the most real, the most honest, in their work. Naming the Stones, the Yardbirds, and the Velvet Underground as examples, she introduced Television as the naked band of 1974:

> The picture they transmit is shockingly honest. And the lead singer, Tom Verlaine (initials TV), has the most beautiful neck in rock and roll. Real swan-like—fragile yet strong. He plays lead guitar with angular inverted passion like a thousand bluebirds screaming. You know, like high treble. And, like Todd Rundgren, he is blessed with long veined hands reminiscent of the great poet strangler Jack the Ripper.

At the Max's shows, Patti continued to attract the attention of the man who would become her most influential supporter after Lisa Robinson, the *New York Times* pop-music critic John Rockwell. He compared her to the poet-rocker Lou Reed for her "absorption with demonic, romantic excess."

With another ardent fan, Stephen Holden, Rockwell helped to propel Patti to commercial fortune. Holden, then working in A&R, tried to sign Patti to a record deal in 1974, and actually went so far as to record a demo with the band, but his taste was just ahead of the times and his efforts failed. Even so, word of Patti Smith was rapidly spreading beyond the confines of downtown New York. In September, for instance, Britain's *Melody Maker* reported that Patti Smith "finally and deservedly made the top billing" at Max's. "Patti is sharp one minute and innocent the next," wrote their U.S. correspondent Chris Charlesworth.

> She's a bitch straining at the leash in most of her songs, all of which are prefaced by some kind of unusual story. Her ability to hold the audience's attention is her main selling point: drift away and you'll miss something you wish you hadn't. Her version of "Hey Joe," recorded by a minor record company, is be-

coming an underground hit in the city even though the radio stations don't play it because of the suggestive remarks about Patty Hearst in the intro."

By the end of the summer, it was clear that Patti and Television were among the key bands in the rock-music revolution that would become punk.

Among Patti's hardcore fans, her move from poetry towards rock 'n' roll was cause for both celebration and concern. The poetry community had come to appreciate the attention Patti had brought to their art with her increasingly popular readings. After performing for three years, Patti was at the top of her form. In fact, many believed that she was at her best and purest when she was simply a poet backed up by Lenny Kaye's guitar. They felt her loss acutely. But the group of people who hung out at CBGB's— soon to be known as "punk rockers"—welcomed Patti's presence on their own raw, new scene.

In November, Patti, Lenny, and DNV went to California to play in a tiny bookstore in Berkeley, and then scored an audition night at Bill Graham's Fillmore West in San Francisco. Patti encountered some of her most fervent fans in California. One of them was Damita Richter, a twenty-year-old junkie and prostitute who wore a Catholic-schoolgirl uniform and knee socks with cowboy boots and a black leather jacket. "Patti came over all flirtatious and asked me who I was. I said, 'I am Damita.' So then she introduced me to Lenny Kaye. I hung out with them for a week, but I would not let Lenny fuck me. I told him I had cancer of the uterus." Lenny was bowled over by Damita's attitude and thought that she was one of the great spirits of the punk era.

After San Francisco, the group traveled to LA to play the Whiskey A Go Go, where they were greeted by another small but enthusiastic audience. These West Coast shows excited them, because for the first time they sensed that they were beginning to connect with a something bigger than just a local, New York scene. There actually appeared to be a burgeoning punk underground all around the country.

"Kids are more maniac in Berkeley than anywhere else in America," said Patti, "even more than CBGB's. It's just so incredible. They'll scream and do interpretive dancing. They don't give a shit about being cool. The East Coast is much more hip, no question about it, but on the West Coast the people have more abandon. 'Ask the Angels' [a song written about San Francisco] is a celebration. See, I think this time around rock 'n' roll is going to get a shot in the arm from New York the way it did from San Francisco in the 1960s. I think all the New York groups will be signed whether they're good or not. I think it will be a big phenomenon. But the thing is, that song, which is about what's happening in New York, is really dedicated to the kids in California. In New York, the audience always tries to be cooler than the performer, whereas in California they give up that right to the performer."

The California trip also convinced Patti and Lenny that they needed another musician to fill out their sound. So, when they returned to New York, "We had fifty guitar players come down," said Lenny. "And it was the first time we actually had to think: What are we doing and who do we need to do it with? Do we want this great blues guitar player? We were working in such weird formats that we needed someone who fitted us rather than [someone who] would take us some more traditional place. We resisted the idea of having a rock 'n' roll band for a long time. We enjoyed staying outside of tradition. We always felt it was important to keep a sense of surprise in the music."

"We had days and days of guitar players, all sorts of maniac baby geniuses from Long Island, kids with nine-hundred-dollar guitars who couldn't play anything," said Patti. "Mother had sent them—in a cab! We'd make them do forty minutes of 'Gloria.' I'd go off on this long poem about a blue T-Bird smashing into a wall of sound or some shit like that, and Lenny would keep the same three chords going, louder and louder. If the guy auditioning dropped out first, that meant he wasn't any good. These kids couldn't believe it, they thought we were nuts. Finally, Ivan Kral came in. This little Czechoslovakian would-be rock star. He said, 'I am here to be in your band.' He was so cute. And we said, 'Oh, yeah?' So we did 'Land of a Thousand Dances,' and it went on so long I though I was gonna puke. But Ivan was so nervous he wouldn't stop, and we figured that was really cool. He ain't no genius, but he's got a lotta heart, Ivan does."

Ivan Kral had actually been playing at the time of the audition with Debbie Harry's band, now called Blondie, and Patti and Lenny were familiar with his guitar work from seeing him at CBGB's. Nabbing Ivan for her own band must have been a special pleasure for Patti, for she and Debbie Harry were never friends. In fact, according to Debbie, Patti had made it clear to her on one of the rare occasions on which the two spoke that there wasn't room for both of them in this scene, and since Blondie didn't stand a chance with Patti around, Debbie should quit now, and split.

It wasn't the last time the two divas—who would both serve as inspirational models for a whole generation of female rockers from Madonna to Courtney Love—would clash. Debbie remembered Patti showing up when Blondie were auditioning drummers. "I had Clem Burke there, and she said [to Clem], 'Hey, you're pretty good, what's your name?' I said, 'Patti, I'm working with this guy.' She just went 'Oh.' You know, instead of 'Oh, pardon me'—like she hadn't done anything. Basically, [Patti] told me that there wasn't room for two women in the CBGB's scene and that I should leave the business 'cause I didn't stand a chance against her! She was gonna be the star, and I wasn't." (At the time, Blondie *was* actually considered the band least likely to succeed.)

The rivalry between Patti and Debbie seemed to be one-sided and of long standing. "If there was one person in New York who could get Patti going, it was Debbie," said Bebe Buell. "I always noticed tension [between them], and I don't feel she [Patti] took

Debbie seriously. Debbie was a great talent, a great presence, and a powerful beauty. Patti just sort of dismissed it. I'm not sure what the thing was with her and Debbie. I noticed that she was always uncomfortable around Debbie Harry–type girls." Ironically, Debbie had all the physical attributes of the women that Patti celebrated in her poetry: blondeness, beauty, and charisma. However, those attributes encountered in the flesh, combined with talent, a voice, and a healthy dose of ambition, constituted a threat.

Patti's animosity toward Debbie, however, was not characteristics of the punk scene, which at that time was generally close and supportive. Not only was there a constant game of musical chairs going on between the bands, as players hopped from one band to another, but it was quite possible that the *fans* of one band would have their own group a month later. Musicians shared histories, apartments, girlfriends, and drug habits. The punk movement (along with the simultaneous but separate disco movement) marked the last scene in which sex played a vital part. In the late seventies, it was rare to go home alone from CBGB's, Max's, or, later, the Mudd Club. "Punk may have expressed a nihilistic point of view, but there was a whole lot of life-affirming stuff going on—everything was just oozing sex," said Deerfrance. "There was still romance, there was still passion, but mainly there was a whole lot of sex. And now there's not. Now rock stars date models and nobody seems to have sex. Back then, if you had one room with no heat you would not be alone at night. The juices were flowing, and it made the bands and everyone want to go out and meet each other. It was real life."

Hard feelings would abound in the CBGB's scene as bands came closer and closer to success—or failure. The demon of competition entered a scene that had been predominantly supportive and friendly. Patti had already experienced a good deal of success before she came to CBGB's, and, apart from Television, she would never really mix or be particularly supportive of any of the other CBGB bands.

horses

1975

"I came into rock 'n' roll for political
reasons, to be like Paul Revere. We weren't
great at the beginning, but we felt like
human alarm clocks: 'Wake up! Wake up!' "

patti smith

In March and April 1975, the Patti Smith Group and Television
played a two-month weekend residency at CBGB's. These performances made both the bands and the club a part of rock history.
"There are many spectacular moments in rock 'n' roll," said Leee
Black Childers, "but few magic ones when you witness the birth of
a great, great artist. Lisa Robinson is one of the toughest critics
you could possibly face, but she and I would sit open-mouthed on
these rickety chairs, in this club that stank and was in a dangerous

neighborhood, because Patti was doing astounding things—with cadence and rhythm and image. She was telling us rock 'n' roll in a different way, and we were astonished that all of New York wasn't already clamoring at her feet."

"Patti had a determination," said Deerfrance. "She wouldn't give up. I remember one time onstage she kept coming back, waiting for that moment. Like, instead of going to bed with someone and just doing it, why not get it right? Why do it at all if you're not going to do it right? Like, hey, something's supposed to happen here! Patti's always had that attitude. Once, she was banging her head against the piano. I was crying . . . I couldn't believe she was making herself more raw, taking off layer after layer. I had never seen anybody that vulnerable. She started banging her head on the piano again and she started bleeding. All of a sudden the music caught up with her, and she was trying to get the band where she was, and they were trying, but they just weren't doing what she needed them to do, and she was destroying herself. I've seen Iggy and all the rest and it was always the boys doing it. I had never seen a girl just do herself in because she really wanted to get something across and she wasn't going to stop until she got it. She was actually bleeding and then she staggered to the microphone and it all came together, this moment—I just couldn't believe it! I was so awed by this tiny girl being so brave. She was just so brave."

"Tom Verlaine flickering his eyelids and doing deep knee bends to 'Little Johnny Jewel,' Patti Smith extending her slender, spidery fingers to weave the lyrics of 'The Hunter Gets Captured by the Game,' Richard Hell running a frantic hand through his fork cut while guitarist Bob Quine (sunglasses, drooping cigarette) loitered on the sidelines, looking like the last word in best bedraggled cool—these are some of the snapshots one carries from the heralded early days of CBGB's," wrote James Wolcott. Patti was not so vivid, recalling the CBGB's residency as "an amplified period of [poetic] exploration" with Verlaine and Hell.

The Television–Patti Smith Group run at CB's helped to

"make" the club by drawing together a notably eclectic audience, CBGB's was only a block away from Robert Mapplethorpe's Bond Street loft, so he frequently dropped by to hear Patti perform on his way to the leather bars. In addition, Blondie lived down the street and the Ramones' loft was only a block away, and many bands hung out at CBGB's even when not on the bill, rounding out the audience with musicians as well as fans. As word spread, people like Lou Reed and Andy Warhol started dropping by, too.

From Talking Heads to the Dictators, from the Ramones to Blondie (which had just lost yet another band member, its bass player, Fred Smith, to Television), a truly diverse group of bands found their core audiences at CBGB's, which became the ultimate rock club of mid-seventies New York. CB's attracted not only punk-rock fans, but also some of the artsy people who were initially drawn there to see Patti Smith. Patti remembered walking to the club during these exhilarating days: "It was never dark, always twilight, and you'd have these old guys warming their hands over trash bins. The place was always so packed, and the feeling so intense. It was like a revival meeting."

The British audience got its first detailed reports of Patti Smith at CBGB's from one of her first champions in the rock press, Charles Shaar Murray, who described a show in the New Musical Express.

She can generate more intensity with a single movement of one hand than most rock performers can produce in an entire set. She's an odd little waif figure in a grubby black suit and black satin shirt, so skinny that her clothes hang baggily all over her, with chopped-off black hair and a face like Keith Richards' kid sister would have if she'd gotten as wasted by age seventeen as Keith is now. She stands there machine-gunning out her lines, singing a bit and talking a bit, in total control, riding it and steering it with a twist of a shoulder here, a flick of the wrist there—scaled-down birdlike movements that carry an almost unbelievable degree of power, an instinctive grasp of the principles of mime that teach that the quality and timing of a gesture are infinitely more important than its size. Her closing tour de force, an inspired juxtaposition of "Land of 1,000 Dances" with a rock-poem about a kid getting beaten up in a locker room, was undoubtedly the most gripping performance that I've seen by a white act since the last time I saw the Who.

Patti, meanwhile, was not unmoved by the experience of playing in such a supportive and welcoming environment. "They were really heightened nights," she told Nick Tosches.

Sometimes I'll see some eight-millimeter footage that somebody took and think, "God, did I have guts!" Because I wasn't much of a singer. But I had bravado, and I could improvise. I would almost burst into tears 'cause of all the stuff that was happening. I'd look out at that long line of neon beer signs over the bar and that dog running around shitting while I'm in the middle of a beautiful ballad, and all these drunks are throwing back shots. It was the greatest atmosphere to perform in, it was conspiratorial. It was real physical, and that's what rock 'n' roll's all about—sexual tension and being drunk and disorderly!

I think all the groups had one similarity in that we wanted to elevate the idea of rock while still trying to keep it simple. It was a real reaction against disco music and the glitter-rock thing. Our lyrics were much more sophisticated, and we weren't into artifice at all. The whole punk phenomenon in England was much more reactionary and more "high style." We didn't comb our hair—not because we were making a political statement, but because we just didn't comb our hair. We were never really a punk band. We were predecessors of that; trying to create a space for people to express anticorporate feelings: Rail against the big arena acts and the glitter bands. Bring it back to the streets, the garage. The people who came after were that genre. We were the grandparents, the first ones to be signed out of CBGB's.

"We helped put CBGB's on the map," declared Lenny. "All of a sudden, the place would be packed out on Friday and Saturday, and it was a pretty good crowd on Thursday and Sunday. And after that, things started rolling on the Bowery. But it helped us too, because playing seven weeks, four nights a week, at CBGB's, all these things that we were working on crystallized. We had Ivan, and Jay Dee Daugherty started playing with us occasionally on drums. By the time we finished CBGB's, we were, much to our surprise, like a band."

Like Ivan Kral, Jay Dee Daugherty was already in a band, Lance Loud's Mumps, when he got the call from Patti. He was gradually eased into the group over a two-month period. Once again, Patti had pinched a musician from another band whose profile was mainly built around its lead singer: Lance Loud had gained renown via *An American Family,* the groundbreaking PBS program chronicling his family's life for a mesmerized American television audience.

It wasn't *all* Patti's doing, however. The position of drummer in the Patti Smith Group was something that Jay Dee had actively sought. After being invited by Jane Friedman to sit in for a couple of nights, he began calling the manager daily, almost forcing his way into the group. When he departed the Mumps, his bandmate and longtime friend Christian Hoffman wrote a thirty-page letter detailing the reasons why Jay Dee should feel bad about leaving the Mumps, and though the letter reduced Jay Dee to tears, he still thrilled at the idea of being part of Patti Smith's band. He recognized that Patti's potential was far greater than Lance Loud's, and he also saw that while the Patti Smith Group took an ostensibly collaborative approach toward their music, it was Patti and Lenny who ran the show. When necessary, Lenny would act as a bridge between Patti and the rest of the band, interpreting her moods, marshaling their energies, but ultimately it was all about forwarding Patti's career. Jay Dee's perceptions would turn out to be correct, but once Ivan convinced Patti that they "should have a drummer," Jay Dee was hired. Upon joining the band, Jay Dee had a lot to learn. "We had to give him a crash course in everything," said Patti. "We'd tell him about the Arabs and sixteenth-century Japan and flying saucers. The poor kid had to carry all these books and records home every night."

Though close in many ways, the members of the Patti Smith Group were separated in others. Patti, Lenny, and Richard Sohl, for instance, smoked grass, whereas Ivan and Jay Dee were more inclined to knock back a few beers when given the opportunity. Patti defined each member of the band as she saw him and pinned them by her way of thinking. To some extent it appeared each member of the band was forced to acquiesce to Patti's image of who he was. She drew out in each of them aspects of their personalities of which they had not been aware, good or bad, but also may have constrained them by not noticing or accepting who they really were.

Patti's spring shows at CBGB's in 1975 could not have been better timed. Dylan was slinking around the Village again, reacquainting himself with the scene and formulating plans that would be realized in the Rolling Thunder Revue in the late fall and winter; Bruce Springsteen was breaking out, and the Stones were touring that summer. Record executives swarmed to CBGB's in a feeding frenzy sparked by the buzz created by Lisa Robinson, Danny Fields, James Wolcott, Robert Christgau, and John Rockwell. One relatively quiet midweek night, the godfather of punk, Lou Reed, escorted Arista president Clive Davis to a show, coaching him through it.

Davis was impressed by the music and especially by Patti herself. Behind her act, he recognized a shrewd, ambitious woman who wanted to be a star. "I have to be in a rush," the twenty-eight-year-old singer told him. "I don't have the strength to take too long becoming a star." Davis was struck by how strong a sense of herself and her destiny Patti had.

Patti felt comfortable with Clive Davis. He had an outstanding record for discovering artists—among his finds was Janis Joplin—and Arista Records was young and growing. She believed that Davis would nurture her and not just look for hit singles. In April, he signed her at $750,000 for seven albums.

"At this point, with the success, everyone changed a little bit," said Terry Ork. "A lot of the Dionysian element evaporated with the pressure of Clive Davis coming down and all that. They [the bands] had to make it, and they weren't making it, they hadn't signed big deals. New wave was dying, and it did die; disco won out. People felt they had sold out because it was the only option. There was kind of a death throe."

Patti's monetary ambitions were relatively modest (she would spend most of the advance on new equipment for the band), but she demanded that an assurance of creative autonomy—which a new artist rarely gets—be written into her contract. This meant, among other things, that Patti could create and approve her own ad campaigns—it was she, in fact, who came up with the famous "three-chord rock merged with the power of the word" line. The clause also meant that she exercised a producer's control over her records, no matter whom she called in to advise her. "My record contract was one of the most unusual contracts of its time," she told William Burroughs, "because although I got a lot of money and a lot of faith put into me, I also got full artistic control of what I did. . . . I don't think even Bob Dylan had that at the time of his first contract."

On June 26, 1975, while the Rolling Stones played Madison

Square Garden, Patti appeared at a small downtown club called the Other End and met one of her idols. Amy Gross, writing a profile of Patti for *Mademoiselle* magazine, described the show:

> She walks in during the first act, greeting friends, touching hands—there's something of the young Frank Sinatra in her now, his con-man cool, his wiry grace. Underneath the black silk shirt is a Keith Richards T-shirt, in honor of the Stones' visit to New York. Also in New York is Bob Dylan, who is perched unobtrusively at the bar. She is exuberant, clowning.

"Somebody told us he [Dylan] was there," Patti told a friend. "My heart was pounding. I made a couple of references, a couple of oblique things to show I knew he was there."

Afterward, a healthy- and relaxed-looking Dylan went backstage to introduce himself to Patti. Though physically unimposing, Dylan can never be separated from his myth, and it was the mythical Dylan—the brooding, volatile poet-star of *Don't Look Back*—that had everyone in the room excited.

Those present noticed a distinct sexual tension in the room and found Dylan to be an intense and compelling provocateur. He had everyone, even Patti, in his thrall just making small talk, though when the photographers' flashbulbs began popping, Patti laughingly pushed him aside, saying to the photographer, "Fuck you, take my picture, boys!" Dylan smiled, made a gesture of prayer toward Patti, and disappeared into the night.

Patti clearly remembered their meeting, and, in true Patti Smith fashion, noted not so much Dylan's effect on her as her effect on him. "He came back to see me, and there was the same kind of sensation that I used to have in high school, like when you meet a guy in the hallway . . . it was just like that—teenage. We were like two pit bulls circling. I was a snotnose. I had a very high concentration of adrenaline. He said to me, 'Any poets around here?' And I said, 'I don't like poetry anymore. Poetry sucks!' I really acted like a jerk. I thought, that guy will never talk to me again. . . .

[H]e kinda saw in me someone who was potentially as strong as him, who has a lot of energy—the kind that makes you totally uncomfortable with the world—and he recognized that. On stage I was into improvising linguistically, and I was especially inspired that night because he was there. But, of course, I learned that [improvising verbally] from him, and yet it was almost like it was a new thing to him. I said, 'You have to remember where that came from!' He started getting really turned on by the idea of the band—my guys following me or pushing me and not faltering or wondering about what musical changes to go into, because I've just spread the song out like a hand. He saw somebody doing something that he didn't think was possible, and he said, 'I wish I would have stayed with just one group—if I'd had the same group all this time, how well we would have known the ins and outs of each other.'

"And the day after, there was this picture on the cover of the *Village Voice*. The photographer had Dylan put his arm around me. It was a really cool picture. It was a dream come true, but it reminded me of how I had acted like a jerk. And then a few days later, I was walking down Fourth Street by the Bottom Line and I saw him coming. He put his hand in his jacket—he was still wearing the same clothes he had on in the picture, which I liked—and he takes out the *Village Voice* picture and says, 'Who are these two people? You know who these people are?' Then he smiled at me and I knew it was all right."

At the beginning of the summer of 1975, Patti and her band went into seclusion to rehearse material for their upcoming recording dates. After a lot of deliberation, Patti and Lenny had chosen John Cale to produce the record. She joked that she was attracted by his cheekbones on the cover of his *Fear* album, but

Cale's association with the Velvet Underground, the sound of his own solo albums, and his production work with Nico and Iggy Pop were more likely reasons behind her choice.

In the beginning, everybody in the band was happy that Cale had been chosen to produce. Jay Dee loved his solo albums, and had met Cale briefly in California in 1969 at the Beverly Hills Hotel, where Cale had a suite while producing the Stooges. Jay Dee thought Cale was great to work with, a great catalyst, and appreciated his eccentric sense of humor. And while Jay Dee agreed that Cale could be difficult in the studio, he felt that Cale respected the integrity that existed in the band and brought his own expertise and musical and technical inspiration to the project.

Lenny was also a fan of Cale's solo work, and was confident that Cale would understand the band's artistic ethos. He was not at all aware of Cale's love for the music of the Beach Boys or his tendency to monopolize any relationship he had, which in Lenny's (and Patti's) view turned out to mean transforming the Patti Smith Group into the Beach Boys.

"We picked John for two reasons," explained Lenny. "The first was that we thought the sound on his Island records, notably *Fear*, was really exquisite. We thought the instruments had a lot of presence and John himself had a lot of presence. Also, we were very concerned about finding someone who could relate to us artistically. At that time, most of the producers we came in contact with wanted to change some aspect of the band's personality. We were interested in John because we felt that he would let us go as far as we wanted to and believe in us."

The band decided to record at Electric Ladyland, where Patti had recorded "Hey Joe" and "Piss Factory" in 1974.

The recording of *Horses* took place through August and into September, and became a battle of wills between John Cale and Patti Smith. After the CBGB's shows in March and April, Patti had felt that her songs were fully ready to be recorded, but Cale disagreed. He made the band rethink all their of material from scratch. Then, Lenny said, "he went right to the songs." This resulted in many days of heated debate in the studio. In the end, "everything wound up pretty much the way it had started," said Lenny, "but we all understood it a bit more." He felt that Cale's main contribution to the project was to set the "psychological aura" in the studio.

"As it turned out, technically he was a wash out," Lenny explained. "He wasn't much interested in the technical aspects of recording. However, as an artist, he challenged us to come to terms with what we were doing. John's conception of how he wanted the album was markedly different than the way we wanted it. But in that conflict of push and pull, the record came out. He really forced us to go out on a limb. . . . I think he would have wanted to make it more of an arranged record. He fought off the live quality of it, and, in fighting with us, he made us so crazy that songs took on a whole new aspect in the studio."

Nevertheless, there was as much camaraderie and laughter in the studio as there was aggravation and tears. The band took to calling Cale "Tarmac," because whenever he entered the studio, he appeared to be skidding around a corner and he would go crashing into things, sending half-empty coffee cups and moldy food and guitar picks flying in all directions.

At his best, Cale was a divinely inspired, courageous worker. At his worst, he was a walking disaster. But that being said, he recognized that his main task was to transform a poet into a singer. "It was not clear what persona this record was going to have until I had her improvise against herself," said Cale. "At that point something clicked. There was a track she did where she read poetry. I had her read poetry against her poetry, and there were two lines going on and I had her mix it. When Clive Davis heard that, he said, 'Hey, you've got a collaborator.' And that's exactly the thing that made that record different. She was really a poet, and you had to respect the fact that she was not a musician but out of sheer bravado and desire was making herself into a rock 'n' roll singer and basically wanted to be Keith Richards. . . . I was awed that she had gotten all that input from Bob Dylan and Lou Reed . . . She had a Welsh Methodist idea of improvisation, in that it was like declamation. Lou was kind of psychological [in his improvisation], but a lot of Patti's impulses came from preaching."

For Patti, *Horses* and working with Cale were "the culmination of all my most heartfelt adolescent desires. All I was looking for in a producer was a technical person. Instead, I got a real maniac artist. I went to pick out an expensive watercolor painting, and instead I got a mirror. It was really like a season in hell for both of us. But inspiration doesn't always have to be someone sending me half a dozen American Beauty roses. There's a lot of inspiration going on between the murderer and the victim. I had to solidify everything I believed in. We came into the studio really half-assed and glib, then I had to pound my fists into John's skull day and night."

The essence of the Cale-Smith collaboration was the fact that each was a committed and original artist. Both were possessed by the desire to have their own way, and both were hung up on competition and domination, regardless of whether it got positive or negative results. The one difference between the two was that when the whole affair was over, John was never quoted saying a bad word about Patti, whereas she took the opportunity on more than one occasion to attack Cale's abilities and insist that it was she who had produced the album—that she had just used Cale when she needed him. Even before the album was released, Patti was publicly expressing ambivalent feelings about Cale's role as producer. When she spoke to Chris Charlesworth of *Melody Maker*, for example she minimized Cale's contribution:

What John did for us was to make us aware of each other. He said that we were really nebulous, and weren't that close, and I thought we were, you know? But after that recording . . . Well, we really broke past everything, got to know each other's fragile stuff. We're like brothers and sisters. I wasn't made to feel guilty or nervous about any of the subject matter. John kept pushing me to improvise and extend."

Later on, she became explicitly dismissive of Cale's role, as when writer Steven Lake criticized the sound of *Horses*. "Forget about Cale," she told Lake. "He had nothing to do with anything. I mixed the record myself, blame me for the way it sounds. The album was spewed from my womb. We ignored all Cale's suggestions."

Perhaps that was wise, for in 1976 Patti said that "production-wise John wanted to put strings on the record and get new musicians. If you're into some Velvet Underground fantasy, forget it. John is into the Beach Boys—totally. He wanted to just get rid of the band and take me into the studio with an orchestra."

Twenty-three years later, though, she had softened a bit, remembering the better aspects of the collaboration. "Sometimes we'd get all excited in the studio. John and I would have a really happy moment together, hugging, then at other times we'd have tears streaming down our faces. It was like two crazy poets dealing with showers of words. But we didn't have any motivation other than to do something really great."

The truth is that John Cale had an enormously positive influence on *Horses*, and without him it would never have had the impact that it did. Cale forced the band to fight for its music, and this had a distinctly positive effect on the album. In the end, John Cale imposed his discipline on the band and the result was that the songs became tighter and the band more confident, which allowed them greater space to experiment. "Birdland" and "Land" were transformed. "We went through all kinds of voyages," said Patti. "Usually [on 'Land'] there's Mexican boys and space guys, weird Burroughs stuff like Arab guys and Christian angels fucking in the sand, pulling out each other's entrails."

Going in, of course, there was no predicting how the sessions would play out. In 1975, recording studios came replete with every

stimulant known to man, from cocaine and marijuana to ampheta-
mines, opiates, and alcohol. The combination of any variety of
these with a minimum of six raging egos was bound to make the
recording of any album, never mind *Horses*, a conflict-prone experience. Lenny had produced records himself, and as their work
progressed he sympathized with Cale's approach, but since it led
almost immediately to a confrontation between John and Patti
(which at least once came to blows), he was torn between his total
allegiance to her and his understanding of Cale's dilemma. The
essence of the conflict lay in Patti's desire to create spontaneously
and Cale's to build layer upon layer of sound a la Brian Wilson or
Phil Spector.

During the making of the album, the continuing triangle between Patti, Tom Verlaine, and Allen Lanier (who both played on
the album) caused friction, yet also spurred creativity. On one occasion, Tom and Allen were in the studio at the same time, and
with Cale there too, there were moments when masculine anger
teetered on the edge of violence. Some onlookers got the definite
impression that Patti enjoyed the tension created by the rivalry for
her attention; others thought it caused her distress. According to
Cale, the most interesting sessions were the ones in which Allen
Lanier felt obliged to flex his muscles. Given Patti's history of
playing her men off against each other, it seems likely that she felt
that Cale's strong presence was primarily positive, even if she did
at one point launch herself at him like a torpedo.

All the songs on *Horses* were cowritten by Patti and a member of
her band, Tom Verlaine, or Allen Lanier. The cuts included one
about her little sister, Kimberly, a rewrite of Van Morrison's "Gloria," and an interpolated "Land of 1,000 Dances" that incorpo-
rated improvisation about the "sea of possibilities." And all except
"Elegy," written for Jimi Hendrix and recorded on September 18,
the anniversary of his death, were long. What made the songs
unique and interesting was the application of William Burroughs's
cut-up technique to the sound and the inclusion of pieces of clas-

sic fifties and sixties rock and pop lyrics. It was, as John Rockwell wrote, this elaboration on rock standards "that provides the most striking songs in her repertory."

Throughout the record, it was the combination of twentieth-century classic imagery with bubble-gum rock that blew the listener into that free space of unlimited possibilities that rock at its best offers.

Patti received her song ideas equally from reading and dreaming. She wrote "Birdland," for example, after reading the *Book of Dreams*, by Peter Reich (son of psychiatrist Wilhelm). "Break It Up" came from a dream about Jim Morrison lying naked on a marble slab with stone wings. Patti plays the part of a small boy repeatedly yelling "break it up" until the wings break and Morrison is free to rise up, like Jesus, and escape.

Near the end of the recording sessions, Patti was down to ninety-three pounds, having lost eleven pounds working in the studio. She alluded to her weight loss in an interview with the writer Tony Glover, telling him, "The thing is, art always wins. Art will survive, and I'm gonna die—so I'm not gonna give art all the best moments of my life. If you live in the moment, nothing comes first—but the energy I have left after my art I save for love. What you have to do is try to capture meaningful moments—and we got some incredible truly frightening moments on this record. 'Land' still frightens me."

Lenny added, "Just as Patti projects personas and refuses to be defined as a woman or a rock 'n' roll singer, she just goes with whatever is happening to the boundary of art—we want to shatter that boundary and get out there."

According to Patti's contract with Arista, she had total control of the album's design along with the content. There was no question that Robert Mapplethorpe would take the picture for the cover; the question was who would choose the image and what would it say.

On the day of the photo shoot, Patti overslept. Robert recalled them eating a long, late breakfast at the Pink Teacup on Grove Street in the village, discussing ideas for the picture. In Patti's version of the day's events, by contrast, she grabbed her usual costume—black pants, white shirt, skinny tie, and a man's black jacket—and headed directly from her MacDougal Street apartment to Sam Wagstaff's penthouse at One Fifth Avenue, which Robert sometimes used as a studio because of its white walls and excellent light.

Robert had chosen a bare wall for a backdrop. Lately he'd noticed how at a certain time each day the sun created a triangle of light on that particular wall, and he wanted to catch that fleeting triangle in Patti's portrait, if possible. Working without an assistant, Robert was nervous but confident. For one shot, he asked Patti to remove her jacket. She tossed it nonchalantly over her shoulder, "Sinatra style," she said later, "hopefully catching some of his casual defiance."

The image Robert captured of Patti in the first few frames of the shoot resonated with a powerful force; it delivered the impact of the first Rolling Stones cover, or of Dylan's first electric foray, *Bringing It All Back Home*.

Patti's image on the *Horses* cover made her an instant icon. All those years of treating clothes as objects of art had paid off. As Tony Hiss and David McClelland pointed out in "Gonna Be So Big, Gonna Be a Star, Watch Me Now!," their *New York Times Magazine* profile of Patti that appeared in December, "Her costume is replete with metonymic significance. Every article of clothing evokes a name and every name evokes a state of mind. For someone who looks rather like the 101st Neediest Case, Patti pays a great deal of attention to the way she dresses." Patti expounded on her look. "A black boy's suit jacket from Saks Fifth Avenue. Once, I went to Saks and watched a thirteen-year-old Catholic boy and his mother choose a suit, then I bought the same one. It's my Baudelaire dress suit. Sometimes a black schoolboy's tie or a black ribbon satin tie. Then white shoes, a tribute to the

Rolling Stones' *High Tide and Green Grass* greatest-hits album. Brian Jones always wore white shoes."

"I saw *Horses* in a record store in Australia," said art critic Paul Taylor, "and immediately fell in love with the picture. I didn't know anything about Patti Smith or about punk, but I bought the album on the strength of the photograph. It was elegant and totally modern, and I remember looking at the photo credit and wondering, 'Who is Robert Mapplethorpe?' "

The record and its cover spoke particularly to women, somehow giving them permission to do and say whatever they wanted, to look and feel however they wanted. *Horses* told the world that men were no longer the only ones selling rebellion in rock.

In its first year of release, *Horses* sold some two hundred thousand copies.

"Patti's great to photograph," Mapplethorpe told this writer not long after the session for *Horses*. "I know that I'm going to have something great out of each session that I do. I guess a lot has to do with our relationship. I think you can get too involved with [someone]. It seems to be better after you're not sexually involved."

It's difficult in the late 1990s to comprehend how strange, how unusual the image Patti presented on the cover of *Horses* was in 1975. At that time, female rock singers were supposed to be glamorous and sexy in the traditional way, with makeup and carefully styled hair. Arista Records' president Clive Davis, in fact, hated the photo and fought to have it changed, or at least airbrushed— to remove Patti's "mustache"—but Patti, having been given artistic control, stood her ground. The cover of *Horses* completely captured the essence of Patti and of the moment, and it offered a new image of a rock 'n' roll woman—ambiguous, androgynous, but strong and in control. In 1991, Rolling Stone included *Horses* high among the one-hundred best album covers of the rock era.

As always, Patti's timing was extraordinary. Everything that was happening worked in her favor, from the kidnapping of Patty Hearst to the return to New York of the legendary Beat novelist,

William Burroughs. By the time *Horses* was released, Patti had gotten to know Burroughs and his amanuensis James Grauerholz well enough to be photographed with Burroughs on her twenty-ninth birthday. She often talked about him in interviews, detailing his influence on her technique of cutting new lines into old songs. Burroughs was happy to accept the free publicity, inasmuch as it drew attention to his books. Despite having little interest in rock music, Burroughs attended several of her ground-breaking New York concerts and seemed to have a genuine affection for Patti.

As the band prepared for the album's November release and rehearsed for a U.S. tour, Patti continued seeing Dylan, with whom she was rumored to have had a brief affair. He wanted her to join his Rolling Thunder Revue that fall. Patti recounted the story to her friend Miles, whom she'd known since her days at the Chelsea Hotel:

> Dylan told me to come to this party. Actually, I thought he was inviting me for a drink—he asked me to come to some bar at Gerde's Folk City, where he first started in New York. So I went, and there's a million people there—well-known people, and I thought he was asking me for a drink, he couldn't have asked all these people—is this a coincidence? But it was a party for a birthday and they were also going to announce Rolling Thunder.
>
> First, him and Joan Baez got up and sang "One Too Many Mornings," which was one of my favorite Dylan songs. I'd seen him a lot in between all this time. Anyway, different people got up: Bobby Neuwirth, Jack Elliott got up, Jim [Roger] McGuinn got up and sang his horse song; Bette Midler got up and sang this song—she didn't do such a hot job. She did this weird thing—she came over and threw this glass of beer in my face! Just walked up! I never met her before. It was like a John Wayne movie! I was real shocked. And then Dylan made me go up there. I had no

band, no song prepared, but I understood that why I had to go up there was to save face. Since I couldn't hit her, I had to do something to maintain my dignity, so I got up there with Eric Andersen, and I said, "Just play a droning E chord behind me." So I just made up this thing. I looked at Bob, and made up this thing about a brother and sister. But while I'm doing it, I start thinking about Sam Shepard—he was in my consciousness—and so I told this story, really got into it, made this brother and sister be parted by the greed and corruption of the system—I did a good job and lots of people liked it. I was real proud.

There was a lot of tension. Phil Ochs was there, and Phil Ochs could always bring out the *Don't Look Back* side of Dylan. Bob wouldn't talk to Phil Ochs. The two of them . . . it was like there was a noose in the middle of the room and they were circling around, trying to get each other to hang themselves. [Phil Ochs would commit suicide by hanging on April 9, 1976.]

Anyway, I'd got everything I needed from him, I guessed it was time to turn the beat around. So I said, "I'll give you one tip. Use your fists." And he says, "Aw, I can't hit the air with my fists or nothing. People will think I'm copying you!" I said, "Well, I've imitated you for twelve years, you can spare a little imitation." So he just laughed. Seeing him laugh is great, 'cause he has a lot of pain. He's like the Duke of Windsor. But he's also got a streak in him that won't give up being a contender. And that streak is what gives him so much life—that streak makes him keep creating, keep putting himself out there. Dylan's such a fucking maniac. He's intense and that intensity has only been successfully revealed through abstract expressionism in rock 'n' roll.

Despite trying to focus on the release of her own record, Patti attended some of the Rolling Thunder rehearsals. As usual her comments about the matter were mostly about herself:

At those rehearsals, I just told him what I always tell him
. . . that I think we could do something great together because
he's such a great improviser. I suppose that creation is improvisation, but I'd like to see him do it onstage. I told him there was
no space for me on that tour. And he knew it, but at that point it
was so early in my career and he felt that I should be exposed to
the public. I thought it was real sweet of him, but he's so restless—at this point we're not chemically suited to be around
each other—both of us have so much electrical energy we need
some kind of calming factor. It's like if you have an electric chair
you need somebody to electrocute, you don't bring in another
electric chair."

The release of *Horses* on November 10, 1975, was cause for celebration. "We wanted it to be so wonderful," Patti said in *Punk*
magazine. "We wanted to make people so happy. I mean, we
wanted to make people as happy as we felt . . . like when *Satanic
Majesties* came out. That was a whole thing. A new Stones album
. . . Dylan. It was so exciting at that time for me, 'cause I was eighteen, nineteen. That year, I got to experience new Stones, new
Doors, new Jimi Hendrix, Jefferson Airplane, oh, God—it was so
great. I want that stuff to happen again, y'know."

Her hopes were not in vain: *Horses* fulfilled her desire to wake
people up to a new form of rock and give the fans a new and exciting album. The album was a manifesto of sorts, and Patti was suddenly thrust into the spotlight as a "rock politician." *Horses*
received excellent reviews and impressed the more literate critics
from *Rolling Stone* to the *New York Times*. In addition, it was the
first record to emerge from CBGB's. A stream of debut albums
from Blondie, the Ramones, and Television would soon follow,
but by getting there first and doing such a swell job, Patti had
snatched the crown.

Patti's longtime fan, the critic John Rockwell, wrote *Rolling
Stone*'s review of *Horses*:

Her first record, *Horses*, is wonderful in large measure because it recognizes the overwhelming importance of words in her work. John Cale, the producer, has demonstrated the perfect empathy he might have been expected to have for Smith, and he has done so mostly by not distorting her in any way. The range of concerns in *Horses* is huge, far beyond what most rock records even dream of. All eight songs betray a loving fascination with the oldies of rock. The homage is always implicit—the music just sounds like something you might have heard before, at least in part—and sometimes explicit.

Patti certainly could not have expected a better response to her first album. *Horses* was trumpeted in the American press as a bona fide musical event. Even the *New York Times* described it as an

extraordinary disc, every minute of which is worth repeated hearings. *Horses* may be an eccentricity, but in a way that anything strikingly new is eccentric. It will annoy some people and be dismissed by others. But if you are responsive to the mystical energy, it will shake you and move you as little else can.

Clive Davis and his staff at Arista could not have been happier: How often does a new contender break big in both the music *and* mainstream presses on a first album?

The British music press, meanwhile, was split. Steve Lake, in *Melody Maker*, was vicious. "Precisely what's wrong with rock and roll right now," he wrote,

is that there's too many academics pretending to be cretins, and too many cretins pretending to be academics. And it's time we started shooting them down in flames. Let Patti Smith and John Cale be the first heads to tumble. There's no way that the completely contrived and affected "amateurism" of *Horses* constitutes good rock and roll. That old "so bad it's good" aesthetic has been played to death. *Horses* is just bad. Period.

At the *New Musical Express,* Charles Shaar Murray took a polar opposite position:

> *Horses* is some kind of definitive essay on the American night as a state of mind, an emergence from the dark undercurrent of American rock that spewed up Jim Morrison, Lou Reed and Dylan's best work, out of Gasoline Alley, to Desolation Row, a thrashing exorcism of public and private demons. Horses is an album in a thousand. God knows, it's an important album in terms of what rock can encompass without losing its identity as a musical form, in that it introduces an artist of greater vision than has been seen in rock for far too long.

While paying homage to rock's great romantics, from Keith Richards to Lou Reed, *Horses* marked the acceptance of the white female voice as a powerful instrument in rock, in a way that no one since Janis Joplin had done. Patti was singing in an instantly recognizable voice that would inspire a new generation of female rockers. "She shocked me the first time I saw her," wrote Amy Gross. "Real old-fashioned shock. This . . . skinny punk who hammered out dirty poetry and sang surreal folk songs. Who never smiled. Who was tough, sullen, bad, didn't give a damn . . . I felt both ravaged and exhilarated."

Another witness, Cleveland-based blues singer Adele Bertei, dropped everything and moved to New York the first time she heard Patti sing:

> At the time music was about divas or rock goddesses. It was nothing to do with boyish little tykes like myself who could sing blues. I didn't think there'd ever be a place for me. Then Patti Smith came out with an album that rocked my universe. She was androgynous, outspoken, obviously well-educated and well-read. She became like a mentor to me. If she dropped references to Brancusi [the Romanian sculptor], I'd go out and find art books. If it was Rimbaud, I'd read him and learn about

the French decadents. Because I didn't have much of an education, Patti Smith in a sense was my first teacher.

In France, *Horses* won the prestigious Grand Prix du Disque presented by the Académie Charles Cros. The album's cover photo
was published everywhere, giving Mapplethorpe's work wide attention. "We had always dreamed about becoming successful together," Patti said. "It was all part of our grand scheme."

Patti's fellow *Creem* magazine alumnus Lester Bangs eloquently
summed up the qualities of the album:

> This is not a spoken-word album, and if you couldn't under-
> stand a word of English, you couldn't miss the emotional force
> of Patti's music. *Horses* is a commanding album, as opposed to
> demanding: you don't have to work to understand or like it, but
> you can't ignore it either. It refuses to be background music, it
> stops the action in a room when it is on, and leaves its effects
> when it's over whether you like it or not.

In the British music paper *Sounds*, John Ingham concurred.
"Ladies and gentlemen, I give you the record of the year. Quite
simply this is one of the most stunning, commanding, engrossing
platters to come down the turnpike since John Lennon's *Plastic
Ono Band*, and for the same reasons." In the *Village Voice*, New
York's most influential rock critic, Robert Christgau, dubbed her
"the first credible rock shaman."

Horses climbed the charts, reaching number forty-six on *Billboard*'s Hot 100, astonishing for an album so completely out of the
mainstream. As it gained momentum, Patti and her band took to
the road for a three-month tour, the opening act a solo John Cale.
Every place they played was sold out. Cale came out every night at
the end of her set and played "My Generation" with the band; the
show culminated with Lenny launching himself into John's arms
and Cale carrying the guitarist offstage.

The Patti Smith Group's first national tour was the most exciting journey she had ever taken. Her ecstasy was infectious as she jumped up and down clapping her hands and rapping away in between songs with feverish intensity. It was *A Hard Day's Night* crossed with *Don't Look Back*, filmed by Godard with Patti as Anna Karina and Lenny as an improbable but willing Jean-Pierre Leaud. As they played into 1976, America's Bicentennial, they too were brand new and red, white, and blue. And the excitement didn't dim with the house lights. Backstage after each gig or in the hotel, Patti got to exercise her love of language in a series of myth-making interviews that stand as little works of art in themselves:

> I think masturbating is a really important function in art. People say I go too far, but there's no too far to go. I can come up to twelve times a day. I can have a lot of brain travel through masturbation. That's where I get a lot my mental images. Besides, when I'm on the road, it means I'm away from somebody I love. It might mean I'm not going to be making love for a month, so I have to get that shot onstage. To me, fucking and masturbation and art are all the same because they all require total concentration.
>
> I want people to applaud too, just like Lenny Bruce. Do you think Lenny Bruce didn't want to be loved by everybody? My goals on stage are no different to Edith Piaf's or Mick Jagger's. I want everybody to love me.

Tony Hiss and David McClelland's December 21 *New York Times Magazine* profile crowned Patti's 1975 achievements. "Patti Smith is having a wonderful time these days," "Gonna Be So Big, Gonna Be a Star, Watch Me Now!" began, with Patti summing things up by declaring that she had "a lot to learn about records and mixing and things like that, but nobody can tell me about the magic. The magic is completely under control."

the field marshal of rock 'n' roll

january–may 1976

> "Where do we work?" Patti shouted.
> "In the fields," the band replied.
> "What do we use?"
> "Marshalls!"
> "WHAT DO WE GROW?"
> "Wheat!"
> "HOW DO WE GET IT?"
> "FREE!"
> "WHAT'S THIS?"
> "WAR!"
> "WHAT'S THIS?"
> "ROCK 'N' ROLL! ROCK 'N' ROLL!"
>
> *the patti smith group's preperformance chant*

In January, Patti played three weekends at the Bottom Line. In the heart of downtown New York, the club was the best rock 'n' roll showcase in the city. Lou Reed had recorded his *Take No Prisoners* album there, and Bruce Springsteen had sealed his stardom with a series of shows at the club in 1974. Now it was Patti's turn to take the room, which she did with all the panache of a seasoned entertainer. She did two shows each night; each set began with the Lou Reed chestnut "We're Gonna Have a Real Good Time

Together." One Saturday's show went out live on WXPN, and an extra show was added on Sunday night. All of the shows were sold out. On the first night, Lou Reed himself was in the audience, as was actor Richard Dreyfuss, singer Peter Wolf of the J. Geils Band with his wife Faye Dunaway, and many other famous faces. It was as if Patti could walk on water. She both charmed and stunned the crowd with her between-song patter, like she was the kid sister of Muhammad Ali: "I am . . . the first . . . Patti Smith," she intoned. "Or maybe the second Anna Magnani! I've been reading all these articles about me, and I'm checking myself out . . . And I think what it is . . . is that . . . I got a lot of . . . posthumous appeal!"

That January, *Creem*, the magazine that had featured her poetry back in 1971, ran a cover story on Patti by Tony Glover entitled "Patti Smith: Sweet Howling Fire." In addition, Nick Tosches interviewed her for the international skin magazine *Penthouse*, a definite sign that she had broken out from the rock 'n' roll and local New York press. When Tosches asked if she had had any encounters with groupies, Patti complained.

Yeah, but they're almost always girls. They're usually pretty young, too. They try to act heavy and come on like leather. I always act as if they're real cool. I never go anyplace with them. They bring me drugs and poetry and black leather gloves and stuff like that. I don't really know what they want. I mean, I think they're actually straight girls. The guys that I get, they're always such great losers. Really pimply-faced fuck-ups with thick glasses, but a lot of heart, y'know? My heart really goes out for those kids 'cause I can still taste what it feels like to be sixteen and totally fucked up. I remember everything. And I figure if I came out of it okay, then these kids are going to be okay, too. They just need to be told that they're going to be okay, that's all.

Patti's roots in rock writing inspired some of rock's most highly regarded writers to pen articles about her, casting her in a highly favorable light: "It's possible to accuse Patti of taking herself too seriously," wrote Robert Christgau, for example, in the *Village Voice*, "but you can't say she doesn't have a sense of humor about it. She knows that her audience—'my kids,' she calls them, more maternal than you'd figure—has the earmarks of a cult. And she knows that her band can be described as a critics' band."

"In January Patti goes on her first full-scale tour outside the [East and West] coasts," wrote Dave Marsh. "If she is as fragile as some think, she will break and run at the first sigh of rejection. If she's as tough as I think, she'll find a way. But what if it all falls through, no more records, no more songs? 'The cornerstone of the little temple Jane [Friedman] and I built is poetry,' Patti replied. 'I always had that. It's like in Hollywood—if you've got good tits, Russ Meyer'll take you. It's the one thing you've got. You can get Lloyd's of London to insure 'em, but at least you've got your tits.' "

Patti spent January to April 1976 touring the United States, performing at an increasingly frenetic pace and receiving great reviews. Richard Goldstein, who chronicled life on the road with the Patti Smith Group for *Creem* in "Rock 'n' Roll Pandora," gives a glimpse of the excitement in his description of Patti's show at Chicago's famed Aragon Ballroom, a "raucous pit stop for weary unwashed rock 'n roll animals":

"When the band hit its stride at the Aragon," Goldstein wrote,

one is struck by a blast of what Saul Bellow calls "the ecstasy of consciousness," while Patti slinks in and out of the shifting spotlight, whirling like a dervish blindly diving into a fetal "Hunchback of Notre Dame" crouch; frugging, jump-romping, arching her back like an alley cat in heat, assaulting Lenny with jungle fervor; first knocking him down, then luring him erect, feigning a leap into the aroused mass of spectators; dangling, then suddenly recoiling an extended foot towards the crowd's clammy, outstretched hands, as if charming a snake . . .

This is no mere performance. As Patti crawls up the mike stand for "Time Is on My Side," hawking wads of phlegm, her glazed mystic eyes darting over the footlights, we gasp for air, shaken by the momentum of abrupt madness, possessed not by some obscure literary text but by a genuine Madwoman of Chaillot offering a fistful of debauchery, a lunatic harangue of disconnected images, a spasm of half-conscious incantations.

At the end of her version of "My Generation" in Cleveland on January 26 (with John Cale on bass; recorded for a live release), she ad-libbed, "I'm so young / I'm so young I'm so goddamn young / I'm so young / I'm so goddamn young / I'm so young / I'm so goddamn young . . . we created it: let's take it over."

"In the seventies, I had a very romantic idea about being out in the world and having a network of people working with me," said Patti. "I thought of it more as a military regiment. I liked to read books about General Patton, Alexander the Great, and T. E. Lawrence, and I had this view of the people I worked with as troops."

"We were happy," said Patti. "We had really great camaraderie. We had a mission." They also had a base. The Patti Smith Group came out of the tradition of white urban street bands like the Velvet Underground, who, like Patti, were diehard New Yorkers.

The "official" public designation of what is today called punk rock came with the publication of the first issue of *Punk* magazine in January 1976. That this movement was so named is in large part thanks to *Punk*. According to *Punk*'s creator and editor, John Holmstrom, "It was pretty obvious that the word was getting popular. *Creem* used it to describe this early seventies music; *Bomp* would use it to describe the garage bands of the sixties; a magazine like *Aquarian* would use it to describe what was going on at

CBGB's. The word was being used to describe Springsteen, Patti Smith, and the Bay City Rollers. So when Legs McNeil came up with it, we figured we'd take the name before anyone else claimed it. We wanted to get rid of the bullshit, strip it down to rock and roll. We wanted the fun and liveliness back."

"Something was going to happen," added *Punk*'s resident punk, Legs McNeil. "No one in New York had any money. The city was nearly bankrupt—that's when President Ford said to the city: 'Drop dead!' "

Patti took the president's statement as a challenge and became one of New York's greatest champions. "I really love this city," she declared defiantly. "New York is like the symbol, the Statue of Liberty. It's a city that takes into its bosom any mutant. It doesn't matter what you look like. New York was the only place I could go where people didn't give a shit what I looked like. New York doesn't judge you. Everybody is unique in New York, everybody is trying. It's a city of personal architecture, with everybody trying to build up their own legend, everybody re-creating themselves. And New York is the art capital of the world! It's the home of abstract expressionism and rock 'n' roll. It's really hard, really dangerous, really fucked up, but I've been in lots of beautiful cities with beautiful streets that weren't hard or dangerous and they were pretty boring."

Patti introduced a new issue into her daily babbles from the stage of New York's prestigious Avery Fisher Hall, protesting that "the people own the airwaves." Patti had already been banned from WBCN, the key FM radio station in the Boston area, an important market for New Wave at the time, and one of the few stations open to playing the new music. On 'BCN, Patti had let loose with a string of "fucks" and "shits" during an interview, knowing that it was live with no delay. American radio has strict guidelines on which words are illegal to say over the airwaves, and radio stations that do not comply, for whatever reason, are heavily fined.

However, in her battle against censorship, Patti was apparently not concerned with who suffered the consequences of her actions. She was looking for trouble.

"We're past the midpoint of a decade now," Patti told her friend Nick Tosches, "and I think a lot of people are ready to take a leap. I think we've had enough mediocrity. There is no way that singers like Elton John or Helen Reddy can ever transport people the way that Jim Morrison or Jimi Hendrix did. I don't feel that people will allow this shit to go on much longer. The heart of rock 'n' roll is integrity."

"The whole point of Patti Smith was beyond gender, beyond politics, beyond, beyond," Lenny Kaye explained. "Any time you were defined, you were caught. I used to use that quote from Mayo and the Red Crayola, one of my favorite sixties albums, where they say 'Definitions define limit.' That was our philosophy. We wanted to have freedom to have a hit single, or to have twenty minutes of abstract noise. And what do you call that? Is Albert Ayler punk? I don't know. On the other hand, we liked the attitude of punk. So, it was kind of a toss-up. I mean, we were feeling like missionaries, carrying the word out there and trying to stir trouble up wherever we went."

On February 20, Patti was quoted in the *New Musical Express* saying, "I'd rather be remembered as a great rock and roll star than a great poet. To reach the highest point of something our generation created." On March 13, Arista released the live version of "Gloria/My Generation" that had been recorded in Cleveland in January.

The single most important event of 1976 for Patti came on March 9, in Detroit, when she met Fred "Sonic" Smith, who had been in Detroit's protopunk band the MC5. Lenny played Cupid, introducing Patti to Fred during a party given by Arista at a tiny hot-dog joint in downtown Detroit called Lafayette Coney Island. "I'm not one much for parties, so I wanted to get out of there,"

Patti recalled. "I was going out the back door . . . I was standing there with Lenny; I happened to look up, and this guy is standing there as I was leaving. Lenny introduced me to him—'This is Fred "Sonic" Smith,' the legendary guitar player for the MC5—and that was it. Changed my life." Fred was standing in front of a white wall wearing a navy-blue coat. The meeting would inspire two songs, "Godspeed" (in which the coat gets a mention), and "25th Floor," about the room at the hotel where they partied that night, after Smith had joined the Patti Smith Group onstage for their encore rendition of "My Generation." Patti was immediately drawn to the tall, quiet guitar player. There was something slightly remote and inaccessible about him, the very qualities that attracted her. The attraction was mutual.

"The first night we met," Patti said, "he [Fred] appeared on stage with us, and I could tell by the way he played what kind of person he was—better than me, stronger than me." After the show they went to Patti's hotel, where she later wrote "25th Floor." The song, which would appear on *Easter*, refers to her "fender duo sonic" and also mentions the Detroit River, which runs behind the hotel where she and Fred spent that first night together.

Fred Smith was in his late twenties, married, and, at the time, led a group called the Sonic Rendezvous Band, which was the hippest band in the Detroit area. According to his close friend and MC5 bandmate Wayne Kramer, "He was an incredibly seductive, charismatic cat, he really understood the dynamics between men and women, really knew how to work it. He was an attractive man, good-looking guy, and Fred was a really smart guy. He was literate, he read a lot, he understood big ideas, ideas of philosophy, the implications of politics, of history; Fred was into a lot of shit, but you wouldn't know that if you didn't know him really well. Incredibly charming, he was a funny motherfucker."

"He was just Patti's type—a tall, brooding blond—the strong, silent type," said Jay Dee. "It was love at first sight for Patti. It was personal chemistry. The MC5 thing was icing on the cake. She loves tall guys with crooked teeth."

Fred Smith introduced a third element into Patti's love life, which still included Allen Lanier and Tom Verlaine. She still felt a connection to them, too, as an episode with Damita Richter in San Francisco shows. Damita had flown in from Hawaii and hooked up with Lenny, but this time "Patti was really mean to me. . . . During a soundcheck she jumped off the stage and started poking me in the chest saying, 'I know you slept with you know who.' She had found out that I had been dicking around with her boyfriend Allen Lanier."

Indeed, back in New York, Patti was still dividing her time between Allen, living with him in their Greenwich Village apartment across the street from the Kettle of Fish, and Verlaine, in whose building she also kept an apartment. The two men satisfied different poles of Patti's personality. From Lanier she had learned everything she could about how to be in a successful rock band, how it was like being in the army, with preparations for tours being boot camp. "Allen brought out something in her that gave her the confidence to execute her music, the strength to be a singer," said Bebe Buell. "He was also open and receptive to her poetry and envisioned music with it, the same as Lenny. That was their bond. He certainly wasn't her physical type."

Allen was a small, wiry man, about Patti's size, with the long hair and standard jeans-and-leather-jacket garb of the heavy-metal rocker. His looks were not striking, neither did he have the charisma of a rock star. However, what he did not have physically he more than made up for mentally and personally—everybody liked Allen; one never heard a bad word about him. Patti's overnight success in 1976 had put her ahead of Allen in the rock-star stakes, adding an element of strain to the relationship. But Allen was always the least dramatic of her boyfriends, the kind of guy who could spend hours just lying around the house talking or playing pool. He had a sharp intelligence that impressed a number of those visitors who would drop by to check in with Patti only to end up spending hours talking with Allen.

Tom Verlaine was the opposite. Terry Ork probably had a better view of the dynamic of the Smith-Verlaine affair than anybody.

They were very competitive in a way, just two kids madly in love, the same physical body type, the same kind of hunger for success, but I also have a real theoretical thing about the whole period. The sixties were about five years dead, but here in the mid-seventies was a kind of "us against them" mentality. Tom and Patti were both very paranoid about the "establishment" ... Patti and Tom both played this dialectic, this us-versus-them thing; they could use it to their advantage if they wanted to or they could drift into this snobbish attitude which would taken them into the mainstream themselves. It was a dangerous line. There was a lot of that kind of politics that would unite them. They would talk to each other about their careers and what this whole thing was about, that was a strong element too. Plus, they were very exhibitionistic, like they would fall down on the floor and mock having sex.

Tom was very paranoid. I spent hours trying to get him to deal with people because he was very uptight. It's sort of symbolic that after her breakup with Tom, Patti went back to Allen, the Blue Oyster Cult mainstream-rock guy, music that was selling and making money. You can see how Tom has struggled ever since.

Once *Horses* took off, Verlaine was intent on making his own band's album, *Marquee Moon*. He needed to go out into the world and put his big hands to his own uses, playing great runaway guitar in seedy underground clubs all over the world. Television already stood out as the most brilliant and beautiful bunch of boys on the block. As an auteur, Tom was as driven as Patti, and he knew that success was not going to wait forever.

In contrast, Patti felt that unlike Allen or Tom, Fred Smith was stronger than she was. Even though professionally she had a more promising future, Patti saw in Fred an inner strength that was all-compelling. Patti's boyfriends had all been champions in their respective fields, from Mapplethorpe to Carroll, Shepard, Rundgren, Lanier, Verlaine, and now Fred. The MC5's 1969 debut album, *Kick Out the Jams*, was a sourcebook for punk, and Fred could certainly still be seen as a musical hero in 1976. When Patti met him, he was married, fronting the Sonic Rendezvous Band, and scuffling to get by, while Patti was about to take over the world. But love would find a way. Though they would not appear in public as a couple for two more years, they began a secret telephone courtship, as they both worked on a way out of their personal situations. Soon she was closer to Fred than to anyone in her life, and over the next four years, Patti would grow more and more attached to him.

In an interview years later, Thurston Moore reminded Patti of an item in *Creem* back then about a love letter she had sent to Fred. "I sent him a telegram: 'Light and energy enclosed,'" said Patti. "I couldn't believe they found out about that."

Fame would mean that "they" would find out not just about Fred, but about everything. In the spring of 1976, an underground paper, *The Daily Planet*, hit the street with a few pages of nude photos of Patti taken three years earlier, captioning them in large type with Patti's remarks from her *Penthouse* interview. "I don't feel exploited by pictures of naked broads. I like that stuff. If it's a bad picture or if the girl's ugly, it pisses me off. Shit, I think bodies are great," the captions crowed, making it seem as though Patti had endorsed the pictures, even though they were obtained without her knowledge or permission, infuriating her. The *Daily Planet* also published the address of the apartment that she and Allen Lanier shared, and accused her of being antilabor for crossing picket lines at NBC to perform on *Saturday Night Live* during a workers' strike. The magazine's reporters followed Patti, staking out her apartment and harassing her in the street in pursuit of a story. "I want you people to stop bothering me!" Patti yelled at them once as she jumped into the chauffeured black Cadillac that waited for her on MacDougal Street. She was beginning to pay the price of fame.

Speaking about the pictures to *Punk*'s Legs McNeil she said that she didn't "give a shit, I mean I ain't ashamed of my body, y'know, it's just that guy was, I mean he was a BASTARD, y'know? I mean, I'm an artist's model, man—I'm not ashamed of my body. I've posed nude for a lotta great artists. It's just . . . the guy was an exploitative sh—. The only reason that I don't . . . that I'd . . . I choose not to see those pictures was outta respect for my old man, y'know? I mean, y'know?"

Despite the hassles with *The Daily Planet*, Patti and the band did make an appearance on *Saturday Night Live*, which in 1976 was the hottest show on American television. *SNL* was in its second season and the one show that everyone watched each week to see the then-daring, and occasionally outrageous, live topical comedy of John Belushi, Bill Murray, Dan Aykroyd, Gilda Radner, Laraine Newman, and Chevy Chase. This was Patti's first appearance on national television, and everyone in the music business would be watching. Perhaps even President Gerald Ford, a constant target of satire by Chevy Chase, would be tuned in.

At CBGB's, the television next to the entrance was turned to Channel 4 at 11:30 so that the staff and patrons could cheer Patti on. The band did "Gloria," and Patti's performance was riveting. Wearing her outfit from the *Horses* cover, a white shirt and black tie, Patti, with her unruly black hair, piercing eyes, and fiery delivery, must have startled most of America. For even while *SNL* was a pretty hip show in 1976, punk and New Wave were not yet part of its vocabulary—musical guests ran more towards sixties veterans like Paul Simon or Joe Cocker. Patti was the first *SNL* musical guest to bring punk rock to American audiences—and also to the show's cast. Soon, Belushi would be a regular at CBGB's, sitting in with the Dead Boys, and Gilda Radner would lampoon Patti on the show as a ditzy punker named Candy Slice.

Radner wasn't the only performer to do a send-up of Patti. Wayne County, the outrageous cross-dressing rock singer who knew Patti from the late-sixties Factory days, fashioned a wicked parody of Patti. At CBGB's one night, dressed in black pants, a white shirt, and black tie, and wearing a black fright wig, he performed a number that began with a long rambling prose poem about following one of Jim Morrison's pubic hairs as it floated through the sewers of Paris. The piece built to a musical climax with County shouting "Horse shit! Horse shit! Horse shit—horse shit—horse shit!" to the tune of "Horses." The contingent of CB's regulars who had long thought Patti more than a bit pretentious cracked up, feeling that the parody was right on target.

Meanwhile, the Patti Smith Group had finished its U.S. tour and was gearing up for the conquest of Europe, where they would play eight cities in seven days. Not a week passed without some interview or review of Patti appearing in the British rock papers. On May 8, the *New Musical Express* ran a short phone interview in which she told Charles Shaar Murray, "I ain't afraid of the Parisians, man . . . I know how to handle the French. I've done so much time in Paris, I've done so much spiritual time, I feel like I'm part French."

In addition to bringing the mission to European audiences, the tour would also serve an important function for the band. Their sets now consisted mainly of new material, and Patti was looking ahead to the all-important second album. This, she was determined, would be a Patti Smith Group album, not one by Patti Smith only.

The European tour climaxed with two performances at London's Roundhouse on May 16 and 17. Like many powerful artists, Patti polarized the British rock press, which at that time comprised three weekly newspapers—the *New Musical Express, Melody Maker,* and *Sounds*—which published detailed accounts of every facet of the British music scene. At the time they were ahead of the American rock press not only in the amount of space they devoted to it but in their stable of writers, which included Nick Kent, Charles Shaar Murray, Miles, Mick Farren, Julie Burchill, and Tony Parsons. The idea was to be as opinionated as possible and to stir controversy. Writing about the London shows, they all had a go at Patti Smith.

Miles went to see her in her hotel before the first night at the Roundhouse, and stayed for the show:

Patti and the band had played the Paradiso in Amsterdam the night before—one of those clubs where hashish is legal and handed round in huge bins and the "Summer of Love" still exists in a time-warp. A few hours' sleep, airports, and a hassle with customs, and here she was, traces of that nervous energy still there, abbreviated stabs at the air while she talks, a highly expressive set of mouth muscles. "Miles knew me when I was just a nobody," she told Lenny. But now she has fame. A huge black limo takes her to the gig, Patti looking tiny and regal in the back while curtains twitch in the street as people peer out to see who it is.

The audience are regular Sunday-night Roundhouse crowd, stoned and shaking sack-loads of dandruff over their Levi's, part Patti Smith cult fans, including a large number of women delighted to have someone female do for rock what David Bowie did for the males. There are also a few fungoids and weirdos who have come to check her out. She comes bouncing on stage like Muhammad Ali jumping up and down on the spot, punchy and laughing, grinning, overjoyed at the cheering, applauding audience, who are all clapping with their hands over their heads. Lenny Kaye adopts the classic stance, legs wide apart, and then that familiar New York music begins. And they are very New York. Patti doesn't mess around. Just grabs the audience and takes them up there. She has tremendous stage presence, not showbiz, not glitter, just a personal magnetism which keeps all eyes beamed straight at her. Patti is not a woman rock and roller as such. There's plenty of sex drive in her act, but it's not specifically male or female by any usual archetypes, it's just a stack of burning energy bursting through. Not even so much sex as love because, for all the sullen street-punk imagery, she is really warm and friendly.

The constant fuzz roar of feedback guitar, the sound of New York City, of the IRT subway taking a curve, the screech of tortured metal, iron on iron, trucks rumbling over the cobbles in Lower Manhattan, transformed into music, organized by the regular no-frills drumming of Jay Dee Daugherty, always on top of it, kicking it into shape. The band eschews solos, functioning very much as a unit to punch out pure positive street energy, raw, bare, naked. Lenny and Patti crouch at each other like playful lion cubs. Patti relates to him a lot on stage. They've been together now for six years and the chemistry must be just right because the strain of playing together in a band is heavy. A rambling spoken intro led into "Horses" and the evening made that magic flip over from being a concert into being an event. I've not seen such audience appreciation in a long time. She returned and encored with "My Generation." They made her come back again and she ended with the very appropriate Stones number "Time Is on My Side." As she left the stage after the second encore, she shouted to the audience, "Remember Keith Relf," but it was lost in the cheers. Backstage afterwards she was exhausted but very up. A roomful of rock press congratulated her. Even later at the Hard Rock Cafe she was still jumping, cruising the aisles, talking to fans, waiters, friends.

Other members of the band, who didn't receive the same level of attention as Patti, were less inclined to accept victory so easily, feeling that the first London show was, in fact, one of the worst of the tour, primarily because they were exhausted. Their circumspection was, perhaps, warranted; not all critics were as kind as Miles.

On May 22, *Melody Maker* had a review of the Sunday Roundhouse show, written by Michael Watts, who, though he called Patti a "poetess," sneered a lot, and concluded by glibly stating that "At last there is a rock star who looks like Nick Kent and not the other way around. Patti Smith is for those who like the idea of rock and roll, rather than its perfect execution."

Steve Lake from *Melody Maker* termed Patti's music "loathsome," and he viewed her stance as entirely manipulative and calculating. The criticism was pointed and hit hard because this was a time when punk rock was a real movement in England and really meant something to a lot of people, including journalists. Patti reacted defensively. In a conversation with Lake after one of the shows, she explained herself:

> I've been a committed artist since I was a child. I do art every day. To me, rock writing is one of the highest professions. Such a high profession that I chose a rock writer to be my lead guitarist. Now, you're a rock writer and you question my integrity. Well, my integrity remains constant through everything I do. Look, I've read *Melody Maker* for years and it's like a lot of rock magazines, it takes a very hard line. It has a very self-important attitude, and rock belongs to the people. The album isn't recorded well. I'll grant you that. It doesn't sound good. We all know that. It's badly recorded. It sounds lousy on the radio. But it's cool, because it's a document of how it was. I mean, I know a lot of famous people. I could have had everybody in rock and roll on my fucking record. But I wasn't interested in that. I wasn't interested in any big-star-syndrome thing. You can call the record fucked-up technically. You can call it a piece of shit. I

call it a naked record. Naked and exposed. And I really don't feel that I have to defend it.

Despite the criticism, the Patti Smith Group soon became aware of the influence the show had on the English scene. The majority of musicians and critics they met during this first groundbreaking visit to the U.K. were, in fact, outspoken in their praise. Chrissie Hynde (still two years away from forming a band) and the Clash's Mick Jones and Paul Simonon (with whom Patti was rumored to have had a brief affair) were particularly friendly, the latter even joining them onstage for "My Generation." Audiences were likewise won over, as some people went so far as to say that seeing Patti that night changed their lives.

"The crowd just went crazy, it was fantastic," Jay Dee remembered. "They just went nuts and we ended up smashing up the instruments." Not all of the praise came easily, however, as Jay Dee continued: "The next night some friend of Lenny's said, 'You guys should come down to this club on Oxford Street and see the Sex Pistols.' I was like, the Sex Pistols? What a wacky name, yeah, okay, let's go. So we get down there and it's this dive and the floor's swimming in beer. This band comes on and before they even say anything Johnny Rotten's onstage, going 'And in we go to the Roundhouse the other night, see the hippie shaking the tambourines, Horses, Horses, HORSE-SHIT.' And I was thinking, 'Fuck, that was a quick fifteen minutes. We're over, we're fucking over already.'"

Nevertheless, Rotten was won over—in a way. "I don't like Patti Smith," Johnny Rotten told Mary Harron, the British correspondent for *Punk* magazine. "Just a bunch of bullshit going on about—'Oh, yeah, when I was in high school!' Two out of ten for effort. I used to hang around the hotel where she was staying. The last night they had to carry her up the stairs. I liked her for that. She was such a physical wreck."

Fan reaction was strong and unapologetic, as Jane Suck, a writer who covered the punk scene for the *NME* and harshly criticized Patti's Roundhouse show, discovered. The week following Suck's review, the paper received a flood of responses to her piece, illustrating the level of devotion of Patti's fans, and how she mesmerized her audience. "I went to see Patti Smith and I have never been through a more ultimate experience in my whole life," wrote Phil Neale of Woodingdean, Brighton. "She is the true Mona Lisa of rock, the real Joan of Arc, the battling crusader who has won. I was one of those stranded outside at 12:30 in the morning after waiting for her to come to the stage door. I had to walk home and I got there at 7:30 in the morning. I came back Tuesday and it was even better, I'd walk a million miles to see Patti. I'm no sycophantic college kid, I work in British Home Stores doing the washing up and I'm seventeen."

Patti Smith had definitely created a stir in England, and she inspired at least one group of girl punks to put together a band of their own—the Slits—right away. Many more would follow.

radio ethiopia

june-december 1976

> "Fucking Ethiopia this, fucking Ethiopia that, you sound like fucking Radio Ethiopia, Patti."
>
> *john cale, on the road*

In July 1976, Patti went into a New York recording studio to make her second album, *Radio Ethiopia*. An artist's second album is traditionally the most difficult. The first album contains a life's history, material that expresses the artist's whole self—all of their dreams, all of their unexpressed desires up to that point—and the material has generally been worked on and perfected for some time.

But if the first album is successful, from that moment the artist has time only to work. Frantically busy—touring, performing, and promoting—they have little or no time for introspection about anything at all. The second album is also made under the intense scrutiny of both the public and the media. It doesn't make things easy, and the pressure on Patti was enormous. Suffering writer's block, she looked for other means of expression to unlock her creativity. It must have been a truly frightening experience to suddenly discover that the river of words that had flowed through her mind since she was a kid had suddenly stopped. This happens to all creative people at one time or another—the novelist, the painter—all are faced with inventing new material, different voices. It seemed, however, to have happened to Patti surprisingly quickly. This was only her second album. Most rock groups turn out two or three before the first creative explosion dries up. Patti bought herself an electric guitar and made a point of not learning how to play it, instead just creating sounds she hoped would express ideas to herself or to the other members of the band.

Her personal situation only increased the pressure. Still living with Allen Lanier, she was in the midst of breaking up with Tom Verlaine. The dissolution of the relationship was difficult, as Terry Ork remembers. One night, he was smoking pot with Patti at her apartment, just before her recording session down the block at Electric Lady was set to begin, when the intercom rang. It was Tom Verlaine dropping by for a visit. "When she heard his voice on the intercom, Patti just flipped out," Ork recalled. "It was way toward the end, and she was clearly back with Allen."

Ork made motions to leave, but Patti grabbed his arm, saying "No! Don't leave!" She begged him to stay. "She didn't want to be alone with Tom," Ork said. "She was very uncomfortable around him by then, because he was still carrying a heavy load for her. It got very bitchy, and I know there were some hard words spoken before they finally separated."

For the all-important role of producer, Patti chose successful mainstream hitmaker Jack Douglas, who had worked with Aerosmith and John Lennon. Douglas was a crack technician with a successful track record, but he lacked the artistic edge of a John Cale—and that was exactly what Patti sought. This time, Patti said, she wanted somebody who would leave her alone, who would work with the band to get the sound required to get her music on the radio. However, despite having announced this as her goal, Patti proceeded to record a set of vocals that on some tracks sounded like the howling of a wounded animal. On other tracks, her lyrics were barely decipherable. She had chosen to have her voice, the band's most distinctive and unique instrument, pushed way down into the mix. As sessions progressed, *Radio Ethiopia* grew increasingly experimental, and ended up being even more of an "artsy" album than *Horses*.

At a press conference after the album was released, Allen Jones of *Melody Maker* asked Patti why she had chosen the very commercial Jack Douglas as her producer. Her convoluted reply is as good an explanation of *Radio Ethiopia* as any of the hundred-odd reviews the album received:

> I wanted to do a record that wasn't just a cerebral experience— it was more of a physical record. If everybody's hung up on po- etry, there's a big fucking poem in the record. Tell them if they're hung up because there's no poem in the record, that when they buy the record it's got the longest poem in the his- tory of man. [Presumably she was referring to the ten-minute "Radio Ethiopia" cut.] It took me four months. The poem, I don't say it . . . everything you don't hear on the record because of the bass and drums . . . I've written the poem. In other words, it's like when you listen to *Madame Butterfly*.

The combination of Patti's military imagery and her newly learned guitar playing evidently unleashed the muse. One night in August when the band was recording, New York was hit by tor- rential rainstorms and high winds, creating a dramatic, noir panorama of dark, rainslicked streets that silhouetted pedestrians in the traffic lights' reflections. Taking inspiration from the heavenly cacophony outside, the band formed a circle and started playing. By the end of the track, Patti was on her hands and knees, convulsed with laughter and "thankful for the privilege of playing in a rock 'n' roll band."

Meanwhile, Patti had taken on a take-charge new persona. As the band gathered momentum in 1975 and early 1976, Patti had begun to see their "mission" in military terms. Then, after buying a Marshall amp for the European tour, she started calling herself "Field Marshal." She identified with the military heroes she'd read about, including General Patton, Alexander the Great, and T. E. Lawrence, and employed military metaphors for her band's musical and ideological assault on the world.

Boxing provided Patti with another source for imagery, one she had drawn from often in the past. Craig Gholson, a writer from *Punk*'s competitor, *New York Rocker*, made note of the inclusion of the words "Ali is still the champ" on the liner notes to *Radio Ethiopia* and saw Patti's recognition of herself as "a heavyweight contender." The boxing metaphor was one that Patti constantly used. Talking about the importance of her technical crew, she said, "It's what helps a performer stay on top, like a boxer with a trainer. You have to know that these people are behind you. Then, when you really start to break and it's happening, a whole new kind of energy is created around you."

Around the time that they recorded *Radio Ethiopia*, Patti changed the billing of the band from "Patti Smith" to the "Patti Smith Group," to deflect attention away from herself as the "poet-performer" and emphasize the idea of the band as a musical unit. This was reminiscent of Chrysalis Records' vain attempt to draw attention away from Debbie Harry as the focus of her band by issuing the promotional slogan "Blondie is a group." No one was fooled.

The name change echoed her hopes for *Radio Ethiopia*, which

(Judy Linn: photo)

....Reading... February 10... 8:30... 1971
Gerard Malanga: POETRY.
patti smith: WORK ___
St. Marks Church-on-the- Bowery... 2nd Ave. + 10th St.

Flyer for poetry reading
at St. Mark's Church on
the Bowery.
(Gerard Malanga)

Portrait of Arthur
Rimbaud (1854–91)
taken in 1870.

Patti across the street
from the loft she shared
with Robert Mapple-
thorpe. *(Gerard Malanga)*

Patti and her younger
sister Linda at a Satur-
day afternoon party
hosted by Terry Ork in
1971. *(Gerard Malanga)*

"I'll be your mirror." Patti and Robert Mapplethorpe on the fire escape of their apartment at 208 West Twenty-third Street. *(Gerard Malanga)*

Femmes fatales: Patti with fellow cast members Jackie Curtis (center) and Penny Arcade (right) in 1971. "Patti always got raving applause at the end of the show."
(Leee Black Childers)

"We wrote one play, *Cowboy Mouth*, together on the same typewriter, like a battle . . . and took it straight to the stage. It was the true story of Sam and me."
(Gerard Malanga)

Patti Smith, Victor
Bockris, Andrew Wylie,
and Gerard Malanga in
front of Kensington
Church in London,
shortly after the Better
Books poetry reading of
February 3, 1972.
(Gerard Malanga)

Two people . . . two big
dreamers: Patti with
Sam Shepard outside
Kensington Church
after their secret liaison.
(Gerard Malanga)

(above, left) Appearing at the trendy downtown cabaret Reno Sweeney, Patti mixed her poetry with Cole Porter and Frank Sinatra songs. *(Danny Fields)*
(above, right) A *Village Voice* advertisement for Patti's performance at Max's.

Patti debuts at the Whiskey A Go Go in LA in the autumn of 1974 with Richard Sohl and Lenny Kaye. Many thought the group was at its purest when it was a trio, a perfect balance of communication and trust. *(Joe Stevens)*

Patti reads from her first book of poetry, *Seventh Heaven*. *(Danny Fields)*

Enjoying the good life after a Rod Stewart concert: Patti (center) with Lenny Kaye and her boyfriend, Allen Lanier. *(Leee Black Childers)*

(*above, left*) Downtown at Mickey Ruskin's Ocean Club in 1975. Patti was already wielding her guitar. **(Dan Asher)**

(*above, right*) 1975: Patti, wearing her Keith Richards T-shirt, works the crowd at the Other End while Bob Dylan sits unobtrusively at the bar. **(Danny Fields)**

Backstage at the Other End in Greenwich Village in 1975, the first time Dylan saw Patti live. Patti joked with the photographers, "Hey boys, why don't you take my picture!?" as Dylan praised her. **(Danny Fields)**

"Secretly I've been trailin' you, like a fox that preys on a rabbit . . . " Patti
sings the Marvellettes' "Hunter Gets Captured by the Game" in 1975.
Later she would record it for the *Ain't Nothing But a She Thing* album.
(Dan Asher)

Richard Sohl, Ivan Kral,
Patti, Jay Dee Daugherty,
and Lenny Kaye at
Mickey Ruskin's Lower
Manhattan Ocean Club,
1976. *(Roberta Bayley)*

Patti appeared on the
cover of the second issue
of *Punk* magazine in
March 1976.

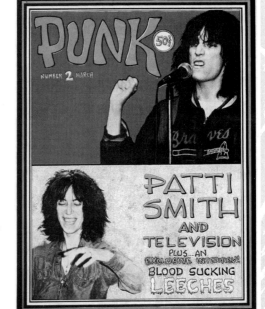

Patti with Allen Ginsberg and William Burroughs at Gotham Book Mart in 1977. *(Joe Stevens)*

Patti's first show after the accident: CBGB's, Easter Sunday, March 1977. *(Godlis)*

Fred "Sonic" Smith with the MC5 in London in 1972. The MC5 "were the guys who chopped down the trees to clear the dirt roads to pave the streets to build the highways so the rest of us could drive by in Cadillacs," said Cub Koda of Brownsville Station.
(Joe Stevens)

The "Field Marshal of Rock 'n' Roll" salutes. Patti with her producer, Jimmy Iovine, and Bruce Springsteen backstage at the CBGB's Second Avenue Theater, December 27, 1977. *(Joe Stevens)*

Patti appeared at the 1978 Nova Convention honoring William Burroughs wearing a $10,000 mink coat that she had recently purchased. *(Marcia Resnick)*

Fred and Patti backstage at the Masonic Auditorium, Detroit, July 1978. *(Robert Matheu)*

(above and below) Fred and Patti playing at Ann Arbor's Second Chance, March 1979.

(Robert Matheu)

Fred and Patti at Second
Chance, 1979.
(Robert Matheu)

Patti waves goodbye,
1979. **(Godlis)**

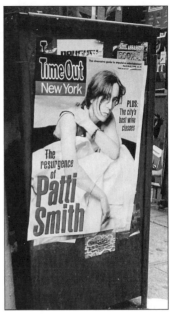

(above, left) Patti back home in New York City, 1995. *(Bob Gruen)*
(above, right) "I'm going to get into all those magazines when I grow up," Patti told her childhood friends in South Jersey, and in 1998 she's still gracing magazine covers around the world. *(Godlis)*

In 1997, Patti appeared with Oliver Ray at the Hoboken Street Fair, Hoboken, New Jersey. *(Godlis)*

she envisioned providing a link between her live shows and her records, especially with its inclusion of the more experimental, improvisational tracks that she felt would evolve over time. She hoped that the album would help to forge an even stronger group identity to help the Patti Smith Group to become "a great band, to become as big as possible, and to gain power." For Patti, the key line on *Radio Ethiopia* was the one in which she speaks of turning God in another direction. In fact, Patti told one interveiwer that it was the greatest lyric in rock 'n' roll. "It's a challenge to God," she said. "I wanna be God's daughter. No . . . I wanna be God's mistress. I'm not willing to witness one miracle and believe. I wanna be fucked by God. Not just once, a thousand times."

"If Jesus was around, if I was a groupie, I'd really get behind that guy," she told Lisa Robinson. "That's why I think Mary Magdalene was so cool—she was like the first groupie. I mean, she was really into Jesus and following him around; it's too bad she repented: she could've left a really great diary. All this stuff about Jesus, how wonderful he was, and how he was gonna save us. All I'd like to know is if he was a good lay. That interests me."

A European tour was scheduled to promote the new album. In September, the band did one warmup show in Chicago, and then took off for Finland. Two days before they were to leave, however, they learned that Richard Sohl would not be accompanying them. He was suffering from complete physical exhaustion, brought on by the endless grind of touring and recording. Patti was very close to Sohl, and she said later that losing him felt like being dropped by a boyfriend—something that had brought her close to suicide in the past. A replacement for Sohl was found in an old friend of Lenny's from Boston, Andy Paley. (Paley would later gain fame as the man who pulled Brian Wilson of the Beach Boys out of retirement, and fortune as a songwriter for Madonna, among others.)

On September 28, 1976, the night before leaving for the European tour Patti wrote in her journal:

the guys are waiting for me in Finland
i got to polish up my weapon . . .

And went on to describe her guitar in loving detail, claiming it once belonged to Jim Hendrix. In the second stanza she addressed the notion that "rock n roll is warfare," citing for examples that rock 'n' roll owned the universe, and on the battlefield guitars strained to reach their notes. Then she lists as footsoldiers the audience ("tender barbarians"), with the aim to unlock an imaginary army of "stampeding angels."

That month, almost one full year after *Horses* appeared, *Radio Ethiopia* was released. The album was anxiously awaited by her tender barbarians as well as those who were now curious as to just who this Patti Smith was. Arista's president Clive Davis was disappointed with the record, fearing it had little or no commercial potential.

The cover photograph for the album, taken by Patti's friend Judy Linn, was unmemorable. On the inside record sleeve were photographs by Andi Ostrowe, Lynn Goldsmith, and Lizzy Mercier, plus a long prose poem written by Patti.

Critical response to *Radio Ethiopia* was not good. Even those who had long supported Patti were disappointed. Charles Shaar Murray wrote in the *New Musical Express* that

The selection of Douglas as a replacement for Cale would suggest what a study of the album bears out: that *Radio Ethiopia* operates according to a significantly different aesthetic to its predecessor. . . .

The problem is that in the move from the uniquely personal and exhilaratingly unconventional territory staked out on *Horses* to familiar ground she treads on *Radio Ethiopia*, she has not so much brought the qualities of imagination, perception, and emotion displayed on the previous album into the hard-rock mainstream, but simply allowed the limitations of the genre to dictate restrictions to her.

John Rockwell of the *New York Times* agreed. "The level of songs seems lower than on *Horses*," he wrote. "And the shift away from declamation and minimal instrumental support to basic rock and roll robs Miss Smith's art of some of its individuality. . . . But recent journeyman rock is no substitute for what she is capable of at her best."

That autumn, Patti moved into the Bond Street loft with Robert Mapplethorpe. She needed time to think: Her affair with Tom was over, but she was unhappy with Allen and unsure about how to handle their relationship. At the same time, her feelings for Fred were getting stronger. She decided that Allen provided her with the security she needed. After some debate, she took her Arista earnings and purchased with Allen an apartment at One Fifth Avenue (where Mapplethorpe's patron Sam Wagstaff had a penthouse), and moved in.

Writer Mick Farren has made the observation that rock, and especially punk, produced a larger and better group of writers than did the hippie movement. Patti Smith, Richard Hell, Lester Bangs, Andrew Wylie, Nick Kent, Julie Burchill, Tony Parsons, Mary Harron, and Jon Savage, among many others, played seminal roles in the creation of punk. It was an incestuous and mutually supportive scene: Wylie had been in a poetry group with Richard Meyers (who later became Richard Hell) and introduced him to Patti Smith. He also published Patti's first book of poetry. Many of the New York musical contingent—Hell, Verlaine, and Smith foremost among them—thought of themselves primarily as writers. Even those in the movement on both sides of the Atlantic without pretensions to aligning themselves with French symbolists, like Johnny Rotten, Poly Styrene, and Debbie Harry, were outstanding lyricists.

Just as record deals were hard to come by, so were outlets for these poets' and writers' written work. As early as 1974, Nick Tosches, a contributing editor of *Playboy*'s hip new skin magazine,

Oui, gave some of his friends—including Andy Shernoff, "Handsome Dick" Manitoba (creators of the fanzine *Teenage Wasteland Gazette* and members of the punk band the Dictators), Richard Meltzer, and Patti Smith, who wrote a record review—work writing for the magazine. Perhaps if there had been a punk poetry magazine at this time, it might have been as influential as *Punk* magazine, which introduced many writers and artists in the seventies. Other than these, though, punk writers had difficulty publishing outside the movement. As a result, the literary output of the relatively short-lived punk movement has been largely ignored.

At the time, no one came close to Patti Smith in terms of recognition as a writer. In 1976, her collaboration with Sam Shepard, *Cowboy Mouth*, was published in his collection *Angel City and Other Plays*, and her poetic collaboration with Tom Verlaine, *The Night*, perhaps her rarest publication, was released in London by Aloes Books and in Paris by Editions Fear Press. *The Night* received all the attention to detail given to the most collectable poets; twenty-five copies of the U.K. edition were signed and numbered, while the French version, though two pages shorter than its British counterpart despite containing the poem in both French and English, was beautifully designed to look like a folded road map.

Another sign of Patti's unique stature in rock 'n' roll was the number of unauthorized bootlegs of her music that were made. According to Clinton Heylin in his history of bootlegs, *The Great White Wonders*, in the years before punk, the growth of the bootleg market was mainly due to a lack of new music from certain artists—Bob Dylan chief among them—whose fans demanded a constant flow of material. It was by going back to "lost" recordings or live performances of their favorite artists via bootlegs that fans could reconnect with their original feelings about the music and about rock 'n' roll in general.

The reason the punk movement came into being was this disconnection—many fans felt that rock had sunken into mediocrity, that it was self-indulgent and complacent, and had strayed far away from its incendiary roots. Live music, in the pubs in England and the bars in the United States, consisted mostly of rock cover songs and blues or country. Few venues showcased original live music. The successful bands touring America were playing huge stadiums and seemed inaccessible to their fans.

Two exceptions in the mid-seventies were Patti Smith and Bruce Springsteen. Both had risen to popularity through the support of their hardcore fans, who saw them perform mostly original material live in small venues. Both artists were heavily bootlegged on both sides of the Atlantic. In fact, Patti actually encouraged bootlegging at her early shows, and sometimes introduced "Redondo Beach" as a song from *Teenage Perversity*, the first such album to appear, which had been recorded at a landmark show at the Roxy in Los Angeles in January 1976.

The Patti Smith Group spent most of October in Europe. With each passing day, Patti's rhetoric was becoming more and more confrontational. In London, she shouted from the stage of the Hammersmith Odeon, "Yeah! I'm a genuine starfucker! I ain't never gotta sell out because my old man is Allen Lanier and he makes the bread in our house! He don't care if I never make a cent! He hopes I don't make a cent!"

Meanwhile, the Sex Pistols had just released their first single, "Anarchy in the U.K.," in England, and the punk movement was reaching fever pitch there. Patti kept repeating in interviews that her job was to shake rock up, to wake people up, to save rock and, from her perspective, it seemed to be coming true. She applauded the explosion of British punk bands from the Sex Pistols to the Clash. It was like CBGB's all over the world now, she said, not just in London but in Brussels, in Copenhagen, in Berlin. Even so, it was becoming obvious that the difference between English and American punk was extreme. Though she tried to be supportive,

Patti didn't really know what she was dealing with. British punk was a whole new thing, a whole new generation, and they didn't really have much in common with Patti Smith.

The British critics were not kind to Patti this time around. "Neither Smith nor her band had progressed beyond the totally inept musical standard displayed at London's Roundhouse in May and on *Horses*," wrote Maureen Paton about Patti's Hammersmith Odeon shows.

> The same embarrassing clichés were still handed out like food parcels to a largely bemused crowd. A lot of women present clearly got off on the idea of having someone up there to identify with. But it's precisely this kind of freak originality that Smith exploits so mercilessly by playing a rock and roll hero. The guitar that she hadn't even bothered to learn to play properly was toted around the stage as a symbol, nothing more.

Around this time, journalist Julie Burchill accompanied Miles to a Patti Smith press conference in London. Burchill was then at the very beginning of her career (she would later write a controversial book with Tony Parsons called *The Boy Looked at Johnny*, a vitriolic—and hysterically funny—diatribe against everyone in rock 'n' roll). At the press conference, Patti lost her temper when asked why her tickets weren't selling, screaming, "Fuck you! You're a drag! Get out of here!" According to Burchill, Patti then reached into a large plate of food and began to fling it around the room. Taunted by another journalist—"Which Beatle newsreel are you acting now?" he sneered—Patti climbed up on to a table, kicking aside whatever was on it. Before stalking out of the room, Patti declared, "I'm the field marshal of rock 'n' roll! I'm fucking declaring war! My guitar is my machine gun!"

"Julie burst into tears, she just collapsed. Patti was her hero," remembered Miles. "Confronted by her heroine, she was horrified, just horrified, to see this person behaving in this incredibly egotistical, stupid way."

"For a two-year-old it would have been a very impressive performance; from the Queen of Rock and Roll it was like watching God jerk off," wrote Burchill later.

The negative reviews angered Patti, but they also spurred her on. The majority of the European dates, particularly the French and Spanish shows, were well received and she felt a good connection with the crowds and picked up a lot of energy.

One thing that stood Patti in good stead was her loyal female following. She had opened a door for all women—both fans and artists—through which to infiltrate and overturn the male dominated rock world. One critic wrote on this topic in the 1976 book *Urban Soundscapes:*

> Punk continued to present itself in masculine outlines. Still, its reactive style, working on an unlikely amalgam of glam-rock ambiguities, stylized differences, and not unaffected by distant echoes of Women's Liberation, also shocked into life a new conflictual female image within white pop. . . . The slightly earlier, largely isolated, example of the American Patti Smith was now replaced by a more collective reconstruction of the white female voice. The disturbance of the "unnatural" voices of the British Siouxsie Sioux, Poly Styrene, and the Slits shattered the existing mold of female singing in pop.

Patti had to cut short her European tour because Andy Paley had other commitments and could not continue. They badly needed to find a permanent keyboard player. Patti was disappointed by the interruption, but not worried. She was strong in her conviction that what the band had achieved was solid.

Soon after they returned to New York, the band brought in session player Bruce Brody as the new keyboardist, and the new Patti

Smith Group gave a three-hour concert in Central Park. Though the concert was a rousing success, no amount of audience enthusiasm could make up for the fact that *Radio Ethiopia* was far away from its projected sales. There was just no way to turn around the bad publicity and negative reviews.

"Everybody thought we sold out," said Patti, who was not ashamed to admit that some reviews reduced her to tears. "They thought we had turned heavy metal. They found lyrics like 'pissing in a river' offensive, they found experimentation offensive, definitely too sonic."

At the end of November, when the band played for a week at the Bottom Line in New York, Patti was in full confrontational mode. "Her performances were getting increasingly chaotic, even self-destructive," Lenny Kaye recalled. "I remember each show getting crazier and crazier. At one point during 'Ain't It Strange,' I ran out into the audience, and Patti chased me and dragged me back, and we were walking on tables. It was just a lot of this adolescent energy and anarchy, and there was something very liberating about it because we were pushing the edge of the envelope."

Bruce Springsteen joined them onstage a couple of times that week. Patti had been introduced to Springsteen by producer Jimmy Iovine at the Record Plant during the making of *Radio Ethiopia*. "That was the period when Bruce was having his legal problems and couldn't record," Patti recalled. (*Born to Run*, released in 1975, had made Springsteen a star, but he would not be able to record again until 1978 due to legal problems.) "He was drifting around. We did 'Because the Night' together, and some English Invasion covers. One night we did this thing where Bruce played piano and I just improvised, sorta sang and talked while he played. That was an especially memorable night."

On November 29, Patti got herself banned from New York's most powerful alternative radio station, WNEW, ostensibly for using "fuck" on the air, but in no small part as a result of her general behavior. Before the broadcast, the show's host, singer-songwriter Harry Chapin, asked Patti not to use any four-letter words, since there was no time delay. Incensed, Patti let loose with a long rant: "How alternative IS this radio? I want to know how alternative this radio is! The first thing that happens when I walk in is that you tell me you don't have a bleep machine and to watch what I say—that's no alternative, that's the same old stuff. You notice I said 'stuff,' being completely professional at this moment, but we have the total alternative to, like, your alternative radio. The radio that I represent . . . it's like we're outer-space people, we're gonna zoom like a leech . . . gonna come in, like, right on a hand . . . take over WNEW right now!"

Patti continued her tirade for several minutes. Any sense she might have been making was lost in her rambling.

"Rock 'n' roll is being taken over by people again," she declared, "by young kids again, who don't want to hear about your digital delay. They don't want to hear about any of this stuff. They don't want to hear that they can't do an Eric Clapton solo. They just want to get out there and just get down on a rhythm. They want to crawl up like a dog or they want to rise up. They just want to feel something."

Chapin was well known as a tireless fund-raiser for world hunger, and Patti also offered her own surreal solution to that problem: "What we should do is just take over the wheat . . . we should look at our power, relax, understand that rock 'n' roll is becoming more and more powerful . . . it, like, indirectly helped elect some guy into the presidency of the United States and we should, like, really exonerate and be happy about this power and do it for the good of mankind, take over the wheat and give it to the people for free. If Ethiopia calls up and says we need wheat, we don't ask them what color they are or what their favorite AM station is—what they're listening to on their radios . . . they don't have to have an AM station . . . or any particular station . . . they don't have to do nothing but be hungry and if they're hungry, you feed the people, that's all."

Chapin was speechless.

Patti's interview did not help world hunger or the sales of *Radio Ethiopia*. In December the album peaked on the U.S. charts at number 122.

On New Year's Eve, the Patti Smith Group performed at the Palladium in New York. WNEW had planned to air the concert, but now refused on account of Patti's on-air obscenity, a violation of federal communications laws that made the radio station liable for huge fines. Upon hearing of the station's decision, Patti wrote a heavy condemnation of "progressive" rock radio in general— "the celebration of 1776–1976 ends tonight . . . we end with the same desires of individual and ethnic freedom of work . . . the freedom/flow of energy that keeps rebuilding itself with the nourishment of each generation."

Though Patti's statement fervently defended First Amendment rights, it also condemned WNEW, one of the few radio stations to have supported Patti and many other punk and New Wave artists, and unfortunately neglected to target the Federal Communications Commission, which made the rules. (Presumably, she did not send them a copy of her manifesto.) The FCC was the real purveyors of censorship, being the government agency under whose dictates any American radio station operates.

Still, the show went on as planned, and was a success, "I was at the best concert of the year, nursing a bad cold and a pleasant high and engulfed by Patti's 'kids,' who looked to average out to college age, juniors and seniors rather than freshmen and sophomores," wrote Robert Christgau in the *Village Voice* of that New Year's show.

> The crowd wasn't as loose as it might have been, but I liked its mix—a few arty types among the kind of intelligent rock and rollers who almost never come out in force anymore, a sprinkling of gay women among the hetero couples. When Patti came on, these sophisticates rushed the stage like Kiss fans, and

eventually two women took off their tops and had to be dissuaded physically from dancing on stage. I hadn't seen the likes since a Kinks concert in 1973 or so, when such hijinks were already blasts from the past. And the climax was better, the true "My Generation." It began with Patti wrestling a guitar away from her female roadie, Andi Ostrowe, and ended with Patti—joined, eventually, by Ivan Kral—performing the legendary guitar-smashing ritual that the Who had given up by 1969 or so.

John Rockwell, Patti's most penetrating American critic, wrote in the *New York Times* of the same show,

Patti Smith's performances are like some cosmic, moral struggle between demons and angels . . . at one point she slumped to the floor and started banging her head against the organ. It was reminiscent of Iggy Stooge's self-mutilations or the excesses of SoHo performance artists, except that it had real fervor to it. She has always walked the line between genius and eccentricity, between the compelling and the merely odd, between art and insanity . . .

the fall

1977

> "There was a moment when I had my fall
> that I felt I could have gone through the
> black tube. I felt myself disintegrating and
> I didn't want to go."
>
> *patti smith*

Then, the once-adulatory music press turned against Patti. This was especially true of the British music weeklies, well known for their habit of building up and then tearing down the latest darling of the pop-music world. In its January 1, 1977, issue, for instance, the *NME* made three mentions of Patti Smith: She was listed as number two of "Last Year's Things," accompanying the piece with a photo of her at Jim Morrison's grave, captioned "Patti Smith went from promise to dementia." In another "looking back" section, Charles Shaar Murray listed her Roundhouse appearance as a "great gig," but said that *Radio Ethiopia* was the "most disappointing album of the year." Tony Parsons, in the same section, cited "the Roundhouse rise and Hammersmith fall of Patti Smith," as if her career was over. Patti's response? "Listen, I'm over thirty. Nobody tells me if I can spit on stage or not."

The New York press was more sympathetic, but acknowledged the problems she faced at this juncture of her career. Robert Christgau, for one, published a piece in the *Village Voice* entitled "Save This Rock & Roll Hero," in which he described Patti as being "caught in a classic double-bind—accused of selling out by her former allies and of not selling by her new ones."

Amid this scrutiny, in the last week of January 1977, the Patti Smith Group began the all-important tour of America to promote *Radio Ethiopia*. The tour involved performing in much larger venues than they had played previously, and also had the band opening up for other acts, which they had rarely done. The tour kicked off in Hollywood, Florida, where the Patti Smith Group opened for Bob Seger and the Silver Bullet Band. The show did not go particularly well: Seger attracted a more mainstream crowd who wanted to hear, as his song put it, "that old time rock 'n' roll," and probably didn't know what to make of the spacey, punky New York poet.

The second date was January 26 in Tampa, Florida, at the Curtis Hixen Hall, a six-thousand-seat sports arena, the largest hall the band had ever played. The band went in determined to win over Seger's fans. Unfortunately, Patti began the show with a vitriolic harangue against the people and the marijuana of Florida.

Although the band played hard and strong, deafening silence greeted the opening number. "They went over like a lead balloon," observed Jim Marshall, a fan and friend who was at the show. Lenny Kaye, however, felt that the band was beginning to move the crowd as they went into their second number, an intense version of "Ain't It Strange." During this song Lenny and Patti would interact in a sort of dance—"a ballet," Lenny called it—until they came to the part in the song where Patti would challenge God, saying something like, "c'mon, God, make a move." Then she would start spinning as the musical intensity built, spinning and spinning until she reached for the microphone to continue the verse. What they did not take into account was that as the opening act, they were confined to using only a portion of the headliner's stage, had to perform around his equipment, and couldn't use his lights.

That night, there was a monitor on the stage near Patti's feet. It was painted black, making it impossible to see on the darkened stage. So, as Patti lunged for the mike, she fell backward over the monitor and off the front of the stage, plunging fifteen feet toward the concrete floor below. "It was like a Bugs Bunny cartoon," she joked later. "When he walks over a cliff into midair and just keeps on walking until he realizes there's nothing there." From his drum seat at the back of the stage, Jay Dee Daugherty thought, "Oh, my God, she's either dead or she's gonna jump back up on the stage." If he had seen the fall from the audience, as Jim Marshall did, he wouldn't have expected her to get up. Patti's brother Todd, who was the head of her stage crew, attempted to catch her, but, according to Marshall, "She hit the base of her neck on some two-by-fours in the [orchestra] pit, then flipped up and hit the back of her head again on the floor. She was twitching and there was blood everywhere, and it looked like she had broken her neck."

Paramedics were called, and an ambulance rushed Patti to Tampa General Hospital. Patti's neck was not broken, but she was seriously injured: she had cracked two vertebrae in her neck and had broken some bones in her face. Twenty-two stitches were required to close the lacerations on her head. Her immediate reaction was one of embarrassment. "I looked like an asshole," she told the band from the hospital.

After two days in the Tampa hospital, Patti was flown to New York to have her medical condition assessed by specialists. Glad to be home, Patti took to her bed, confident that two weeks of enforced bed rest would take care of any damage caused by the fall. But the injuries were more serious than she imagined, and she soon began having trouble with her vision, as well as difficulty walking. The doctors were not optimistic. Though she was assured that her vision would return to normal, she received conflicting reports about the paralysis in her legs and different recommendations about how to deal with it. One doctor told her that she would not regain the full use of her legs without undergoing spinal surgery. Another doctor, from the Nautilus Sports Institute, felt that rigorous physical therapy would correct the damage. The thought of major surgery on the delicate spinal area under full anesthesia scared Patti, and so she chose physical therapy. It was the more demanding course of action, but also the one in which she would feel more in control of the outcome.

Forced off the road by her accident, Patti gained time to work on new material for another book. Earlier in the year she had signed a $5,000 contract with Putnam to produce a collection of her poetry, which would be called *Babel*. Patti dictated the book from her sickbed, to a new assistant, Andi Ostrowe. Ostrowe was a fan who had written Patti a letter. Patti recalled the moment well: "Everybody was standing around Electric Ladyland, just hanging out, and the secretary hands me this fan letter. The envelope had all this Ethiopian writing on it and a stamp of Haile Selassie so I opened it up and inside was this heavy letter. It was like a lightning bolt, like instant karma."

Ostrowe had worked in Ethiopia as a volunteer for the Peace Corps; Patti was obsessed with the country because that was where Rimbaud had done his early exploring, back when it was called Abyssinia. Patti saw in Ostrowe an opportunity to get closer to Ethiopia and Rimbaud. "I needed a guide, and I get this fan letter from a girl who can do all that stuff—a guide who can interpret, who knows the language fluently, who knows all the shortcuts and where to buy the dope," Patti explained enthusiastically. Ostrowe started off as a roadie and then, after the accident, offered to work for Patti without pay. She would stay with Patti through thick and thin until Patti's retirement in 1979, and resume working for Patti in the nineties.

Of the time immediately following the accident, Patti said later, "I was able to clean up a lot of loose ends and best of all, I wrote a book—which I'm really proud of. I was able to do a lot of work I hadn't been able to do for a long time. The other books were like very spontaneous efforts. I haven't published anything since early '73, because I was so intensely involved in performing and verbal expression that I lost contact with the word on paper. *Babel* is entirely different. It's mostly prose pieces, they're longer and there's much more voyage."

Informing those voyages, she realized, was the Percodan she was taking for her pain. "I wrote a lot of it [*Babel*] in a very unusual state of mind because I had special prescriptions from doctors, so I think it deals with a very subliminal landscape," she told a journalist.

During her convalescence, Patti rarely enjoyed being alone. A regular visitor at One Fifth was Legs McNeil from *Punk* magazine, who spent a lot of his time shooting pool with Allen Lanier. Legs was a cartoon character, the walking embodiment of a punk. Soon Legs was arriving at One Fifth every night at 6 P.M., like clockwork, clutching his breakfast of a six-pack in one hand and holding a Kool in the other. Patti eschewed alcohol, but she smoked pot enthusiastically, and as soon as she was high she would launch into long Burroughsian rambles, speaking of spaceboys called Johnny and describing Venusian landscapes that only she could see. Sitting at the foot of her bed guzzling a Bud, Legs did not understand a single word of what she was saying, but as long as the beer held out, he was a good audience, and that was all that Patti required.

Miles was another visitor at One Fifth during Patti's recuperation. He remembered the apartment as being big, with lots of expensive rock-star stuff lying around. "What really struck me was her bedroom," he said. "She had a little altar by the window, just below the window sill. There was a low table with a cloth over it, on top of which was arranged a first edition of *Naked Lunch*—the original Olympia Press edition—a portrait of Rimbaud, some crosses, and a rosary. We talked about Rimbaud and Burroughs, and about a dream she had about Dylan's dog. She went on about that at some length. She was definitely speeding or coked up. At that time you couldn't call her before three o'clock in the afternoon. This was a very very strict rule: you should never call Patti before three o'clock because she was sleeping."

After leaving Television, Richard Hell had continued to collaborate with Patti. During her recuperation, they decided to do a book together. While Hell and his new band, the Voidoids, were recording *Blank Generation* down the block at Electric Ladyland, he would visit Patti at One Fifth Avenue. "I'd go up there and we'd pass the typewriter back and forth," Hell remembered. "It resulted in a few good poems, but I finally had to drop out because I just didn't have enough time." Although he was fond of Patti, he was also somewhat uncomfortable around her: "She was just too 'on' for me," he confessed. "I felt like it was a competition when you were around her. She's so lovable and charming with her 'little girl' stuff and her sweetness. . . . [But] we just didn't mix very well. Patti's so much a performer that she's always superconscious of making an impression. It's not a criticism. I think most great performers tend to be that way—that's what makes them great. They're so conscious of the impression they're making all the time and they want it to be a strong impression. It may be my own fault—she may be different with people who are more comfortable with her. But I couldn't deal with it."

On another afternoon, Bruce Springsteen dropped by. He and Patti played each other old 45s and compared favorites. Both from New Jersey, the two songwriters had a camaraderie touched with friendly rivalry, and their relationship would later result in a hit single.

Even as her visitors came in and out, Patti thought about her place in the punk pantheon as she lay in bed recuperating. When she and Lenny began their crusade, she had always insisted that she was only going to play rock 'n' roll as long as it took to wake up the masses so they could return rock music to the revolutionary, boundary-pushing medium that it had been in the beginning. By 1977, punk had garnered national attention, but was still not a commercial force. It didn't look like there was going to be a punk revolution, at least not yet. Seeing this, Patti could have used her fall as an excuse to make a graceful exit from a scene that was about to self-destruct. But instead of abandoning the fight, Patti trained hard to get back in shape so that she could play live again and continue the struggle. She was addicted to the adrenaline rush of being onstage, as well as the fame, money, and prestige that went with it, things she had always believed she deserved. She also kept up with the scene, and her competitive drive remained undiminished. One night Lisa Robinson came by, having just returned from Toronto, where Keith Richards had been arrested on charges of heroin trafficking. As Lisa described the scene, Patti hung on every word, but when Lisa started talking about Debbie Harry and Blondie, who had played Toronto the night of Richards's arrest, Patti demurred, casting aspersions on her colleagues. Lisa took that in, then said, "Debbie's really nice." Legs McNeil was also present, and he saw that Patti was seething. Her debilitating fall had come at just the moment that Blondie began its own meteoric rise.

Meanwhile, out in Detroit, Fred Smith's Sonic Rendezvous Band was at the height of its powers, and was receiving a good deal of attention in the local press. "Sonic Smith, magnificent wearing a torn black silk shirt, led the band through a crack set of Detroit hard rock," wrote John Koenig of one of their shows in the spring of 1977. "When Smith returned to the dressing room, he had blood running down his hand from the ripped fingers. He attacks those strings. It's an amazing rock 'n' roll performance." And Mike Taylor wrote in January 1979, "There is a primeval, earth-shaking quality to this music. . . . Its beauty can't easily be defined."

It was during Patti's recovery that the affair with Tom Verlaine finally ended. Deerfrance was angry with him for leaving Patti, even though she could see how their personalities clashed. Verlaine was detached and analytical, even cold, while Patti "always had the strangest energy," said Deerfrance. "If you were in a room with her, it was nerve-wracking. You didn't feel comfortable. She had a kind of tornado energy that was very nervous and made you uncomfortable. But she always had a great presence."

Deerfrance thought Patti lucky to be with Allen Lanier instead of Tom. "I think Allen was really good for Patti, he really took her up to a better level of living," she said. "He was almost more like a father than a boyfriend. We talked about Patti as someone who had to be protected. Even though when you were in Patti's presence she seemed like the last person in the world who needed to be protected."

During her recuperation, Patti also separated from her long-time manager Jane Friedman. The two had been together since the beginning of Patti's career, and the split was painful for both women. But Jane was now living with John Cale as well as managing him, and some speculated that Patti felt Cale had taken her place as Friedman's top priority. In Jane's place Patti hired lawyer Ina Meibach to handle her affairs.

In March, Patti began a rigorous course of physical therapy at the Nautilus Sports Clinic. Patti took on her physical therapy like an athlete in training, "like Mr. America or Muhammad Ali, somebody who can't let a day go by that they're not rebuilding or maintaining themselves," she said at the time. "It has given me a new kind of discipline—it has put my life in better form."

A show of her drawings at the Gotham Book Mart was scheduled to coincide with the release of *Babel*, the manuscript of which was now completed. Around this time Patti was also offered another art exhibition at the prestigious new Robert Miller Gallery on Fifty-seventh Street, which had a new owner. Patti decided to turn the show into a collaboration with Robert Mapplethorpe. The idea of doing an exhibition together had been one of their earliest dreams, and now it would actually happen—and at a prestigious uptown gallery. Despite the accident, things were coming together in a positive way.

She set Easter Sunday, April 30, as a goal for her "comeback" performance at CBGB's. "One day I was at the door of CBGB's," said Deerfrance. "It was a bleak Monday night, I saw this little face looking in through the window and it was Patti. I ran out and said, 'Patti, come on in,' but she was being really shy and really adorable, and said, 'No, no. No one would know me.' 'No one would know you?' I said. 'God, everyone here is just trying to pretend to *be* you! For God's sake, come on in!' But she got all shy and said, 'No, no.'

"Later she did some shows there and I always worked the door for her because I would get every dollar from every person who walked in. She did one show on Easter and told me, 'Everyone has to pay, no exceptions.' I said, 'Okay.' So Clive Davis comes in and I say, 'That'll be six dollars,' and he walks right past me. I stood up and repeated, 'It's six dollars,' and he said, 'Do you know who I am?' and I said 'Yes, and I know you have six dollars!' I'm very protective of my friends. Then Ian Hunter walks in and just personality after personality and I just kept saying, 'That'll be six dollars,' and they kept saying, 'Do you know who I am?' and I would say, 'Yes, and that's six dollars!' Even the staff [of CBGB's] had to pay! So that's why I would work the door for Patti. She would give it away free to someone who didn't have it, but if you have it, hey, you know . . . *pay*."

Patti's roll continued when the first show after the accident happened as planned, at CBGB's on Easter Sunday. Fans lined up around the block to see Patti's return, which followed a matinee performance by Cleveland's Dead Boys and the British punk band the Damned, the final show in a three-night stand. The house was cleared after the matinee and a separate admission was charged for Patti. William Burroughs was a special guest, and a youthful Thurston Moore (who would later go on to form Sonic Youth) was in the audience.

The show was an event, and Patti took the opportunity to demonstrate how to turn weakness into strength, by making a theatrical prop of her neck brace—wearing it onstage for the first half of the show, then dramatically ripping it off in the second. In the end Patti made the fall work for her, using her recovery and comeback to gain attention and publicity. In a later conversation with Burroughs, Patti was candid about her feelings about being onstage again:

> When I was first trying to learn how to be on the stage again, I was not only afraid, but I was concerned about my energy. I couldn't really move around so much. I mean, you were at one of those performances when I started to get back. I hadn't been able to get out of bed for a few months, and I was addicted to pills, or whatever, and had to be carried onto the stage. And I had them put a chair on the stage. Well, those nine days that I spent with the people, doing a couple of sets a night at CBGB's, around Eastertime in '77, was the best therapy that I had. I took my [neck brace] collar off by the end of it. I don't quite understand it myself, but I don't find it overtly mystical.

Jay Dee Daugherty felt that Patti had gone through a change after the accident, coming to grips with her own religious or spiritual system. As evidence, he points to the fact that the band cut "Gloria," with its line about Jesus having "died for somebody's sins, but not mine," from their set. "She changed," stated Jay Dee. "She didn't feel that way anymore."

Her shows also changed as she continued to perform over the next few months, doing shows at CBGB's in June and at the Elgin Theater and Village Gate in July. The shows were becoming increasingly accessible, "shorter and faster," Patti said. "It's still improvisational, but it's shorter, stronger and it's not so much groping around."

She also appeared with William Burroughs and Allen Ginsberg for a joint book signing at the Gotham Book Mart in September, and, before going into the studio to record her third album, Patti played a benefit for the Museum of Natural History at the Hayden Planetarium. There, she introduced two new songs, one being "Till Victory." Despite the steep ticket price of $35, many of Patti's devoted fans showed up and cheered her on.

Patti chose Jimmy Iovine as the producer for her next album, which would be titled *Easter*, continuing her theme of resurrection. The band was friendly with Iovine, having met him in the recording studio at the end of making *Radio Ethiopia*. He had worked with John Lennon and Bruce Springsteen, and had encouraged Patti's band in their songwriting. Early on, too, he'd had the idea of getting Patti and Springsteen together. Bruce had recorded a demo of a song called "Because the Night," but there were no lyrics other than the chorus. He gave the tape to Iovine, thinking that the song was perfect for Patti's voice. When Patti finally listened to it, she was immediately struck by its commercial potential, though she also questioned whether doing a song written by an established artist so different from herself would conflict with her band's vision. In the end, however, the strength of the song won her over.

Patti wrote the lyrics to "Because the Night" in a flash of inspiration. Late one night, as she paced the room waiting for Fred's call from Detroit, she glimpsed a cassette lying atop a colorful piece of cloth. Picking it up and popping it into the tape deck, she found herself listening to Springsteen's song over and over, hearing the chord changes anew. The lyrics fell into place rapidly. "It was an easy song to write," she said, "and the easiest song we ever recorded. Bruce was right—it was written in my key and it suited my voice perfectly. I knew exactly what to do with it." She brought the completed song into the studio the following day.

The completion of *Easter* marked the end of Patti's convalescence. The time out of the spotlight had certain benefits for her: while resting, she'd read a biography of T. E. Lawrence, smoked a lot of pot, and had a chance to rethink the basic precepts of her mission. Thus, when *Easter* was released and "Because the Night" became a hit, she was fully prepared to handle the charges of "sell out" that were sure to come. Ever defiant, Patti simply said, "We took our hit and our rock 'n' roll nigger stance and hit the road."

r e s u r r e c t i o n

1 9 7 8

> "Being great is no accident."
>
> *patti smith*

In January 1978, the Patti Smith Group mounted another American tour, performing in many of the same clubs that the Sex Pistols would play a week later. The Pistols' incendiary tour and messy breakup at Winterland in San Francisco in February would signal to many in the music business the lack of viability of punk rock as a commercial force, and few punk bands would be signed in the following years.

During this tour, Patti's secret two-year telephone affair with Fred Smith finally became public knowledge.

Fred had been born in West Virginia and moved to Detroit as a child. He met Wayne Kramer in junior high school, and in 1965, with Rob Tyner, Mike Davis, and Dennis Thompson, they formed the MC5. Fred Smith eventually became one of the best guitar players in rock 'n' roll, a naturally gifted musician whose talent was never fully recognized. The MC5 strongly influenced both the punk and heavy-metal bands of the seventies, but commercially they went nowhere. "The importance of the MC5 can't be overestimated," Cub Koda of Brownsville Station told writer Ben Edmonds years later. "There would have been no Michigan scene without them. The Five brought focus to the whole thing, a sense that it meant something to be from here. They were the guys who chopped down the trees to clear the dirt roads to pave the streets to build the highway so the rest of us could drive by in Cadillacs." By the mid-seventies, the MC5 had been gone for half a decade—with Fred forming the Sonic Rendezvous Band—and Wayne Kramer was in prison.

When he first met Patti, Fred was married to a woman named Sigrid. The couple later separated, and Fred began spending time with Kathy Asheton, the sister of Scott Asheton, who had been in the Stooges with Iggy Pop. Though they weren't a regular thing, Kathy still thought of him as her boyfriend. So, while at first Kathy thought it was "kinda cool" that Patti was interested in Fred's Sonic Rendezvous Band and had them open several shows in the Detroit–Ann Arbor area, she found it less cool when she saw Patti moving in on what she considered her territory—Fred.

Meanwhile, Patti told her friends that she'd "found the man I love, all I've been looking for all my life." In addition to her strong romantic feelings about Fred, Patti also felt that they could collaborate on an artistic level. "Fred and I had always worked together," she later recalled. "We wrote songs and pursued individual ideas. It had been that way since I met him in 1976. He instilled in me confidence and clarity, a calmness that made me believe I could do anything." The relationship seemed to have a quality of inevitability, and, shortly before *Easter*'s March release, Patti surprised everyone she knew by leaving Allen Lanier and New York to live with Fred Smith in Detroit. "She'd met God!" exclaimed one friend. "It was as simple as that."

In 1978, New York was in every way the cultural capital of the world, having undergone a rebirth of sorts after its brush with bankruptcy. Detroit, on the other hand, had never fully recovered from the race riots of the sixties, and there had been a mass exodus from the inner city over the following decade. With the decline of the American auto industry, by 1978 it was one of the most depressed cities in America, vexed with a soaring crime rate. Detroit was certainly not perceived by the outside world as a desirable place to live. It did, however, have a long and illustrious musical history, first as one of the hottest jazz spots in the country, and then in the sixties, as home to Motown—"the sound of young America." And, while they would not have the commercial impact of Motown, the Detroit rock bands of the sixties, such as the MC5 and the Stooges, would be models for punk rock. Even in 1978, there was a vibrant local music scene, full of energy and creativity, but it was self-contained, with musicians tending to keep their own counsel, avoiding the hustle of New York or Los Angeles. Not only was Patti choosing this over New York but she was also leaving Allen Lanier, who was supportive, successful, and financially secure, for someone who appeared to offer little. Fred Smith was an anomaly in the music business: He was not a driven self-promoter, but rather a talented loner who walked his own path, fitting more comfortably into the role of artist than rock 'n' roller. He looked cool, too.

"Fred was one of the classiest dressers," noted his friend Freddie Brooks. "Even if he was wearing jeans, he always had a nice cotton shirt. He prided himself on looking neat."

The couple moved into Detroit's tony Book Cadillac Hotel and began their life together. Although to the outside world Patti's move to Detroit defied logic, for her there was no other choice. Such is the power of love.

Always given to creating myths around her life, Patti would later describe her move to Detroit, and especially her union with Fred, in highly romantic terms. "To leave New York was a very tough thing," Patti told William Burroughs in 1979. "But it was a great joy, too—you know, like a pioneer. It's like you have to 'Go west'! I've always been a very East Coast girl. I was raised in South Jersey, Philly, Camden, all the coolest cities. Actually, though, when I was a teenager I thought that the coolest city wasn't New York, it was Detroit, because Detroit had Motown. But the thing is, I'm very happy because I have met the person in my life that I've been waiting to meet since I was a little girl. For the first time I'm not pursuing—the person has opened up to me another way to express myself truly, which is music."

Upon leaving New York, she acknowledged what the city meant to her, but didn't look back. "I've always loved New York, and I did miss the light of the city and how good it had been to me and my friends," she told Lisa Robinson. "But I never for a moment had any regrets. I just felt I did everything I could have done in my twelve years in New York. It's my spiritual home, where I flourished as an artist and gained confidence as a person. But I've never been afraid of change."

Patti, in fact, looked forward to her move and defended it to writer Gerrie Lim: "I'm not burnt out. I may be thirty-one years old but I've just begun. I feel like it's new and fresh . . . I'm just starting! I believe that we, that this planet, hasn't seen its Golden Age. Everybody says it's finished . . . art's finished, rock 'n' roll is dead, God is dead. Fuck that! This is MY chance in the world. I didn't live back there in Mesopotamia, I wasn't there in the Garden of Eden, I wasn't there with Emperor Han, I'm right here now and I want now to be the greatest time. This is my Golden Age . . . if only each generation would realize that the time for greatness is right now when they're alive . . . the time to flower is now."

Around the time of Patti's Detroit shows, Wayne Kramer was

released on parole, and he sought Patti out. *Radio Ethiopia*'s back cover had carried the slogan "Free Wayne Kramer," and he wanted to let Patti know that he had been surprised and touched by the show of support. When he tracked her down, though, he did not find the champion he had expected, and also was disturbed by the dynamic he saw developing between Patti and Fred. "When I came out on parole, I went to a Patti Smith show in Ann Arbor to thank her," said Kramer.

It was awkward because I was with my girlfriend and Fred's ex-wife Sigrid. Fred had just started courting Patti in public. We're watching Fred go get a pitcher of beer, pour her a drink, it just seemed really insensitive. The idea that this guy was fronting off his wife with this other woman rubbed me wrong. I thought, "This ain't cool."

I went backstage afterwards, and as Patti walked by, I said, "Hi, Patti, I'm Wayne Kramer and I just wanted to thank you for mentioning me on your record." She looked at me kind of blank and drifted away, leaving me talking to the wall—she moonbeamed me! Later, backstage, I could see Fred in the dressing room, but I wasn't allowed in the dressing room. The whole thing was just awkward. When Fred met Patti, it was like he cut himself off from his life before and all of his friends from before and all of his associations with his old band.

I finally realized that her putting my name on the record didn't have anything to do with showing solidarity with me, it had to do with giving credibility to her! Turns out it was Lenny's idea anyway.

Patti seemed to have made Fred pull away from his old friends; similar things were happening to her. The professional ramifications of Patti's new relationship with Fred were not immediately clear, but the band could not but hear the distant death knell of the Patti Smith Group. They tried to make light of it, making cracks like "It must be love!," but inside they had to face the possibility of being out of jobs. Patti was their director, their inspiration, their leader, and their role had been to support her. Without Patti, there would be no band. How long could they carry on with their leader a thousand miles away? And how long could they write songs over the phone and expect satisfying results? Perhaps Mick Jagger and Keith Richards could do it—they had been for years—but could they? The final break would not come for some time, but, in a way, the slow deterioration of a band that had been like a family was more distressing than a sudden break might have been. The uncertainty caused by Patti's move to Detroit would be hard on Lenny, Jay Dee, Ivan, and DNV, but had they seen the clues, they could pretty easily have seen the future.

Patti had indeed talked about the possibility of leaving the rock stage before. In a January 1976 *Punk* magazine interview, for instance, she told Legs McNeil that she gave herself "one or two years maybe. I'll do as much rock 'n' roll as I can and I'll transcend to something else. I did as much painting as I could—I transcended to poetry—now I'm into this period of my life . . . I wanna keep transcending." Moreover, the liner notes to *Easter* included a quote from the New Testament letters of Timothy: "I have fought the good fight, I have finished my course . . ."

Easter was released in March. For the first time, the cover, by Patti's friend Lynn Goldsmith, was in color. The image of Patti was softer and more feminine than the stark androgyny of the *Horses* cover or the ambiguous image on *Radio Ethiopia*. The lyrics to "Because the Night," which implore her lover to "come on now, try and understand/ how I feel under your command" foreshadowed Patti's deferential relationship with Fred Smith. Reviews of the album were mixed. Interestingly, Allen Lanier, who had been badly hurt by Patti's abrupt departure, liked the record, and praised it in an interview appearing in the March 4 issue of the *New Musical Express*. "*Easter* goes right at you. It has none of the idiosyncrasies which prevented people from deciding whether they really liked her or not. Her band is so improved that the ambivalence has gone." In the same issue, writer Paul Rambali was less enthusiastic: "We find Miss Smith still plagued by the problem of getting her stream-of-consciousness raps in synch with the hard pumping rock of her band, and of getting it down with the ferocious energy it possesses live," he wrote in his review.

The American reviews were generally more positive though tinged with ambivalence as well. "Christ gains admission to Smith's eccentric pantheon of 'Rock n Roll Niggers,' beside Jackson Pollock, Jimi Hendrix, and unless my ears deceive me, Smith's grandmother," wrote Ken Tucker somewhat sarcastically in the *Village Voice.*

> But even though "Rock n Roll Nigger" has pretty silly lyrics, it's also the album's best rocker, with a sublime found guitar riff that Lenny Kaye and Ivan Kral throttle with skill and delight, and Smith's most concise, magnetic hook yet: the refrain "Outside of society," sibilants exquisitely hissed by Patti and Lenny. Other pleasures include "Ghost Dance" and an American Indian chant that is every bit as haunting as it is meant to be.

Tucker, however, went on to compare Patti to Willem de Kooning, Neil Young, and the Three Stooges, for her ability to "pile everything on too thickly."

"Musically, this is Smith's best album," wrote Daisann McLain in *Crawdaddy.* "What was implied on *Horses* is filled in on *Easter,* and improved." McLain found Patti's religious preoccupations unsettling, though: "It's as if any minute she'll come out with 'I am the way and the truth and the light' over the E chord."

"After Patti started changing the band I didn't like it so much anymore," said Deerfrance. "Even when she played CBGB's. I didn't see her as a rock goddess like Pat Benatar. When Patti started getting pulled into that 'rock goddess' thing, I think that's when she somehow began to lose interest. When she brought out 'Because the Night,' I thought, No, no, no! Patti do your thing, go explore those unknown places—that's what she was so good at doing. And transforming those corny songs every once in a while, like 'You Light Up My Life.' Always so hilarious.

"I think she got into the big, heavy-rock stuff to please the guys in the band," Deerfrance continued. "That's more like boy music. The guys wanted to be rock stars, as guys always do. Patti was more like a high priestess. I think she went along with them 'cause they'd backed her up for so long and now it was her chance to give them something. But it really wasn't what she could live with for very long."

On the strength of *Easter* and the band's live performances, Patti was determined to reestablish herself as a force in rock. They embarked on an extensive tour, but, as with *Radio Ethiopia*, critical backlash followed her. Some of the criticism seemed to be provoked by Patti herself. At a New York press conference, for instance, she exhibited some of the in-your-face punk behavior of her past (and which she was soon to deride in others like Sid Vicious). She entered the room "from the back to the front," remembered Bebe Buell.

> She walked across tables to get to the stage, and in the process anything in her way—human, glass, or alcoholic—ended up on the floor, so it was just a shocking moment, truly shocking. Now, when somebody does that, you go, "Oh, fucking asshole, go back to Des Moines." But on her part it was definitely rebellious, she was the real thing, and you truly wondered: Could she snap? Could she hit me? Maybe. You weren't sure. In Patti, there was some real element of danger that's not present any more.

In 1975 Patti had impressed Clive Davis by being aware of how little time she had to make it. Now that she had succeeded, she was not sure that she could sustain it. "This line of work is tough," she admitted in a radio interview with KSAN. Like Keith Richards, who kicked heroin at thirty-three, she could not help identifying with the ultimate rock star's paradigm: "Look at Christ—he only lasted thirty-three years!"

The European tour began in March and the writer Chris Brazier spoke to her in Berlin just before she took the stage. He asked about *Easter*'s intimate relationship with Christianity, Patti replied:

The myth of Christ is still exciting and stimulating to me, whether he's a real guy or not doesn't really matter any more. I did say "Jesus died for somebody's sins but not mine," and I still believe that. I wasn't saying that I didn't take responsibility for the things that I do—I didn't want some mythical or ethical symbol taking the blame or the credit for what I do. When I steal, if I commit murder or adultery, whatever I do—I believe that the crime goes hand in hand with art. It's bad enough being a Smith, 'cause the word Smith means Cain, and being a true Smith means I came on the Earth marked anyway, and marked once is enough. Also, I'm a very Old Testament kind of person and in the Old Testament man communicated with God directly; in the New Testament man has to communicate with God through Christ. Well, I'm a one-to-one girl and I have always sought to communicate with God through myself.

And I feel that was one of the reasons I fell off stage. I'm reevaluating my state of being, I'm learning to accept a more New Testament kind of communication. So as part of that acceptance I have to reevaluate exactly who Christ was. And that's why on "Till Victory" it says "God, do not seize me, please, till victory" because I felt like my work wasn't done.

To me, the greatest thing about Christ is not necessarily Christ himself but the belief of the people that have kept him alive through the centuries—the guy must have had powerful magnetism. I mean to me, Christ, Jimi Hendrix, Brian Jones, Jim Morrison, they're all the same. All great men. I'm into the war manoeuvres of Alexander the Great, I'm into Popeye, I'm not just into neo-Christianity. Right now I'd rather be a little less satisfied 'cause I really love being an earthling. But like Alexander, I'm gonna go after all the territory I can.

Even with the help of Alexander and Popeye, Patti's march on Berlin was of mixed success. The audience was silent and still during most of the set, which made the band uptight. Patti was frustrated and she took the offensive: "I ain't impressed with you," she taunted the crowd. "I sang in front of fourteen thousand people so two thousand don't mean shit to me!" Luckily, most of the German audience had no idea what she was saying, and at the end of the set they applauded for over fifteen minutes, demanding an encore. The manager of the theater told Patti there would be a riot if she didn't return to the stage, and the mystified group returned for an extended version of "Land." The British critic Paul Morley described one of her performances in Germany as "a mesmerizing, sucking hole in time . . . honouring the vibrant spirits of destiny, anarchism, surrealism." He felt the band was strong as well: "The Patti Smith Group have grown—matured as their audience has expanded. The group played strong rock and roll, and Smith is finding her way back into performing. They are at a transition period: one more effort and they are truly great, truly special. Classical." The Berlin paper (whose writer perhaps spoke English and had heard Patti's insults) was less kind. He complained about the hype, said the music wasn't much "fun" to listen to and the lyrics were indecipherable, but that Patti "had a good voice." Berlin was a good example of Patti's ability to confound, infuriate, and mesmerize all at the same time.

During her European tour Patti performed one of her rarely publicized acts of charity when she ran into a down-and-out Nico in Paris. "Patti was very kind to me," Nico recalled.

Early in 1978 my harmonium was stolen from me. I was without any money and now I couldn't even earn a living playing, without my organ. A friend of mine saw one with green bellows in an obscure shop, the only one in Paris. Patti bought it for me. I was so happy and ashamed. I said "I'll give you back the money when I get it," but she insisted the organ was a present and I should forget about the money. I cried. I was ashamed she saw me without money.

As good as the European shows were, many observers saw the toll that touring was taking on Patti. Dave Ramsden of *Melody Maker* saw Patti's show at the Rainbow in London and noted that even though the fans loved her, Patti was exhibiting signs of rock 'n' roll burnout. "She has none of the bounding excess of energy, the sheer childlike exuberance that used to crackle through her performance," he wrote. "She often stands stock still or goes through stagecraft motions where before she'd leap up and down excitedly. Hand in hand with that is a drastic reduction in her communication with the audience—she seemed unable to think of anything more to say than 'I'm really happy to be here.' " The writer Paul Morley commented that "she looked weary, was in fact very ill and running to a tight doctor-imposed schedule . . . the bubble was soon to burst."

Patti herself had no use for most rock critics and instructed them to "put more integrity into your writing" instead of "writin' a bunch of gossip and bullshit of [your] own twisted ideas of what we're doin' . . . I think a true hero can only be criticized by himself. A true hero is his own highest critic. What he needs is support, he needs confidence, he needs the energy and the strength of the people. He doesn't need criticism."

"She's a very strange woman," Paul Morley wrote, "hopelessly impractical, breathtakingly wise, energetic, polite, mentally acrobatic and perversely perceptive. Crudely, she had a vision and rock 'n' roll was best equipped in terms of its endless range of emotions, its potential audience, its ecstasy factor, its possible pureness."

Tony Parsons in the *New Musical Express* criticized Patti's guitar playing, describing her as "crouched over her dull axe like Qua-

simodo on a Bert Weedon course for butter-fingered beginners."
He wished that a few more people had "the common sense to call
her out when the going gets unbelievably corny."

"Because the Night" was the first single from *Easter*, released on
March 29 while the band was on tour in Britain. The track was immediately picked up by radio stations and was one of the signature
songs on the airwaves that season, becoming the biggest hit of
Patti's career. In Britain the single went to number 5 while the album went to number 16. In the United States the single peaked at
13, the album number 20. The band was finally succeeding in its
mission to reach a large audience. Patti was thrilled:

> Charts are charts. Our whole point of doing work is to commu-
> nicate ecstasy or joy, but now we're communicating to a lot more
> people.
>
> I think the reason we got such heavy airplay this time was
> mostly on our own steam. But the song is really good; Bruce gave
> me a structure that really fits the kind of singing I used to do
> when I was younger. Of course, I think that FM radio playing the
> single more than the album is pretty gutless. I think that it's
> taken a lot of guts and foresight for AM stations to play our sin-
> gle, because when you play something by my group, you're not
> just playing a piece of music that's abstract, but a whole political
> outlook. But FM . . . it's like they'll play the single so they don't
> have to deal with my saying "fuck" or "nigger." I was banned for
> a year and a half on WNEW because one night I came on and
> criticized them for being pseudoliberal.

Chris Brazier called "Because the Night" "the first entirely successful conventional rock song that Patti Smith has created—this
doesn't carry her hallmarks of extremism or adventure, but it's so
good that it doesn't matter." Patti faced a catch-22 that all artists
who achieve commercial success must deal with. Blondie's *Heart of
Glass* would hit the same year, but Blondie had not been touted as

an art rock band. "Patti got a little frustrated when people thought of it as a total Bruce Springsteen song," said Lenny Kaye. Patti also felt that all the attention to the single drew attention away from the album. She later told a longtime friend, the writer Ben Edmonds, "*Easter* was strong, and some recognition of that was lost. Also, people imagined that now we were really huge and hugely prosperous. But that never actually occurred. The Patti Smith Group never had much financial success. And the record didn't even go gold or anything."

The popular success of the single placed enormous pressure on her. While she publicly ridiculed the song as "commercial shit," it allowed her a measure of recognition that she had not previously had. And, though it didn't make her rich, it did allow her to fulfill one dream; to buy her father a car. "He walked outside," she told Edmonds, "and when he saw the car—a shiny black brand-new 1978 Cordoba—he just sat down on the front step and stared at it. . . . Is there a gold record in the world that can compete with a moment like that?"

For herself, Patti made the seemingly incongruous purchase of a mink coat, and wore it on stage at the 1978 Nova Convention, which honored William Burroughs. "This coat cost $10,000," she told the crowd. "I sleep in it. I live in it." Such a display cannot have endeared her to the wannabe Beats in the audience. But Patti's love of the finer things in life was nothing new. In 1973 she had done a fashion show at Saks Fifth Avenue for Revillon. "I like Fernando Sanchez, who designs furs for Revillon," she said at the time. "He makes me feel like Anouk Aimée—I would love to dress in Balenciagas. When I was a kid and going nuts over Bob Dylan and Rimbaud, I was also reading *Vogue* and *Bazaar*. I thought the whole Saks show was an honour." In 1976, *The New York Times Magazine* quoted a close friend describing Patti's secret love of "Bergdorf Goodman and little lace panties." But while her actions may not have been inconsistent, they annoyed those on the punk scene who had been her champions. Trashing Patti became an increasingly popular pastime. Given so much ammunition by Patti herself, it may have been like shooting ducks in a barrel, but that didn't stop anyone from taking aim. For somebody who had compared herself to Paul Revere to use the moment of her highest profile to date to prance around in a ratty-looking fur coat belting out the refrain "the night belongs to lovers, because it belongs to love" begs at best a surreal interpretation.

However, as it turned out either Patti had nine lives or she was very clever, because the success of the Springsteen collaboration helped her escape the death of punk, which came rapidly on the heels of the Sex Pistols' January to February rampage across the United States. As bands with any of the punk stigma desperately scrambled to become new wave, *Easter* received terrific reviews in the American press. Dave Marsh's *Rolling Stone* rave titled "Can Patti Smith Walk on Water?" best summed up what she was doing.

When she played her hometown's Palladium, located on the great dividing line between downtown and the rest, Fourteenth Street, the answer was very apparently, Yes. "Watching the crowd rise out of its seats when Patti walked onstage, you had to clench your fist for her," wrote Fred Shruers. "Patti Smith is the Gunga Din of a certain kind of rock magic, trumpeting so hard and bravely that even the false notes become poignant and powerful."

When Patti appeared on Stanley Siegal's popular, controversial morning TV talk show, and was confronted by a jittery host who could not figure out what was supposed to be threatening about her, Patti came face to face with the conundrum she and other artists, like Talking Heads, the Cars, and, most spectacularly, Blondie, breaking out of the underground were in. Her decision to play it straight and charm her host was perfect.

Patti had graduated from being a punk rocker, if she ever was one, and was now, for the most part, treated as a popular entertainer. Not that she would never have another problem with an interviewer. In fact another TV spot on the *Today* show royally pissed her off:

I don't like people introducing me like they [the *Today* show] did, as "outlandish" and "crazy." 'Cause it sets me up, like I'm a rat. They back me up against a wall, and I'm not really a hard person to get along with. By the same token, there's not much difference between being introduced as a crazy on the *Today* show and the rock press calling me "the Queen of Punk."

Steve Seimels of *Stereo Review* marvelled at Patti's "unswerving faith" in herself and her work. "Only a supremely confident artist could continue to maintain, as she does, that everybody's least favourite Patti Smith song, 'Radio Ethiopia,' represents her finest achievement to date in any medium." He was also struck by her professionalism and ability to control her image despite "the seemingly anarchic quality of her act on stage and off . . . she is thoroughgoing pro in the most traditional show-biz sense: she knows exactly how to present herself at all times."

Patti did countless radio interviews that summer, wearing a polyester lizard jacket, a gift from Fred Smith, who had worn it onstage in the MC5. "I do everything with the same fervor, whether it's writing a poem, doing a drawing, or playing electric guitar," Patti told a DJ.

Personally, I feel that playing electric guitar is the heaviest thing I can do; it's the most exploratory, it's the most daring, the most risky. And I don't feel that's opposed to Art. My definition of Art is much more advanced, I think, more futuristic than most critics. I said in *Babel* that in another decade rock and roll would be Art. But when I say a decade, I mean for other people. For me, since 1954 or something, it has been Art. Since Little Richard, Elvis Presley, Jimi Hendrix. I mean, these guys are masters. And I'm an illuminated apprentice who seeks to go beyond my masters. Being great is no accident. Little Richard wasn't an accidental phenomenon; he knew what he was after. He might not define it with intellectual terminology, but he was defined by what he did. I didn't think Jackson Pollock wrote a manifesto first and then did all his painting according to it. Now, as for what I'm trying to do as an artist. . . . Well, the highest thing an artist goes for is communication with God. Which is universal communication. I've always spewed out my subconscious through improvising poetry, language. Now my language is being extended into sound, which I find much more universally communicative. People respond to it. I mean, what makes opera communicative?

"Y'know, the same girl that takes Jimi Hendrix as a master has learned a lot from Debby Boone this year," she said to the Hong Kong–based DJ and writer Gerrie Lim.

I've watched Debby Boone sing "You Light Up My Life" maybe fifteen, twenty times. Each time . . . perfect. Each time with total, focused, concentrated commitment to delivering that song. Which I think is real good. Now I ain't a Debby Boone fan, specifically, and I ain't gonna start wearing chiffon tent dresses tomorrow. But I did learn something by watching that. I've got to be able to deliver "Because the Night" with all the strength and integrity and clarity that I was able to deliver it with in the studio. And if Debby Boone can do it, I certainly can do it.

And she did: Patti actually added "You Light Up My Life" to her 1978 concert repertoire.

I have changed, though. I've learned to relax. When I first started performing, if it wasn't real every second, if it wasn't magic, I would get desperate. I didn't want to cheat anybody, that's my morality. I'm not moral in many ways, but I'm a very responsible person.

It's very hard to peg me down because my body encases a soul split and contradictory, I run, like Leonardo da Vinci, on many rhythms, good and evil, disciplined and maniac. I offer no excuses or explanation, I am still a physical architect. Building a temple of experience. I am not dead, finished, or nearly finished.

Asked her opinion of her peers, she replied, "I love the Clash, and I really love the Sex Pistols" (who had broken up but were still the most famous punk group).

I think Johnny Rotten's great, I have a real crush on him. All those kids were my friends before they had bands, so it's real gratifying to me to see them up there. I don't like Elvis Costello. If you ask the fan in me you're gonna get a pretty narrow view. Basically, if there isn't somebody I want to fuck in a band, I couldn't care less. Unless it's such great abstract music it carries me away. Otherwise, if it's a rock and roll band, there better be somebody fuckable or forget it.

"We're not all one, we're not equal, who wants to be equal?" she told a fifteenth DJ.

That's a totally absurd idea, it's against creation, against sexual tension, against seeking of wisdom. Nobody wants to be equal. But there is something that makes us not equal but of one great rhythm and that's our most ancient source of communication which is belief. I'm sure the ultimate way to get to it is relaxation but me being a true American the only way I can get there is to first blow myself out, which is why I play electric guitar. . . . I feel like Ernest Hemingway.

Andy Warhol had known Patti since 1971, when she appeared in the Tony Ingrassia plays with Jackie Curtis. By 1978 he viewed Patti with some distaste, mainly because of what he saw as her blatant social climbing. Patti in turn was suspicious of Warhol because of the way he had treated Robert Mapplethorpe in the past. In his diary entry of May 29, 1978, Warhol wrote:

I walked over to have lunch at One Fifth [a fashionable restaurant located on the ground level of Patti's apartment building] and on the way I saw Patti Smith in a bowler hat buying food for her cat. I invited her thinking she'd say no, but she said, "Great." When we walked in, there was the number-one bestseller Fran Lebowitz sitting with Lisa Robinson.

Patti didn't want to eat too much, so she ate half my lunch. She said she only loves blonds and that she wanted to have an affair with a blond. All I could think about was her b.o.—she wouldn't be bad looking if she would wash up and glue herself together a little better. She's still skinny. She's with a gallery now, doing drawings and writing poetry. The Robert Miller Gallery. She reminds me a lot of Ivy [Nicholson, a Warhol superstar from the sixties]—everything was put on. She said she didn't take drugs in the sixties, that she'd only started recently, and just for work.

On June 12 she opened for the Rolling Stones in Atlanta, Georgia. "One of my dreams," she told Nick Tosches. "Now all I wanna do is open for Rimbaud. Why don't the Rolling Stones play the Apollo? We could play it together. I'll call Mick up. We're friends now, ya know. He's a really great guy. I mean, he's really a nigger. If anyone qualifies to be a nigger, it's Mick Jagger." This casual use of the word "nigger" would cause Patti some problems later on.

In June, the Robert Miller Gallery presented Robert Mapplethorpe and Patti's joint exhibition, "Films and Stills." The opening was a bona-fide media event, with overflowing crowds and television news cameras. Patti and Robert arrived together, obviously ecstatic to be finally realizing their long-held dream of "making the big time" together. Reviewing the show for *Art in America*, the poet and critic René Ricard wrote:

Their friendship is their masterpiece. What's on show, the works, is documentation or artefact; its importance is that it was made by these people. This works doubly. Mapplethorpe photos are always beautiful, but a Mapplethorpe photo of Patti Smith is, well, history. By the same token even if Patti had no talent for drawing (it's only gravy that the drawings are fine) the lovely drawings of Rimbaud in the show would be something to have, the way a Verlaine or Rimbaud would be something to have. . . . Verlaine, Rimbaud, Smith, Mapplethorpe: we are dealing here with a network of homage and swapped destinies, like Piaf and Cocteau, people who would die within minutes of each other.

Patti Smith had returned with a vengeance from the setback of her accident seventeen months before. In July, she was featured in *Rolling Stone*, and adorned the cover as well, in a striking photograph by Annie Leibovitz. In the portrait, Patti stood in front of a wall of real flames, wearing a see-through white blouse that revealed a black bra underneath. The story inside, by Charles Young, was titled "Patti Smith Catches Fire" and was the most widely read piece on Patti so far. "This woman can sing rock and roll," wrote Young. "Power, passion, sex appeal, unique style, enough control for professionalism, enough lack of control for suspense—it's all there. She is, at the age of thirty-one, a star." The article, however, turned out to be highly ambivalent. "Her personal charm, when she wants it to be, is enormous," Young continued.

Her followers are increasing every day, and they are among the most ardent anywhere. She is a poet for the people. Patti Smith's detractors think Radio Ethiopia, a loosely defined organization of her supporters, amounts to a Kiss Army for intellectuals who like to be mystified by poetry without capital letters. They think she is a fool. Because she cultivates the look of a possessed poet, she can say things like "the word *art* must be redefined" and get away with it. Her fans, in fact, eat it off a stick. And she is happy to feed them, so long as they don't question the menu too closely.

Young also took Patti to task about recent comments she had made explaining her use of the word "nigger," sex, and religion.

The other day you said [to Nick Tosches] that if anyone was qualified to be a nigger, it was Mick Jagger. How is Mick Jagger qualified to be a nigger?

SMITH: On our liner notes I redefined the word *nigger* as being an artist-mutant that was going beyond gender.

REPORTER: I don't understand how Mick Jagger has suffered like anyone who grew up in Harlem.

SMITH: Suffering don't make you a nigger. I mean, I grew up poor too. Stylistically, I believe he qualifies. I think Mick Jagger has suffered plenty. He also has a great heart, and I believe, ya know, even in his most cynical moments, a great love for his children. He's got a lot of soul. I mean, like, I don't understand the question. Ya think black people are better than white people or sumpthin'? I was raised with black people. It's like, I can walk down the street and say to a kid, "Hey, nigger." I don't have any kind of super-respect or fear of that kind of stuff. When I say statements like that, they're not supposed to be analyzed, 'cause they're more like off-the-cuff humorous statements. I do have a sense of humor, ya know, which is sumpthin' that most people completely wash over when they deal wit' me. I never read anything where anybody talked about my sense of humor. It's like, a lot of the stuff I say is true, but it's supposed to be funny.

REPORTER: You were quoted in [*Rolling Stone*'s] Random Notes as saying you jerk off to your own photograph. I'm trying to figure out if you're actually that sexually attracted to yourself.

SMITH: No, it was just one of those moments, ya know? It was the photo for the cover of *Easter.* I thought if I could do it as an experiment, then fifteen-year-old boys could do it, and that would make me very happy. Ya know, people say to me, "Aren't you afraid of becoming a sex object?" Especially a lot of writers are obsessed with making you feel guilty or upset because you might become a sex object. Well, I find that very exciting. I think sex is one of the five highest sensations one can experience. A very high orgasm is a way of communication with our Creator.

REPORTER: You jerk off to the Bible too?

SMITH: Definitely.

Patti's comments in the *Rolling Stone* article about redefining the word "nigger" incensed many of the magazine's readers, as well as its editors and writers. The magazine's own review of *Easter*, by Dave Marsh, questioned her appropriation of the inflammatory word. " 'Rock n Roll Nigger' is an unpalatable chant because Smith doesn't understand the word's connotation, which is not outlawry but a particular kind of subjugation and humiliation that's antithetical to her motives, " wrote Marsh. This controversy would dog her throughout the year, but Patti stood unmoved. "If I wanna say 'nigger,' I'll say 'nigger,' " she proclaimed. "If somebody wants to call me a cracker bitch, that's cool. It's part of being American."

On August 4, the Patti Smith Group released an EP in the U.K. that mixed old, new, and live material. It led with "Privilege (Set Me Free)," a song originally recorded by former Manfred Mann lead singer Paul Jones for the classic rock movie *Privilege*, and "Ask the Angels" from the *Radio Ethiopia* album. The flip side was a live version of "25th Floor" and a reading of "Babelfield" from *Babel*, her new book. The EP peaked at number seventy-two in the British charts. The band followed the record to England on August 27, when they headlined the Reading Rock Festival in Berkshire with the Tom Robinson Band, John Otway, and Sham 69. Like most of their 1978 shows, this gig earned mixed reviews. "Gradually the sound improved and the band tightened, but Patti increased her unsettling line in chat between numbers," wrote Ian Birch in *Melody Maker* of the show. "Maybe it was designed to be acidly witty, but it didn't come across that way to me. Rather, it lay somewhere between the infantile, the slightly removed and a nascent showbiz stance. All this wouldn't have mattered so much if she had appeared to be as intent on entertaining as the rest of her band, who worked and worked and worked."

Graham Lock, reviewing the show for the *New Musical Express*, thought the show was lackluster. "She never gave the impression that her heart was totally in it . . . [it was] a thoroughly entertaining, if surprisingly unadventurous, hour and a quarter."

Justifying the unevenness of the shows to Paul Rambali of the *NME*, she said, "We're not like a male band . . . in that the male process of ecstasy in performance is . . . building and building until the big spurt at the end. We're a feminine band, we'll go so far and peak and then we'll start again and peak, over and over. It's like the ocean. We leave ourselves wide open for failure, but we also leave ourselves open to achieving a moment more magical."

She evidently took such risks with her books, too, for Patti was also thrown on the defensive by British reaction to *Babel*. Published in the States back in March, it had been reviewed in the prestigious *New York Times Book Review* by critic Jonathan Cott. "If Patti Smith lacks the range of poets such as Diane Di Prima, Anne Waldman and Carolyn Forche," he wrote, "she must still be praised for her insistence that one 'never let go of the fiery sadness called desire,' for her striving to attain the kind of vision Rimbaud nicknamed 'voyance'—and this at a time when many writers settle for simply being voyeurs." Patti considered *Babel* to be "an extension of what I used to do onstage." At a press conference in London in September to promote *Babel*'s publication in England, Patti elaborated on that thought: "I spew out a lot of stoned spaced-out meanderings of the sort I'm well known for spewing."

Later, talking to Rambali about *Babel* and her writing in general, Patti said that "while I'm very intelligent, I'm no intellectual. All my beliefs, political and otherwise, are very romantic. It's like me having a crush on Prince Charles. I don't know anything about him, I just think there's something sexy about him."

Some critics remained unmoved. Ian Penman, who reviewed *Babel* for the *NME*, was merciless:

Most of us were writing better that this in the lower Sixth, with or without expensive drugs, friends or book deals. I hate this book, actually. All it'll ever give people is confusion and ignorance. This is self-conceit, and it should have been burnt out or burnt years ago. This is semi-literature, and I hate it even more when I realize that it's probably the only book of "poetry" a lot of impressionable young people will buy this or any other year.

Allen Ginsberg was philosphical. "I was surprised by Patti Smith's rise," he mused. "It's sort of heartening to see how somebody else could get ahead. I wonder how she'll do. I was reading Rimbaud's last letters, when he was dying, about how miserable life was and 'all I am is a motionless stump' and I'm wondering how she'll deal with that aspect of heroism."

After the British publication of *Babel*, Patti withdrew to work on songs for her next album, *Wave*, and to be with Fred in Detroit. She told many of her friends that she found the transition hard. When Legs McNeil visited friends in Patti's building, he knocked on her apartment door, only to come face to face with a surly Fred Smith, who said that Patti was not in. Legs left a message, but he never heard from her again. It would also be hard for her band to communicate with her, separated as they were by a thousand miles. This was the beginning of the end for the Patti Smith Group.

Part of her defiance—and developing rock-goddess self-image—may have been encouraged by her fans. Yet in doing so, they may also have encouraged her to abandon the role, too. "I think Patti attracted a lot of fans who were into worship, like she was the Messiah, like she was going to cure all their ills, like she was God," said Deerfrance. "Here you are with a whole front row of crazies looking at you like you're the answer. They're like vampires, taking all your energy. I don't think she could deal with that anymore. She had a desire to preserve herself, a survival instinct, which all the great ones have. That's why they can take on the weight of so many people who are looking to them for all the answers for their whole life. They take on the artist's life instead of having one of their own. I think after a while that gets really tiring."

the end

1979

> "In the seventies, I actually enjoyed the
> privileges and the excitement and some of
> the danger of being a rock 'n' roll star. It
> was very intoxicating at that time in my
> life. But it wasn't enough."
>
> *patti smith*

Patti's life was now in Detroit with Fred. As their relationship
grew, they discovered that they shared more than just a last name.
In one conversation, Fred revealed an awakening to rock 'n' roll
that closely resembled Patti's, right down to the performer: "Ever
since I saw Little Richard on the tube many years ago, this black
man playing wild, crazy music, I knew what I wanted to play." The
couple's musical tastes were similarly wide ranging. Fred liked
"anything that's high-energy expressive, from John Coltrane to

209

Patti Smith to punk rock." Rather than any genre, he gravitated toward feeling. "I like high-energy music," he said, "people kind of exploding musically. I like to feel it, that they're coming apart and just letting everything out." Perhaps unsurprisingly, then, Fred also shared Patti's appreciation for people who literally challenged death: one of Patti's big heroes was escape artist Harry Houdini, while Fred admired Karl Wallenda, patriarch of the great tightrope-walking family, who, in fact, fell to his death from the highwire that year. Patti and Fred each seemed to have met their match in the other, so much so that Patti entrusted her affairs to him. Now, everything she did had to be approved by Fred, and while it was a virtual about-face for her, Patti seemed to welcome his control. The choices they made, however, began to put distance between her and the boys in the band.

The decisions they made about the Patti Smith Group's next album and its recording show this. When Patti and Fred decided on Todd Rundgren to produce the next album, it made sense, but it also meant that the group and their entourage of assistants, roadies, and families would have to move to the tiny upstate–New York hamlet of Bearsville, where Rundgren had built a world-class studio. Then, upon arriving in Bearsville, they were surprised to discover that the preproduction period, in which, normally, the band would get to know the producer and the producer would familiarize himself with the songs, had been cut: they were to start recording right away. It was as if Patti did not want to spend an hour longer than she had to with them, and maybe this was true. Patti confided to Todd that this would be the last Patti Smith Group album, but she swore him to secrecy, and didn't even inform Lenny Kaye, her collaborator since her start in music, of her intentions.

Tensions stemming from the relocation and truncated preproduction period were exacerbated by other circumstances. First, there were Patti's medical problems. After her fall, she needed to see chiropractors and doctors regularly, and she had lost the indefatigable cheerfulness that had characterized her in 1976. Despite this, the band continued to work, sometimes quarreling over arrangements and production choices, perhaps sensing the unspoken feeling of finality. But just as they were getting into a groove, word came from New York that ex–Sex Pistol Sid Vicious had slashed Patti's brother Todd's face with a beer bottle at the uptown music club Hurrah. "That was actually quite frightening," Patti told Gerrie Lim. "My brother is a tough kid, but he's very pacifistic. Sid Vicious just went crazy and my brother almost lost his eye. He didn't provoke him or anything." Todd survived his injuries, and the band went on with their recording sessions.

They called the album *Wave*. In between its completion and release, the band played a few warm-up shows, and Patti did a few select interviews. One of them was with William Burroughs. On a cold night in early March, Patti visited Burroughs at "the Bunker," his famous residence on the Bowery six blocks south of CBGB's. The two were alone that evening, but though Patti had always professed to idolize the esteemed sixty-five-year-old writer, Burroughs, a world-class raconteur, barely got a word in edgewise. Patti had a lot to say about a lot of things.

I look to my future with so much joy, because I am in the most wonderful position. When I entered rock 'n' roll, I entered into it in a political way, not as a career. After the death of a lot of the leading sixties stars, and after the disillusionment of a lot of people at the end of the sixties and early seventies, I felt that people just wanted to be left alone for a little while. But when '73 and early '74 came around, it was just getting worse and worse, and there was no indication of anything new. I felt that it was a time for me to do something. All I really hoped to do was initiate some response from other people. I didn't have any aspirations of a career. I look at the world, I get very brokenhearted about what happens in the world. I hate to see people hurt. I see what's happening with Iran, and I'm mostly worried that Iran will lose its culture, or that somebody will destroy [the

Sufi poet] Rumi's grave. I worry about things that are not, I suppose, really so important to anybody. But the things that I was involved with politically in America were very simple things having to do with the minds of teenagers, and how they were being shaped. I feel that in my own way, I was able to at least put a stick in the coals a little. Now it's 1979 and I'm still involved in this thing, but it's come to a point in my life that, like you said, I have to stop and say, "What am I doing?"

I was actually very heartbroken in the last few years, because I had to accept a lot of things about our planet and about, you know, realities. But still, like I said, just as we have the temptation to be corrupted we have the strength not to be corrupted. I like to think of those forty days when—[Here Patti interrupted herself and began speaking about Jesus.]—The idea of Jesus. I haven't completely accepted that thing in my mind. The day that I totally accept him is going to be a very wonderful day, if it happens, but I have to think about it still. I'm still exploring that guy. One of the stories that I really like is when he [Jesus] went into the desert for forty days and wrestled the Devil, they actually had a verbal and physical battle. Forty days of someone woodpeckering your spirit is pretty—

"Yeah, it's pretty harrowing," said Burroughs, finishing her thought. Yet she went on undeterred.

And he came out of it. And so for me, whenever I think that I have it tough because I have to fight radio stations, or a record company or anything, I get pretty ashamed of myself when I think that this guy had to spend forty days without food or drink in the middle of a desert with the Devil. But it does get to you.

Initially, all I wanted out of life was to do great work, and thus communicate with myself, but most of all, to be able to honestly, totally communicate with another person, totally. Telepathically, or whatever. I've no desire to be like some movie star and leave a trail of husbands behind me, you know?

Our credo was, "Wake up!" I've said this before, but just to tell you, in case you haven't read it or anything—I wanted to be like Paul Revere. I didn't want to be a giant big hero; I didn't want to die for the cause. I didn't want to be a martyr. All that I wanted was for the people to fuckin' wake up. That's all I wanted them to do, and I feel that that's what happened.

"Well, as you say that this is what happened," said Burroughs, finally getting a chance to speak, "you have the whole punk generation, essentially, who are antiheroes. See, they're rejecting the old values, because having been woken up, they realize that all this nonsense that they've been brought up on is nonsense. And all these standards. And they're rejecting those standards. So we could regard them, if you will, as something that you have been instrumental in creating."

Burroughs's implications were clear, but Patti wasn't going to be blamed for creating nihilistic, drug-worshipping punk rockers. "I don't agree with these kids," she objected. "I believe in heroes. See, I love these kids, but I think they've spawned a lot of little monsters. I don't feel the same way they do. I don't think it's cool to shoot yourself up with heroin at twenty-one years old and die. I don't think it's cool to die at twenty-one, you know. I don't want to be dead. I would exist forever.

"What's important is that there are—I hate to call it this—more impostors, than ever," she continued, and then, in a rather shocking statement, gave her views on who should "do art":

I never think that anybody should do art unless they're a great artist. I think that people have the right to express themselves in the privacy of their own home, but I don't think they should perpetuate it on the human race—at least in a pleasurable kind of manner.

It used to be that art was unquestionably art. And I think that we have to get back to that frame, but that can only happen again by the eruption of like at least ten great people at once. I want to live in an illuminated time.

I wouldn't talk to you about gender, if we were talking about performing properly, or the act of doing work. I understand that it's important to go beyond your gender in that process. I know that women, by the basis of our makeup, we perpetuate civilization, and we have to be optimistic. We have to believe in the future, or else. Since we're the ones who bear the children of the future, we have to feel we're not setting them to light on a volcano. You don't want to bear a child and then drop it in a volcano. You want to bear a child and put him in paradise. I don't believe in having nine kids at this point. I'm not a Mexican Catholic. I desire for the planet to go on, and not see swans go extinct, and all that stuff.

When *Wave* was released on April 27, 1979, Robert Christgau was one of the few critics to defend the album:

A lot of folks just don't like Patti anymore, and so have taken to complaining about the pop melodicism ("AOR sell-out") and shamanistic religiosity ("pretentious phony") she's always aspired toward. But this is an often inspired album, quirkier than the more generally satisfying *Easter*—especially on the sexual mystery song "Dancing Barefoot," quite possibly her greatest track ever, and, yes, the reading for the dead pope that she goes out on.

More typical were Simon Frith and Julie Burchill, who criticized the record on its production as well as content. "The crucial component of *Wave* is Todd Rundgren's production," Frith wrote in the *Melody Maker*, "He has his own theory of rock, a technological, engineer's theory, and it's his sound rather than Patti's that dominates this LP. Now they're an American rock band—double guitar breaks, synthesized sustenance—and she is an American rock singer, filling in the spaces the musicians leave."

Burchill was merciless:

[Patti's] story is that of the Emperor's New Clothes in reverse; Patti has the gear, but there's nothing inside it. Is this the blandest record in the world? Even old Todd's lack of talent in the production can't be blamed. I thought Patti Smith had got what she wanted, but she is obviously a very disappointed person. She has babbled and jived herself into a corner where two mirrors meet and seems set to stand there examining herself for the rest of her career, wishing that she could be like Stevie Nicks.

Wave reached number eighteen in the U.S. Top 20, and forty-one on the U.K. charts. On May 16 Patti publicly announced plans to stay in Detroit with her new man, Fred Smith, whose influence on Patti could increasingly be seen in the two areas which she had previously made her domain: the interview and the stage. Journalists trying to track Patti down for an interview were given the runaround and finally put away with the line, "Could you come back later, or call me tomorrow 'cause it's all up to Fred, and he's busy." Any intrepid scribe who attempted to breach this barrier was met with a firm refusal. Meanwhile, when Patti played New York's Palladium in May, John Rockwell reported that her performance, while not up to her greatest, was more controlled and effective than many recent efforts. He withheld his praise for an encore, on which Patti was joined onstage by Fred. "Lots of rock performers play self-indulgently with the mind-blowing aspects of feedback," Rockwell wrote, "but what Mr. Smith wrought in that regard—soft, bending filigrees of sound alternating with rich, grating onslaughts—was the most interesting use of feedback this writer has ever heard."

Onstage she may not have shown it, but though Patti had

agreed to do a long tour of the U.S. and Europe to support *Wave*, in the interim she had lost her enthusiasm. The tour was thus filled with stress and its resultant problems. Patti turned on her closest associates, including her devoted personal assistant Andi Ostrowe. For Ostrowe the tour marked the low point of her relationship with Patti, whom she had virtually deified. As the tour neared its end, the two women were not even speaking.

The stress of being on the road was taking its toll on everyone, but Patti was especially affected, since, as the frontwoman, the focus was always on her. Doing seemingly endless interviews and radio-station visits while being constantly catered to by an ever-growing entourage of employees and hangers-on made it increasingly difficult for Patti to remember her original precepts for being a rock 'n' roll singer. And on top of everything, she was plagued with recurring bronchitis throughout the tour. The novelty of touring had worn off—plus she also had other things on her mind.

"In the seventies I actually enjoyed the privileges and the excitement and some of the danger of being a rock 'n' roll star," Patti later remembered. "It was intoxicating. But it wasn't enough. Basically, I had fallen in love with Fred, and I didn't like being parted from him. When we [the Patti Smith Group] started performing, I really gave everything to it. I gave my time, my energy, my love. But my feelings for Fred were so strong that when I was on tour and away from him it didn't mean anything, and I felt extremely false being on stage."

"Actually, when I think about it, my happiest memories of that time weren't about performing," she said years later. "I think about sitting on the edge of the stage at the end of the night, talking to the kids who don't leave and answering their questions or listening to their philosophies."

The *Minneapolis Tribune* described Patti as "dispirited," and she herself acknowledged her weariness. From a stage in St. Paul she told the crowd, "If you don't like the tired aspect of it, go get your money back and leave me the fuck alone. I am extremely tired."

Deerfrance saw it as a case of burnout. "After a while the crowds really overcame Patti," she recalled.

She used to come to CBGB's shows, and she was always really cool. She always bought everybody's records and was very supportive, but I think after a while she didn't really like what she was doing. She didn't want to do the big rock thing. She had a lot more on her mind than that. She withdrew, and when that happened, I just didn't see her anymore, she didn't come around. After the accident, she really withdrew, and then she went out to Michigan. I sensed that she wanted to be left alone. She had given so much, supported so much. It was all on her little shoulders for so long. I was happy she'd gotten away from it all because it really wasn't what she wanted to do; I think she had much greater interests. I think she wished she'd done more. Patti has a lot to say, she has a tremendous fascination with life. Rock 'n' roll wasn't really for her. Rock went right down to the sewer, whereas Patti wanted to elevate everybody. Like, let's all think big thoughts. But we all said, "Noooo!" The audience just wanted her to rock on and deliver. I think Patti wanted to get a little quieter, a little more esoteric, and to enlarge her sphere. Instead, we all settled for so little and beat it into the ground. She just had to withdraw, and she did. There she was, just one girl on tour with a bunch of guys going from town to town, playing huge arenas. She knew there was more.

The summer shows in Europe were mostly in large arenas. The band had prepared a set for those huge spaces, rolling out some cover songs that they hoped the European audiences would respond to, including "Mr. Tambourine Man," John Lennon's "It's So Hard," the Who's "The Kids Are Alright," Manfred Mann's "5-4-3-2-1," and old chestnuts like "Jailhouse Rock" and "Be My

Baby." They organized the set so that each member of the band could take a vocal, to give Patti's voice some rest. "Radio Ethiopia" was dropped.

Still, critics picked up Patti's attitude and in Europe the reviews were scathing. *Sounds*'s Phil Sutcliffe reported, "Atrocious axe-womanship! Patti Smith is a wonderful gift of the late seventies, an inspiration to me, but this is the wrong time and the wrong place. I could only think that after a lot of experience and intellectualizing she still doesn't know why she goes on stage and so her efforts are rather aimless and dependent on the prevailing winds for their success or otherwise."

The band, however, had worse to worry about, and the chaotic final shows in Italy were emblematic of the whole experience. It was the closest Patti came to her own Altamont.

First, in Bologna, the concert promoters had been forced to accept the "protection" of the Italian Communist Party, which turned out to be no protection at all. Fans were breaking down the venue's barriers and getting in for free, and there was no backstage security. Attempting to take the stage, the band got lost in a maze of corridors and occasionally ran into threatening-looking "guards" who confronted them and instructed them to "obey orders." When they finally got onstage, they were in a state of angst and confusion hardly conducive to playing music to eighty thousand people. This was the second-to-last show of the tour, and they were all exhausted, particularly Patti. The band did its best, each member taking a turn at the mike as planned so that the burden of singing would not rest solely on Patti.

After the events in Bologna, Patti's manager, Ina Meibach, confronted the promoters, demanding protection for the final show and insisting that nothing like this assault on the stage be allowed to happen again. The Italians assured her that everything was under control.

The following day in Florence, the tour's last stop, Patti came face-to-face with the price of her fame. Strolling out from the hotel hoping to pick up some last-minute souvenirs for Fred, she seemed to see her face on the cover of every other magazine on the newsstands. Soon gangs of teenage girls wearing white shirts with thin black ties began gathering and chased her back to the hotel in a scene reminiscent of one in Tennessee Williams's *Suddenly Last Summer*, in which a character is literally devoured by a crowd of young boys. Patti was becoming a prisoner of her own success; fame was her jailer.

The show in Florence would be the last straw. Throughout the tour, Patti had been hounded by the press, constantly surrounded by live TV crews and reporters, as well as besieged by representatives from various political factions petitioning her for her support. It was a highly volatile setting, full of mounting pressure, made all the worse by her state of mind. Beat poet Gregory Corso had joined their caravan for the Italian tour, and he mischievously advised Patti to play the media for her own gain. Patti, as always ready to push the envelope, took him up on the suggestion. So, despite knowing nothing about the political situation in Italy, she decided to ignore the advice of Ina Meibach and fly the American flag during her Florence concert.

Florence, then, by the end of the show showed her something new. For the first time, Patti faced a crowd that she could not tame. The concert ran its course, building until that moment in the last three songs when, if she had done her job, the crowd would be on the edge of madness. She was used to this, but now, suddenly, she felt a foul, uncontrollable force driving the fans to that edge, a force the Greeks call *sparagamos:* the rending of a hero into pieces, limb by limb. To take an audience to this height is an extraordinary achievement: Elvis could do it, Jagger could do it; maybe Morrison on a good night. But for Patti, it was something that she had not encountered before—the knowledge that the crowd could have gone either way, with her or against her, that it was no longer her choice.

As the band careened through this last show, Patti knew that it would be the last time she would be singing "My Generation." When she cried out "We created it, let's take it over!" the audience took her at her word, descending onto the stage in wave after wave. Some of the more brazen fans commenced to bang on Jay Dee's drums and thrash away at Patti's guitar. For a brief moment, the heat of street politics flared as the fans "liberated" the stage and became the performers.

As the concert neared its end, what appeared to be a full-scale riot broke out, as even more overeager fans broke through the flimsy barricades and charged towards the stage. It was an extremely frightening moment, but, as it turned out, Patti's Italian fans were so enamored of her that they simply wanted to sit on the stage, to be as close to her as they could.

Florence was the last time Patti Smith would confront a rock audience for sixteen years. The next time she went out on tour, the single most pronounced aspect of her shows would be control.

Afterward, back at the hotel, Patti told the band that she had had it, that this was it, the Patti Smith Group was over. Ivan and Jay Dee were devastated, feeling that after working their way from the bottom of the barrel to almost within reach of the pot of gold, to quit now was insane. Despite Patti's claims that she was going to settle down with Fred in Detroit and devote herself to having a family, she was a star, and there were many ways that she could continue her career. In contrast, none of the other band members stood a chance of attaining this level of success or renown on their own. Still, Lenny defended Patti to the end, and they all told themselves that this might be a temporary decision anyway, brought on by exhaustion and the craziness of the last two nights. Like Dylan after his motorcycle accident, maybe Patti would return.

dream of life/the outrageous lie, part two

1 9 8 0 - 1 9 8 8

> "It was a happy, J. G. Ballard existence—
> if a J. G. Ballard story was ever happy."
>
> *patti smith*

Just how private Fred and Patti wanted to keep their lives was illustrated by their wedding ceremony in Detroit on March 1, 1980. In a country where rock stars are treated like royalty, the marriage of the house of Smith to the house of Smith passed almost without notice. The couple had a small, private wedding, attended only by their parents.

At first, Patti enjoyed "civilian" life in Detroit, away from the chaos of rock 'n' roll. Despite its economic decline, Detroit had a rich cultural heritage, and the city's inhabitants possessed their own blend of soulful toughness, battling hardship with humor. "Detroit people are my favorite people in the whole world," Fred said. "They have good hearts and feelings. Europeans are always interesting, but nothing like here. I always want to get back. It's more than just home."

Still, even as she settled in, Patti didn't leave performing completely behind. In June 1980, the Patti Smith Group, which had not yet been formally disbanded, performed at a benefit for the Detroit Symphony Orchestra at the city's Masonic Temple. "I love classical music, but it always seemed inaccessible," said Patti, explaining her reason for doing the benefit. "And then Fred and I started watching the Beethoven series on television and listening to Antal Dorati [the DSO conductor] talk. We started looking forward to it the way we might have looked forward to a Rolling Stones concert. Having lived in New York where the orchestra is very aggressive and flamboyant, there was something inspiring for me about the way Dorati presented the Symphony. We just want to help support the Symphony in our own way and get more people to share the experience of listening to the Symphony play." Fred concurred: "It makes you feel good, the music. It inspires you. It extracts the feeling out of you, and we want to help pay back the Symphony for that enjoyment."

The show Fred and Patti put on together had enough angles to confuse anyone trying to look for a new direction in her career. First Patti took the stage alone and gave an inspired reading. She was then joined by the angelic DNV, who accompanied her on a big pipe organ for an outstanding rendition of "Hymn," from *Wave*. When the song ended, a screen was lowered behind Patti, and Fred joined her onstage. Then, as a silent black-and-white film of Jackson Pollock executing one of his famous action paintings played behind them, the Smiths improvised an "abstract expressionist" soundtrack, Patti on clarinet, Fred on sax, and a

Fender Duo-Sonic leaning against an amp on feedback. Next Fred left the stage and Patti was joined by Lenny, Jay Dee, Ivan, and DNV. They started with three jazz-influenced oldies, taking Patti back to her childhood. Next, harking back to the days of *Radio Ethiopia*, they launched into an experimental improvisation pointing to an excursion into the heady avenues of "Afghanistan."

In an interview he gave shortly after the show, Lenny sounded as if he believed they might develop in this direction. In that case he must have been as upset as Jay Dee and Ivan when that same month Patti called a business meeting of the band in New York and formally told them it was over. Considering how hard they had worked for six years and had just started making the big money, they were to say the least, frustrated by their benevolent despot of a leader. "The official end of the band came when we were in our accountant's office," reported Jay Dee.

I don't think Richard was there, I guess he already knew. It was me, Lenny and Ivan. Patti basically said, "The group is no more. We're going to go out gracefully—we're not going to announce that the group is breaking up." I know that it was very hard for her, and I know that she probably thinks that we think badly of her. Deep down inside, I hope she knows we don't. I wasn't angry, but I was devastated. I mean, for like the last year of the Patti Smith Group she was living in Detroit with Fred, so it was something I had feared might happen, on a purely selfish kind of level. But I didn't realize at the time that the group was my identity. That's who I was—I was the drummer of the Patti Smith Group. I wasn't anything, I wasn't me, I was a thing. So it was just like, "Wow. Now what?"

"We started out playing in front of 250 people at St. Mark's Church, and finished up in front of 70,000 in a Florence soccer stadium," concluded Lenny Kaye years later.

You can't invent a better narrative than that. Patti was extremely inspirational. She had a great enthusiasm for the creative energy of art. There was the personal side of her, which was very warm and funny. We used to giggle a lot and tell jokes and sit around and have good times. There was something very little-girlish about her. She also had very set ideas about pushing herself and making sure that neither she nor anyone else she was working with was content with what was. She was working for what could be. That's why the band split up. When there was nowhere else to go we decided to go on to new things. I first got into Patti as a fan when she was an actress in a Jackie Curtis play at La Mama. I still remained a fan throughout my association with her. She's one of the great creative minds of our generation. Music was not the foremost thing on her mind right then, I supposed, but I was sure we had not heard the last of Patti Smith.

When asked what she thought of Patti's decision to withdraw from the field, Debbie Harry, the lead singer of Blondie, who were at that moment the number-one bestselling pop group in the world, answered wisely and without malice that she thought it was probably the most sensible thing that Patti had ever done. Debbie, after all, was in a better position to judge the dangers of the game both she and Patti had been playing. Of course, Debbie did not know Fred, or Detroit, or what strange engines ran Patti's emotions. Though Patti and Debbie had emerged from the same scene and had traveled a lot of the same terrain, like Elvis and Jerry Lee Lewis they never had been and never would be friends. But Debbie was the more generous of the two, and she understood Patti's decision.

Deerfrance, on the other hand, was baffled: "I'd been in Detroit and had met all those guys before Patti knew them," she recalled. "I could never understand how she wound up with those guys. The boys from Detroit were old for their years. They lived hard.

They'd been around the block a few times; they'd be drinking booze by the case. I always thought it was interesting how she ended up with someone like that."

Patti's "disappearance" from rock 'n' roll would become as much a part of her legend as her fiery rise. Indeed, James Grauerholz pointed out that in "disappearing," Patti had died a rock 'n' roll death without actually having to die: she had preserved her legend while continuing on with her life. Patti had always wanted to be a shaman, but had never wanted to be a sacrificial victim like her heroes Brian Jones, Jimi Hendrix, and Jim Morrison—they were heroes, not role models. Patti wanted something different for herself.

"I didn't even think of it as retiring," she said.

I mean, I've read everything—that I burned out, that I was on drugs—which was totally untrue. I was actually at the top of my game. But the reason I left was because I had met a man who I deeply loved. Who had been through all of that. Who wanted a quiet life, to raise a family. I found it really unacceptable to be parted from him. And everything lost its meaning. When I began to perform, I did my work with my group with all my heart. It took all of my energy. I put it before everything. And I could no longer do that. And so when I worked, I felt not like a phony, but I just felt like I wasn't giving what the people deserved to have. And I just didn't want to be parted from Fred. I felt good when I left because I felt my initial reason for being involved in that world was to create space for some kind of idealistic minority—you know, if you felt like an alien, whether that was a black, a homosexual, a thief, a female. I know we made a certain difference, we had an effect on people and it was positive. The idea is to create a space for yourself and leave one for the people coming. You want to leave room for other people to work, not to fly a flag and say, "This is mine." I feel that my group achieved that goal. And we didn't start work to achieve fame and fortune.

That wasn't supposed to be our goal. And that was where it was heading. So I felt it was an honorable leave taking.

Fred broke up the Sonic Rendezvous Band around the same time that Patti dismembered her group. And while Patti constantly referred to starting a family with Fred, she also believed that they would start a band, or at least make music together. She was perhaps inspired by ex-Beatle John Lennon: after withdrawing from the music business in 1975, Lennon was making a big comeback in 1980 with his wife, Yoko Ono. Given Patti's timing and her flair for attaching herself to the mythos of rock legends, it would not have been surprising if, rather than wear the widow's weeds that she'd handed to Lenny, Jay Dee, Richard, and Ivan, Patti took her chance to grab the gown of matrimonial rock and become the new-wave John and Yoko (or, as it were, Yoko and John). It did make some sense, for Yoko was an oft-cited influence on some of the first female punk and New Wave singers, and was finally getting some recognition, thanks to her songs on *Double Fantasy*. Why not try a hip version of that?

Patti was driven by other forces as well: the music she and Fred made would show everybody back in New York just who the real queen of punk rock was. Lydia Lunch and all those no-wave jerks who were already putting her down had better watch out. Patti was hot as a pistol. She would redeem Detroit! She would make it the Motor City again! Whatever the motives—which could have, of course, been no more than a desire to make music together— Patti and Fred booked time at a Detroit studio and started working on a new album that they tentatively titled *Dream of Life*. Before the end of 1980, Patti and Fred had recorded five songs, but then suddenly dropped the project without explanation.

When Patti walked off the stage in June 1980, one of the strongest reasons was the fear of being consumed by her fans, of becoming a creature dependent upon their approval and vulnerable to their madness. Patti knew she could have died in Florence at her show at the soccer stadium; John Lennon's murder in New York that December confirmed her worst fears. However, now even as she retreated, the writing she wanted to do about her experiences would not come, and she was not making music, either. For the first time since she left New Jersey for New York, Patti was definitely off her spot.

Meanwhile, after her stint as a "big star," Fred thought that Patti needed some humbling. Her everyday existence in Detroit, cleaning and doing laundry, was certainly that. "I didn't do it for that reason, but Fred knew it was necessary," said Patti. "I learned all those things from him, and I'm extremely grateful to him. It wasn't an easy task to teach me, either. Fred's motto around the house was, 'fame is fleeting,' . . . To strip one's self of all that is quite interesting. It's somewhat humiliating and painful at first, but once you do it, it's liberating."

Patti confided to friends that she deeply missed New York, that the transition to life in Detroit was difficult. As she stayed relatively out of touch and out of the public eye, rumors floated back to New York that Patti had retreated into the arms of Morpheus—that both she and Fred were junkies. These rumors were never substantiated, but since they were out of the studio and not seeing anybody or doing anything, for a lot of people that was the only explanation that made sense.

The world went on, however. An indication of how quickly even the most compelling figure can disappear from rock's memory came like a spear shooting through the roof of Patti's brain when the 1981 *New Musical Express* readers' poll didn't even mention Patti Smith. To make matters worse, during this rough transitional period, Debbie Harry, whom Patti had dismissed, was at the height of her popularity; and Chrissie Hynde, the tough, talented guitarist and band leader who in the eighties would take Patti's place as rock's leading female singer-songwriter, made her debut.

It must have been difficult for Patti and Fred, both proto-punk innovators, to stay outside the action. The American rock scene continued to change beyond their comprehension particularly with the advent of MTV. Debbie Harry's dramatic fall from grace in 1982 may have given Patti a little satisfaction, but she couldn't have taken much pleasure in the inexorable rise of Detroit native Madonna Ciccone—if indeed Patti thought of these things at all.

In the art world, there was a new explosion of work by young artists who had been partly inspired by Patti and the punk and new-wave music of the preceding decade. Artists like Keith Haring and Jean-Michel Basquiat were internationally acclaimed and became major stars. Elsewhere, some of her former running mates were making names for themselves as well. Patti's old flame Sam Shepard became a full-fledged movie star, appearing in such films as *Days of Heaven* and *The Right Stuff,* and Jim Carroll signed a contract with Rolling Stones Records and made a critically lauded album of his music.

Had Patti's reputation depended on the rock press, it might have dwindled and died, but by the early 1980s, she had achieved enough notoriety to be a reference point in the mainstream press. For example, when Cher appeared on Merv Griffin's television show in 1980 wearing her version of the punk look, the *Los Angeles Herald Examiner* commented that "when Cher talked, she mumbled incoherently, sort of like Patti Smith, but as if she had paid Patti Smith a huge weekly salary to teach her these mannerisms."

She also remained a touchstone for women in rock, but opinions on her role in the rock-music world were divided. In *She Bop*, Lucy O'Brien mused, "Was she a rock 'n' roll saint, an asexual hero, or a feminist sell-out?" There was no consensus on that question. When the *New Musical Express* got a panel of female rockers together, including members of the Slits, the Raincoats, and the Au Pairs, they seemed to concur that Patti was more of a threat to feminism than women who openly sold their sexuality in rock music. Panel member Barbara Black of the Passions pointed out that

Patti actually denied she was a feminist. She said, "Oh yes, it's over there somewhere, but it's nothing to do with me. I'm here because of my merits." That is simply not true. When Patti Smith came to the U.K., there were thousands of women who went to see her because of the way she was, her way of performing. And to deny her association with them, to me, is cowardly. I think she's lying to herself when she says the women's movement has nothing to do with her.

Patti had always described herself as someone who didn't like labels and movements. "Part of the reason I was so obsessed about women, and acting so like a snot all the time, saying 'Women are stupid, I don't like women's lib' was because I was afraid of the woman in myself," she had told Nick Tosches. "And I didn't want to admit to myself that I really didn't know nothing about how women are held back. I never felt held back. I was like a little animal all my life. I was given free rein."

And although Patti cut herself off from the scene that spawned her, her mission—as articulated in her final interview of 1980—to make a place from which others could take off, a rock 'n' roll launching pad, was being realized, quite literally. On June 18, 1981, a band formed by two Patti Smith Group fans, Thurston Moore and Kim Gordon, decided to call itself Sonic Youth—a combination of Big Youth, a late-seventies reggae band, and Fred Smith's Sonic Rendezvous Band. "Fred loved that," Patti recalled. "He always said, 'They got that from me!' I'd say, 'Well, you don't know that.' It was a source of pride for him. He was Sonic."

With all of this going on, Fred and Patti were more than happy. In the carefree early days of their marriage, they dreamed up a paradise: free of any demands and financially independent as long as they lived frugally, they set themselves goals and aided each other in completing them. Patti worked at her prose writing, while Fred learned how to fly a plane and got his pilot's license. Patti wanted to write about a man who explored beaches, so Fred took his flying lessons at small aerodromes around the Great Lakes region and the Gulf of Mexico, as well as places on the East and West Coasts. Packing lightly, the couple would take off on these adventurous trips, staying in cheap motels for weeks at a time. The Smiths' life was exactly the kind of "beautiful, simple, nomadic" existence that Patti had imagined an artist having. After spending the day with her notebooks, she looked forward to quiet evenings with Fred, when each gave the other an account of their day. Ironically, however, after Fred got his pilot's license, Patti only took one flight with Fred—she was scared of heights and often experienced nausea in the air.

"Fred was gifted at driving motorcycles and race cars," Patti recalled. "He had great instincts; he was quick—the same way he was on guitar. If he put himself into a weird corner, he'd get out of it in ways other people wouldn't even think of."

In New York, people heard from Patti less and less. Penny Arcade came back to the city in 1981 and heard that Patti had gone into virtual seclusion. "Everyone who ran into me thought that I was in touch with Patti, that I could get a message to Patti. It was bizarre. I would say, 'Look, I haven't been close to Patti for years. I don't have her phone number, I don't talk to her, I don't write her, she doesn't write me.' "

In addition to their life as a couple, Patti and Fred by now had also settled into a comfortable musical collaboration. Neither they, nor anyone who knew them, ever doubted that they were gearing up to record an album together. "We write songs together and pursue individual ideas," Patti said of their working relationship. "It's been that way since I met him in 1976. We have been writing and working on songs together for ourselves. I never stopped writing. Working with Fred is very important to me. We have a lot of other ideas and songs we haven't done yet. Many songs. We're looking to the future with some other works. What we wanted to do was a piece of work together that addressed the things we care about." "People Have the Power," from 1978, rose out of a typical Smith-Smith collaboration, One afternoon, Patti was doing some basic housework when Fred said, "People have the power. Write it." Patti dove into the subject and came up with an anthemic lyric.

Some greeted such statements with skepticism. "Almost every woman artist I've ever met has this ideal of being in a partnership working situation with a man that men don't seem to share," noted Tom Verlaine when asked about working with Patti. "John Lennon ended up in it briefly with Yoko. They [women] seem to want this ideal thing, that we'll always be together and work together."

Verlaine's comment, however, belies the reality of the punk movement (and certainly that of John and Yoko, whose collaboration lasted for over ten years, ending only with Lennon's death), which saw successful and long-lasting collaborations both early on, with Debbie Harry and Chris Stein, and later, as in the cases of John Doe and Exene Cervenka, and Thurston Moore and Kim Gordon, among others.

In late 1981, Patti became pregnant. By the time she gave birth to a son, Jackson Frederick, in 1982, the phone calls to New York had stopped completely. When friends tried to reach her, they discovered they could not. Her number was unlisted, and when they moved out of the Book Cadillac Patti left no forwarding address. To her friends, it seemed as if Fred could not afford to share any of her. On top of that, along with the drug rumors, there were rumors of domestic violence.

"Fred was beat as a kid," Wayne Kramer asserted.

He was an abused kid. His dad beat him pretty good. Lots of times Fred didn't come to school because of it. Sometimes I'd go over to his house and he'd have a black eye. His dad was from the South and had that kinda down-home ignorance—you beat your wife, you beat your kids, when they don't do like ya say. That syndrome gets passed from generation to generation, unless you interrupt it with a lot of hard work.

James Wolcott, one of the earliest writers to cover the CBGB's scene, interviewed Patti for a *Vanity Fair* article around this time and got "a spooky vibe about Fred and Patti's relationship," particularly from Patti's conduct afterward. She phoned Wolcott the day following their interview, asking him to omit any mention of her affairs with Tom Verlaine and Sam Shepard. When he pointed out that those relationships were a matter of public record, Patti replied, "I know, but Fred gets upset when he reads that stuff." She also requested that Wolcott omit other facts from the interview. "She didn't sound like a considerate spouse trying to spare her husband's tender feelings," Wolcott wrote in the never-published piece. "She sounded nervous, fretful—cowed."

Whatever the case, what was becoming apparent was that Patti and Fred were quite different people. Initially, she and Fred had done everything together, but three years into the marriage it became clear that, much like Patti's parents, in many ways they were polar opposites. While Patti thrived on a communal environment and enjoyed working in physical proximity to her collaborators, Fred needed isolation to do his work. In the studio, for instance, he was a stickler for hitting the exact note at the exact time, but Patti was much more interested in the feeling of a song than its technical perfection. "She could have driven him crazy a lot of times," commented an engineer who had been in the studio with both of them for some abortive 1982 *Dream of Life* sessions. "She can be a very frustrating person to work with, asking for something and then by the time you get it for her she's changed her mind and wants something different. She can really piss you off." Both she and Fred were strong personalities, too, and for somebody who had been allowed to be a benevolent despot for so long it was hard to accept another musician's opinion as equal to her own.

Accept it she did, though. In the twelve-step jargon that would become so prevalent in the eighties, Patti would be called an enabler, one who was in deep denial herself, maybe even a codependent. She loved Fred, and couldn't help deferring to him. It did not help their collaboration, particularly with regard to Fred's drinking. She could not stop him from drinking, yet by allowing it to escalate, she made it impossible for Fred to work with her.

The truth was Fred's health problems, combined with his drinking, had rendered him nearly incapable of performing. Getting him into a studio had itself become a major production, and then, when he got there, he would insist that without just a little taste, he couldn't play. However, by the time he had consumed the two bottles of wine he required before playing a note, he really couldn't play at all. Patti, who used to kick Lenny in the ass if he repeated the same solo on the same song, was understandably frustrated.

Despite the obviousness of the problems, Patti seemed paralyzed, unable to act. In reaction, she turned her attention to bringing up Jackson, who would see his mother change over the next ten years from a vibrant thirty-six-year-old to a careworn, gray-haired mirror image of her "old man," whose own decline was so marked that his former bandmates from the MC5, meeting up with him in the early nineties, would hardly recognize him.

As of 1983, neither Patti nor Fred had released any material to the public, and they had virtually become recluses. Learning new rhythms and ways of working would dominate their life for the next few years. Motherhood, much more than marriage to Fred, would change Patti's day-to-day existence, but with those responsibilities she was still able to dedicate time and energy to her artistic pursuits. With Jackson's birth, late nights sitting at the typewriter vanished as she was forced, like any new parent, to adapt to the demanding schedule of an infant, rising early and being available for his every need. Patti rose to the challenge, focusing on staying healthy and maintaining her flexibility as she grew into her new role as mother. Fred, too, was a devoted and caring father. Old priorities evaporated for the couple as Jackson became the center of their existence.

"I really love my kids," Patti said. "I love having them around even though they are a big responsibility and can drive you nuts. But one of the pluses of advancing through life is how your spectrum widens. In being a parent, your spectrum widens even further. You become real aware of how everything affects your child. I know Fred and I, individually and mutually, have always been concerned about the state of the planet, but somehow when you have children, it becomes even bigger."

Shortly after Jackson's birth, Patti and Fred purchased a one-hundred-year-old house on an acre of ground half a block from Lake St. Clair in the suburb of St. Clair Shores, about forty miles outside of Detroit. Buying the house brought a renewed focus to Patti's family life and took her another step away from her past.

St. Clair Shores is a peaceful place, and just sitting on the edge of the lake gives one a feeling of centered solitude. Unlike any of the other houses in the neighborhood, the Smiths' house looked somewhat like a small castle. It was made of dark-brown brick and wood, and was topped by a small turret. There was even a small swimming pool on the property—which, not being swimming-pool types, Patti and Fred broke up, hauled out, and filled in, so well that it was impossible to tell that a pool had ever been there. In the backyard sat a picnic table, a symbol of the family life they were now living.

In place of her colorful New York friends, Patti now claimed to have her closest relationship outside her family with a pet fish called Curley. She took pleasure in watching television, which she called "studying." "I went through different phases, such as a *Kung Fu Theater* phase—it aired every Sunday night. Everybody had to be quiet so I could have my cup of sake and sit there and watch it.

And I used to watch the original *Route 66* at night. When they took both shows off the air, I was brokenhearted."

Despite such travails, Patti looked back favorably.

It was hard to stop working in public, but I balanced myself in the early eighties. It was slow in coming at first but very rewarding. I had never been much of a drug taker, but I did smoke a lot of marijuana. I gave that up and was drug-free, which required a lot of concentration. I had to learn to work again, find my own time, usually before six A.M., when my baby woke up. Eventually, I found that my faculties had really sharpened. I find that the things I did in this period are far more extreme than the things I did in the seventies.

Keeping up with current trends in music was of little interest to Patti; her exposure to new music was limited to what she heard on the car radio when driving around with Fred. Though the Smiths owned a brand-new sedan, Patti, whose eyesight had been damaged in the 1977 fall, remained one of the few people in Detroit without a driver's license. This left her trapped at home and completely reliant on somebody to drive her wherever she wanted to go. "I'm the only person here who doesn't drive," she admitted. At home, the couple tended to listen to classical and jazz, exploring Beethoven and Puccini, Coltrane and Ayler. There was always some new gem from Bob Dylan to treasure, but, for the most part, music ceased to be the compelling force it was in Patti's life in her teens and twenties.

Fred was a little bit more attuned to what was happening. Though Fred despised the business for the way it used up and exploited young talent—an attitude that had a strong influence on Patti, even though her own experience had been fairly positive— he also missed playing. It was difficult for him to reconcile this dilemma, and some felt that he never really did. But Fred was still

full of ideas for songs, and though no longer ambitious for himself, he still was for Patti. He watched the rise of female performers with great interest, encouraging Patti to keep in touch with
what was developing. "I am getting such a multifaceted education
from Fred because I am privileged to learn so much of what he
knows—which is a million things," she said.

Fred's longtime friend, the producer Freddie Brooks, concurred with Patti's view of her husband. "Fred was a really smart
man," said Brooks. "I just basically soaked up whatever knowledge
I could from him. We were equals but I was totally under him—it
was like a study program. If there were two opinions about a way
to do something, Fred would always come up with a third way, he
would just invent a whole new thing. I was just in awe of him. Fred
was a great guy." Like the Rolling Stones' Brian Jones, Fred had
the capacity to quickly master almost any instrument. "Fred
played the piano and he played the saxophone," said Brooks,
"Fred could play just about anything, he could figure anything
out. He was a real musical guy."

When she wasn't doing the chores and errands of suburban
life, Patti's favorite place in the house was the music room. Fred's
upright piano stood flush to one wall, with a bust of his idol
Beethoven atop it. "The narrow, pointed lancet windows, the
whitewashed walls and the dark wood ceiling," suggested to
one visitor "the mood of a secular monastery." The sparsely
furnished space was decorated by a scroll of a Buddha on one
wall, a Mapplethorpe sculpture of knots and beads on another.
Two tiny Hanuman books, William Burroughs's *Painting and
Guns*, and Jean Genet's *What Remains of a Rembrandt*, were also on
display.

The eighties were a very creative period for Patti. She cherished
writing as her main task and spent every day working on it, eventually completing five books, of which three—*Woolgathering*, *The
Coral Sea*, and *Patti Smith Complete*—have been published.

I actually worked harder in the eighties than I ever had. I spent time as a wife and mother, bearing and raising two children. There's a lot of sacrifice and very intense responsibility. I've grown and expanded as a human being in that way. That's permeated into the work. And a lot of the other work I've done over the past years hasn't been shared yet. I think it's some of the best work I have ever done. It's the most articulate, and I'm pleased with it. Fred and I have done a lot of work together. A lot of writing and exploring in a lot of different areas. It wasn't like we sat at home not doing anything.

Patti and Fred rarely went to the movies, but they rented films to watch at home on the VCR, and found inspiration in the works of such master directors as Kurosawa, Bertolucci, and Godard, as well as those of Woody Allen, whose *Purple Rose of Cairo* Patti watched ten times.

Though Patti later said that "nobody really cared about Fred and me during the eighties," they were the ones who had cut themselves off. According to John Sinclair, the MC5's manager, "they never went out, they never had people over, they didn't perform, they didn't record, they never even went to local shows. Nobody could figure out how they were surviving." Friends did wonder how they were supporting themselves, since neither Patti nor Fred was doing any income-producing work. Patti did receive regular royalty payments on her albums and publishing rights as bands began covering some of her songs, and Fred collected occasional minor royalties from MC5 rereleases. They had some financial difficulties, but they also had the occasional windfall, too, such as when Bruce Springsteen recorded "Because the Night." Patti put a positive spin on it all by pointing out how living frugally helped make them a closer family, and she romanticized their occasional travails—like the time the house flooded and they had to pull together and sandbag to save it, a situation that she compared to that of the TV family on *Little House on the Prairie*, citing the common necessity of joining as one against the odds, out on the new frontier. "An artist may have burdens the ordinary citizen doesn't know," Patti declared, "but the ordinary citizen has burdens that many artists never touch."

After Jackson's birth, Patti and Fred scrapped the tapes from their 1980 *Dream of Life* sessions and began anew. Later, these sessions, too, were scrapped. They went back into the studio for a third shot at *Dream of Life* in 1986. This time they recorded in New York, with Richard Sohl, Jay Dee Daugherty, the producer Jimmy Iovine, and a revolving team of bassists that included Kasim Sulton from Utopia, Todd Rundgren's band. Lenny Kaye was conspicuously absent, apparently at Fred's insistence.

Patti characterized *Dream of Life* as an "extremely difficult album to create, with two highly self-critical people trying to please themselves as well as each other." It would, of course, have taken four tries, but Patti had nothing but glowing praise for the recording experience: "Jimmy Iovine was wonderful to work with as producer. Fred and him really collaborated well on this project. . . . all the musicians were properly represented. It was a real collaboration on everyone's part, from Richard Sohl to the assistant engineer."

Wayne Kramer saw things from a different angle. "Fred's roadies, the Hurley brothers, told me how hard it was to get Fred up for rehearsals for the recording sessions for that record," said Wayne Kramer. "That they had to go over to his house in the morning and drag him out and drive him to the rehearsal studio, drive him to the recording studio, drag him in, tune his guitar for him and then they recorded an album that didn't exactly burn everybody up with enthusiasm because there wasn't that much enthusiasm that went into it."

Enthusiastic or not, the band had finished laying down the tracks and were slated to record the vocals when Patti discovered that she was pregnant again. This time the project would have to be put off for almost a year. Patti and Fred soldiered on in the studio until it became too much for the pregnant Patti. The sessions went on hold until Patti's second child, Jesse Paris, was born in 1987.

Robert Mapplethorpe was Patti's choice to do the cover of this all-important album. When they met in New York in the coffee shop of the Mayflower Hotel on Central Park West to discuss the image, the two had not seen each other for several years, during which Mapplethorpe had achieved considerable notoriety. In 1985, he enjoyed a brief stint as the most famous artist in the world when his portfolio of photographs of black male nudes became a bone of contention on the floor of the U.S. Senate in a debate over federal arts funding. Mapplethorpe became a whipping boy of the Reagan administration, the quintessential "rebellious artist working outside society," and a target of born-again Christian conservatives. His cause was taken up not only within, but also outside the art world, serving as the subject of countless editorials defending him on First Amendment grounds. Ten years after Patti was featured in the *New York Times Magazine* with *Horses*, Robert Mapplethorpe made an even bigger splash with the *X Portfolio*, hitting the headlines and editorial pages around the world. As a celebrity, Robert, in fact, had become everything Patti had wanted to be. At times like these Patti Smith may have felt as forgotten as Memphis Minnie. Yet, though Robert's career was soaring, he had contracted the AIDS virus and was beginning to feel its ravages. By the time that *Dream of Life* was released, he was hospitalized at St. Vincent's.

Patti, meanwhile, had been married for seven years and had given birth to two children, and Robert was shocked by the drastic change in her appearance. Her hair, which had always been the crowning glory of her image, was now long and straggly and streaked with gray. Her face looked tired and drawn, and her eyes stared out with an almost frightened look from behind schoolmarm glasses. She seemed no longer in control. Moreover, Robert was uncomfortable with Jackson and Jesse's constant demands for attention, and stunned by her constant deferral to Fred on every question about the album cover. The situation was awkward for Robert in every way.

Getting a successful image was obviously not going to be an easy task. The first session was a disaster, producing a glamorized image of Patti wearing makeup. Three months later, in Los Angeles, Mapplethorpe finally captured an image of Patti that they both liked, a black-and-white shot taken outdoors in natual light, her hair twisted into tiny Frido Kahlo–inspired braids.

To Robert and to her old friends, Patti seemed to be a different woman. When she wrote *Cowboy Mouth* with Sam Shepard, she had been the equal of her male collaborator, but now she deferred to Fred on everything, seemingly incapable of doing anything without his OK. The question was, who or what changed her? Was it her devotion to Fred? The isolation of life in Detroit? Was it the slavelike servitude of being a mother? For people who had known Patti over the years, it was a mystery.

Wayne Kramer saw Fred at the root of it. "Fred was a real traditionalist, he wasn't into 'modern' relationships," said Kramer. "He was a 'You're my wife, and the wife does this and the man does that' kind of guy. As much as Patti eloquently repainted him as a gifted artist and a saint of a man, he had his roots in this Kentucky redneck attitude, and I think that fed into their disconnection with the outside world. The wife's job is to stay home and raise the kids—keep 'em pregnant and barefoot."

Patti, however, insisted that she was happy in her life with Fred. "Fred wanted a family, a son and a daughter, and that's what I gave him," she said.

He was a great father, a really loving, compassionate father. He was a complex man: warm, generous, and gentle. He was extremely soulful, but he was also exacting in his philosophies about relationships, marriage, and work ethics, and he was extremely private. Our communication was limitless and if we had difficult times, we rode them out together. Sometimes it felt like we were together in the same car while it was crashing, surviving it together. . . .

Working with Fred is very important to me. Our album represents us working together. We have a lot of other ideas and many songs we haven't done yet. We're looking into the future with some other works. We have achieved what we wanted with this album.

In the spring of 1988, Patti and Fred finally finished *Dream of Life*. An organic album, it grew out of the life they shared—and that, more than its actual release or the time it took to finish, was most important. "What interests us most in the entire process is the work aspect," said Patti. "For me, releasing an album is never as exciting as working on the music. We strive to do the work that we want, and we don't want any outside type of pressure or motivation that could shift the quality or direction of our work. Ever."

Released that summer, the album was greeted warmly by rock critics, who generally all bought Patti's mythologizing about her new mature, married self. "Patti Smith's nine-year absence from the music business has been a positive experience for her, a time of emotional healing and personal growth," wrote Mary Anne Cassata in *Music Paper*. "She spent most of her time raising her two children, Jackson Frederick (now five) and Jesse Paris (now two), drawing much inspiration from them. *Dream of Life* is a celebration of family unity and of the love Patti and Fred share for each other, their children, and the world."

"*Dream of Life* is an inspiring piece of work," wrote Brett Milano in *Pulse!* Milano also observed that

the phrase "Fred and I" turns up often in conversation—that's who wrote the songs, that's who made the record, that's who's in for the long haul. Most of all, she emphasizes that the Patti Smith of the Patti Smith Group and the Patti Smith of "Fred and I" are two different animals. "People Have the Power" caught a lot of Patti Smith's old fans by surprise. The hippie-ish sentiments were odd enough, but the kicker was that Smith expressed them convincingly. "That's a gift type of song," she said. "I meant it to give some kind of positive energy and hope to people in a very difficult time. The song addresses itself to the various dreams that mankind has and reminds us that perhaps we can achieve those dreams if we work together. It's not intended to incite so much as to remind people." Asked if she would have believed those sentiments at the time of *Horses*, Patti replied, "Sure. I was never a pessimistic person. I questioned many things and had a growling nature, but that doesn't mean pessimism. Art is by nature optimistic. If one keeps working one has hope for the future. If one didn't feel that, one would crawl into an opium den and pull the covers over their heads.

"It is time to make things better. We have to help our fellow man, we have to address problems like AIDS, we have to amass the money to find a cure. We have to make people aware of the dangers, we have to clean up this world. I mean, every time I fill a water glass for my son, I'm thinking, is there too high a lead content in this water? We need to get a great cosmic broom and sweep up the planet. I've had millions of dreams of the great collective, of the whole planet rising in prayer."

Some of Patti's old friends were amazed by her apparent transformation. Reading a piece on Patti in *Vogue*, Penny Arcade, for one, was shocked. "I just wanted to kill her," she said.

I'm reading this thing, and it was very reactionary. She struck me as a reactionary person. I didn't know where her politics were and then toward the end of the article she says this thing about, "Well, I'm a married woman and I would always change my name to my husband's name and the only reason that I didn't change it is 'cause his name is Smith, too." I was like, what is this? The article probably really colored my not wanting to see Patti. I don't understand her and I don't understand who she became, but on another level, I feel like, Patti became a fantasy, as opposed to becoming who she was gonna be.

In New York doing publicity for *Dream of Life*, Patti promoted the album relentlessly, giving interview after interview, reinforcing her new persona as New Age mom and benefactor of the planet.

Unfortunately, the long, often difficult creation of the album and the flat-out publicity push all came to nought for the simple reason that the Smiths flatly refused to tour, or even do one show on the East Coast and one on the West. Suddenly taking refuge with Julie Andrews in *The Sound of Music*, Patti claimed it was because of "the children." Nothing could have been further from the truth. Either set of Smith grandparents, aunts, or uncles could easily have watched over Jessie and Jackson for the two to three weeks an efficient U.S. tour would have taken. The Smiths' Achilles heel, all too evident here, was Fred's inability to perform the gruelling task (due to illness and alcohol). As a result, *Dream of Life*, eight years in gestation, died a quick, silent death as Patti's cult reputation washed up against the hard new world of MTV.

Years later, Marianne Faithfull, one of Patti's role models, spoke about *Dream of Life* and the limitations put on women artists in the music business. "It made me really angry when Patti Smith's *Dream of Life* record was rejected," she said. "She changed her opinions and fell in love and got married and had kids and made a tender record and her record was rejected because she wasn't the raging junkie anymore. I don't know her that well, but I know she was incredibly hurt by that."

Patti had envisioned *Dream of Life* as the pinnacle of her long collaboration with Fred, yet when the record failed, it was Fred who was the most affected. According to Patti, "People have this idea of me as a sensitive soul, but Fred was much more sensitive and soulful than me. I was always the more practical of the two."

"The fact that the album was not successful was very depressing to Fred," said Freddie Brooks. "I think breaking his heart would be the right expression, that's really what happened. It just broke his heart."

dreams of death

1989 – 1994

> "First Andy died. Then Robert. And then, quite suddenly, without a word, Richard followed."
>
> **patti smith, *"february snow"***

In late February 1989, Robert Mapplethorpe telephoned Patti in Detroit to say that he was going up to Boston for a series of experimental treatments for the AIDS virus that was rapidly destroying him. Patti asked Fred to drive her from Detroit to New York, a ten-hour trip, so that she could spend some time with Robert. Though her friend had maintained a cheerful stoicism over the phone, Patti knew that Robert was dying.

The two "enfants terribles" spent one long afternoon alone together, the way they used to be. Patti would remember looking at a photograph of a desert scene that graced the cover of an old *Life* magazine bearing the date of Mapplethorpe's birthday. "We stared at the picture for a long time," Patti told Patricia Morrisroe. "It was like the photograph had opened up and we had entered the scene."

After a while, Robert began experiencing severe gastric pains and had to be helped to the bathroom by his nurse. He was in bad shape. When he emerged he looked at Patti. "I'm dying," he told her. Patti began to cry, sobbing and sobbing until finally Mapplethorpe was able to calm her. In their last conversation, he made her promise that she would write the introduction to his forthcoming flower book—even in the face of death, their artistic collaboration was the thing that mattered most. Robert rested his head on Patti's shoulder, and, after a few minutes, she realized that he had fallen asleep. For the next two hours she sat with him, quietly listening to the beat of his heart.

The next day, Patti and Fred returned to Detroit. As it turned out, the doctors in Boston were unable to administer the special treatments to Mapplethorpe because of other complications he was experiencing, and on March 9, 1989, Robert Mapplethorpe died. He was just forty-two years old. "I was sitting up all night in vigil because I knew he was dying. His brother called me at 7:30 in the morning to tell me that he had finally passed away," Patti said. "I wept for him so much while he was still alive that I found when he died I was unable to weep. And so I wrote. Which I think he would have preferred anyway, because Robert liked to see me work."

That day, Patti began a long prose poem about him, which she would publish as *The Coral Sea*, the title taken from a grainy Mapplethorpe photo of a huge gray sky pressing down upon an aircraft carrier—the U.S.S. *Coral Sea*. In the text, Patti imagined Mapplethorpe as a sailor taking passage on a ship, "venturing to Papua to secure for his soul a legendary butterfly, which he would tack to his chest as [Peter] Pan had attached his shadow to his wild little feet." Although the writing's near-biblical formality, old-fashioned usages, and relentless mythologizing was sometimes overrich, many deemed the book Patti's most beautiful and moving work, and felt that it truly "rings the bell of pure poetry," as William Burroughs said on the back of the paperback edition, quoting from Tennessee Williams.

"What I was trying to do was conjure up a portrait of Robert as I knew him, in a way that I knew him," Patti explained.

"If our friendship is legendary, that's because it's a fine example of friendship. Robert and I went through a lot of things. We met when we were twenty. We experienced puppy love. We were girlfriend and boyfriend. Robert opened up and found himself to have a calling more toward homosexuality, and we went through that together and stayed close. We collaborated together, we went through many artistic processes together and remained loving, caring friends until his death. I think any story of an everlasting friendship is worthy of legend."

In a prescient 1974 interview, discussing the phenomenon of Patti Smith, Allen Ginsberg dramatically posed the question: "How will she deal with suffering? How will she transcend suffering and become a lady of energy, a sky-goddess, singing of egolessness? Because so far her proposition has been the triumph of the stubborn, individualistic, Rimbaud-Whitman ego: but then there is going to be the point where her teeth fall out and she's going to become the old hag of mythology that we all become." The coming years would provide plenty of opportunity for Ginsberg to find his answer.

On June 3, 1990, barely fifteen months after Mapplethorpe's wrenching death, thirty-seven-year-old Richard Sohl suffered a cardiac seizure and died. "He was wonderful and I was actually quite heartbroken," said Patti, who would describe this period as "the youth of my grief."

Penny Arcade went to DNV's memorial service, and the Patti she saw there was a far cry from the woman she had once known.

There were seats reserved in the front row. I knew that Patti was probably going to be sitting on those seats, so I went and I sat on the side facing those seats. Finally Patti showed up, with her husband, and an entourage, her lawyer and whoever. She came in and sat down and they started the memorial. She got up and spoke, and I was looking at her, and she looked horrible. She looked weird and she was deferring constantly to Fred. I didn't know Patti like that. I knew Patti as a fiercely independent person. I didn't know this person the last time I saw her. She was like this eclipsed moon.

At the end of the memorial, I wanted to split, I didn't want to go up to Patti, but Danny Fields was looking at me, so I finally walked over and said hi to her, and she goes 'Oh, Penny, hey man, you look exactly the same, man,' which was always the first thing she'd say. I'm looking at her and she looked beat. I mean, like, *really* beat. And there she was going "Oh, man, you look exactly the same, you look great, you really do." What could I say? So I said, "Patti, you really look great too."

Fred was a changed man as well, and friends remarked upon it when he and Patti made one of their rare public appearances, such as at a 1990 AIDS benefit at Radio City Music Hall, where they performed a powerful acoustic version of "People Have the Power." At another AIDS benefit in May 1991, at the Nectarine Ballroom in Ann Arbor, Michigan, Freddie Brooks saw Fred for the first time in ten years. Brooks thought that Fred "did not seem all there. I'm not putting Fred down or anything," he said,

> but they were playing some of his old songs and he just didn't seem to remember them. Some people attributed it to his being drunk, but it was obvious to me that it wasn't just drinking. I know that for a fact. I attribute it to health problems. The drummer in the Sonic Rendezvous Band said Fred was always taking Rolaids. His condition was probably pretty painful, and

when things are that painful it's conceivable that you might be doing something to try and alleviate the pain, whether it's the right thing to do or not. His whole family had illnesses that passed through their lives. You don't go from being a powerful guy like Fred to looking as frail as he did at the end for no reason. He had bad stomach problems all his life. I think there was something going on there that no one will ever know because they didn't delve into it when he died.

In addition to the health problems, the fact that his work—including the MC5's output—never received the attention and appreciation that he felt it deserved ate away at him. To make a record as strong as *Dream of Life* and have it fail was the final straw. *Dream of Life* wasn't just a Patti Smith record—it was also in large part a Fred Smith record, and its rejection broke him.

Later in 1991, the MC5's vocalist, Rob Tyner, died of a heart attack, in Detroit at the age of forty-six. In the aftermath, Wayne Kramer had his first close dealings in many years with Fred Smith, his old bandmate. "Rob didn't have any insurance and he had left three kids and of course being in the MC5 had not left any of us independently wealthy," Kramer recalled. "So they started to get this whole thing organized in Detroit—it was gonna be four-day tribute to Rob Tyner in four different clubs all over the city, climaxing with this big tribute show at the Michigan Theater." The two were to perform, but disagreed on how to approach the gig. "I didn't wanna go up there and jam," Kramer continued. "I wanted to rehearse and have something together, but Fred was being real obstinate about it."

Kramer was shocked at the changes in Fred, who, despite their estrangement, was one of his oldest and closest friends. It was difficult to get Fred to do anything, and Kramer thought a lot of it had to do with drinking. "He looked like his skin had drooped down like he had palsy, and all his teeth were rotted. He looked scary. Afterwards, me and Michael [Davis, the MC5's bassist] went out to dinner together and said, 'Man, did you see Fred's face? Oh, Jesus, man, what happened to the guy?' " Still, determined to pull off a good show for the Tyner benefits, Kramer, Davis, and Dennis Thompson, the MC5 drummer, set up a rehearsal.

Thompson was first to show up, soon to be followed by Kramer and Davis. Two hours passed. "We jammed and we were having fun, and finally Fred showed up," said Kramer.

The roadies scurry out and they carry in his gear for him, and here comes this frail old guy and he sits down. These other guys are tuning his guitar for him and plugging everything in. He sits down with two bottles of wine and commences to knock one off before we start playing! And then we start to rehearse what we're gonna do, and he can't play his guitar—he don't remember the parts! "Wayne, what did I play? You know what I used to play." "Yeah, I think it went like this, it's seventh fret, doo-do-da." He said, "Oh, oh, I don't remember anything, after the band broke up I, I don't remember anything."

"Fred commenced to get plastered," Kramer continued.

Dennis got so angry at one point he said, "Come on, can we get on with it? I have more fun at the dentist." Finally we finished the rehearsal. We might as well not have rehearsed for the good it did. The next day we got to the gig and everyone's waiting for Fred to get there. He arrived late, and then it was time for us to play. The stage was dark and the gear was ready and we were waiting, sitting backstage, and Fred would not go on. Fred was drinking more wine out of a coffee cup, and waiting. Michael and Dennis both kept coming in saying, "Come on, let's play, let's play, let's play," and Fred wouldn't play. At one point they left the room, and Fred looked at me and said, "Fucking amateurs!" which was an old joke. We went on and played. Fred told the audience, "Well, if we know anything, we're only here for a minute and you've got to make your mark and Rob certainly made his mark." Patti was not around at all. She never showed up, not even for the gig. Fred didn't play well, I've listened to the tapes a lot and he was really out of sync with everything. He wasn't on the beat. And then he disappeared into the night. I didn't talk to him again, didn't see Patti . . . until Fred died.

The Tyner benefit would be Fred Smith's last public appearance.

Meanwhile, in the midst of all of this death and the growing problem of Fred's health, Patti continued her artistic rebirth. In 1992, she published *Woolgathering*, a pocket-size volume of new writings produced to be part of a series from Hanuman Books that included volumes by Bob Dylan, Allen Ginsberg, and Richard Hell. *Woolgathering* is a collection of nine short, poetic prose pieces, most of which are evocations of Patti's childhood in rural New Jersey. It presents a serene and meditative Patti, one seemingly far removed from the aggressive, willfully provocative rebel of her youth. The book presents a Patti who appears to have traveled back to her childhood in order to remove herself from any contact with a reality that might be painful. It is so sickly sweet and wistful that you're never sure whether it's going to evaporate into thin air or float away like a helium balloon with its banal thoughts that compare, for example, the mind of a child with a kiss and the frosting on a cake as poisonous yet sweet.

The only music Patti and Fred released in that year was a song, "It Takes Time," which appeared on the soundtrack album for the Wim Wenders film *Until the End of the World*, but Patti began cropping up in the media with some frequency. In December, Patti's picture was included in a collage on the cover of an issue of *Life* magazine dedicated to the history of rock. While this spoke well for the public perception of her importance, the only reference to her in the accompanying article was a snide, dismissive comment: "Patti Smith, who didn't shave under arms, was a punk goddess." At least REM's lead singer, Michael Stipe, was quoted in the issue speaking of her influence, saying, "Patti Smith was the one who said anybody could sing . . . and I thought, yeah, I can do that."

Shortly after the *Life* mention, *Rolling Stone*'s twenty-fifth anniversary "Portraits" issue featured her in a famous seventies nude portrait by Mapplethorpe, and additional shots showed her in what the magazine's writers termed "Rimbaud manqué menswear." In *Spin* magazine's cover story on its band of the year, Nirvana, Courtney Love asserted that "Patti Smith saved my life." In a *Details* article on Sonic Youth, Patti was named as one of the band's idols. In fact, a young generation of musicians, many of them female, were increasingly citing Patti as a major influence.

"I realize that I first heard Patti Smith out of context, and was very lucky that way," wrote Kristin Hersh of Throwing Muses, who first heard Patti's voice blaring from her father's turntable as a child, and then later rediscovered her via a tape of Patti she listened to on her long walks to rehearsal as a fledgling musician. "It was her bubble I heard. I didn't hear it as seventies rock, or as coming out of a scene. I just heard a voice. It didn't seem so much of a 'fiery rebel' thing to me, and by the time I grew up, I'd seen so many rebels that it'd stopped meaning anything any more. She was so delicate, and her voice was so thin. She seemed kind of breakable, which is great. I mean, that's a planet!"

Cover versions of Patti's songs appeared, too, though none became hits except for the 10,000 Maniacs recording of the Springsteen collaboration, "Because the Night." This song was the most often covered; "Dancing Barefoot" came in a close second with at least seven versions. U2 and Johnette Napolitano were two of the notables to record "Dancing." "I found it very wonderful to hear different interpretations," Patti said. "It helped keep the music alive."

Seeing her work remain vital was indeed gratifying, for both

Patti and Fred, for during the years they were married they kept a wary eye on the music business. Even as his own ambition ebbed, Fred placed increasing emphasis on the importance of Patti not being forgotten. He thought that she had a successful future ahead of her, even despite the time she had taken out to raise their family. To prepare for and encourage her future work, Fred began giving Patti guitar lessons and taught her how to write songs on guitar. For while she had long toted a guitar onstage and in the studio, Patti had really only used feedback and random strumming, never really attempting to master the instrument. Now, however, night after night while the children slept, the couple sat in the music room and painstakingly studied chord and song structure. "I wanted to learn chords so I could sit down and write melody lines," Patti explained. "So he gave me guitar lessons every night after the kids went to bed. I was slow, but he was very patient. He taught me chord after chord and how to structure songs. He used to tease me and tell me I wasn't allowed to tell anybody! I'd play a song really poorly, and I'd say, 'I can't wait to tell people my guitar teacher is Fred 'Sonic' Smith, and he'd say 'Don't do that, Patricia!' "

At first the guitar lessons were filled mostly with intimate laughter, because Patti's progress was slow. She persevered, though and gradually the idea for another album was taking shape. Patti had loved Dylan's 1992 return to folk on *Good As I Been to You*, and, in response, wrote a batch of acoustic songs with the intention of doing a folk album. Fred insisted that she make a rock 'n' roll album, realizing that was where her real strength lay. Folk or rock, they felt that this proposed album presented a chance to comment on the times, and they both had a lot to say. However, as "Fred's health deteriorated that year," Patti noted, "we spent less time writing songs."

Patti kept up with her own writing. In early 1993, her short essay "February Snow," memorializing Andy Warhol, Robert Mapplethorpe, and Richard Sohl, was published in *Interview* magazine, accompanying photographs of winter scenes by Bruce Weber, Kurt Markus, and Margaret Durrance. The essay described the night in 1987 that Warhol died, when Patti was recording *Dream of Life* and pregnant with her second child, and mused on the fleeting nature of life, reflecting that everything disappears in the light of dawn. She lists the deaths of Warhol, Mapplethorpe, and Sohl, which lead her to walk across a field on which the impress of her shoes would soon be covered by snow. Just as nobody will ever know she passed this way, she concludes, so are the dead "but a shroud of snow stained in memory, graced with mourning light."

On the hot steamy evening of July 8, Patti made a dramatic return to the New York stage with a remarkable public reading in Central Park. Though nervous and uncertain as to how she would be received after so many years away, she nevertheless gave a strong performance. "It was one of the happiest nights of my life," she would say. "I couldn't believe how great these people were. The whole atmosphere—not just the audience, but I had my brother there, and Fred was there, so I have really happy memories of it."

Patti's audience seemed to look to her for a way of understanding all of the negative things going on around them, including the AIDs plague, which had claimed so many young lives. "A lot of people in the crowd had all gone through that," said Patti, "and all the rough experiences in the past decade join us together."

Death remained close, too, as in April 1994 Patti was deeply affected the suicide of Nirvana's leader, Kurt Cobain. She wrote a song, "About a Boy," in his memory, drawing on Cobain's own "About a Girl." "Fred and I wept when that kid did that," she recalled. "I loved that *Unplugged* record, but we didn't weep for him like fans. We wept like parents. We mourned the loss of someone who was so gifted and obviously in so much pain . . . and we all know there are lots of kids in that same pain." Patti expressed admiration and concern for Cobain's widow, Courtney Love. "I think she's done really good work . . . I just think it's important that even for artists that move toward the edge, you have to maintain some balance or you won't live. I hate to see anybody throw their life away, so I hope that a lot of these younger people will try to keep some balance."

One of the few bright moments in 1994 was the W. W. Norton Company's publication of *Early Work, 1970–1979*, a collection of Patti's poetry. The book made generally available, in elegant form, the writings that first brought Patti acclaim. Sadly, however, while Patti seemed to be gradually returning to her audience, Fred's condition worsened. Word spread among his associates; Wayne Kramer heard from his Detroit friend Joe Hurley that Fred had been hospitalized for stomach trouble, and Ben Edmonds, who was writing a book about the MC5, told Kramer that it was still "drinking central" at Fred's house in St. Clair Shores. There was even talk among Fred's friends about doing an "intervention," in which friends and family members would confront him in an attempt to get him to acknowledge and deal with his problem, and get treatment. "One of the Hurley brothers was involved in therapeutic community work, he was a counselor or something," Kramer remembered. "They loved the guy [Fred], so they're saying he don't need to be onstage, he needs to be in the hospital. At one point they were going to pull an intervention, but there was a fear that Patti would not allow it, so the idea went no further." It looked to Wayne Kramer that Fred might be the next to die.

No one can know what would explain Patti's apparent acceptance of Fred's self-destruction. Perhaps she was just tired and didn't see any way out of the situation but to let him die. And he did indeed appear to all who saw him to be dying.

Indeed, on November 4, 1994, which would have been Robert Mapplethorpe's forty-seventh birthday, Fred Smith died in a Detroit hospital. The cause of death was listed as heart failure. He was forty-six. A memorial was held for him on November 8. There, the Rev. Inglass of Mariners' Church, who had married Patti and Fred in 1980, remembered Fred as "gentlemanly and de-cent. There was a sense of values" in Fred, he said, even "when the pull was so strong in other directions." Another friend said, "I always remembered him as a really solid guy. The stuff he did with Patti Smith, 'People Got the Power,' was brilliant. My only wish was I could have gotten to hear more of that."

As Wayne Kramer sat staring at Fred's coffin, he could not help but see the irony. The situation perfectly summed up Fred's life: here Fred was lying on his ass in this box, doing nothing, while everyone was talking about him! Moreover, Kramer said, "It really struck me at the funeral that there was no grieving."

> Patti was gracious and kind and more down to earth and accessible than the first time I met her, but she wasn't weeping. She didn't look like she'd been through hell; she was very bright-eyed and bushy tailed. Then at the service at the church, it was like a Patti Smith gig. She was on, she did a performance, she told a couple of stories about Fred, she was witty and charming and funny, she sang a song a cappella. It was a gig.

In the last year of Fred's life, Kramer, acting for the MC5, had persuaded Elektra, their old record company, to agree to pay each of the band members $5,000 in lieu of royalties not paid over the last twenty years. He knew that it wasn't a great deal, but at least they would get something, and they all needed the money. However, the deal would not go through unless each member of the band signed off on it, and Fred had refused because he thought the money was too low.

Important as the matter was, though, the last thing Wayne wanted to talk about was MC5 business at Fred's funeral. But Patti brought the subject of the deal up, telling Wayne that she was going to her lawyer, Ina Meinbach, and would take care of "all that business." "We're gonna straighten it all out," Patti told him.

"I didn't think it was the appropriate place or time," Kramer recalled. "We can talk about that stuff on another day, this is Fred's funeral, we're here to grieve today, but she was just like, 'Let's take care of this—all right, Ina Meibach is here, have you met Ina?' She was going on and on about how Fred really believed there was a better deal to be had and he really just wanted to do the right thing for the band." (Eventually, a better deal for the MC5 *was* negotiated by Ina Meibach.)

Kramer noted a lack of grieving at Fred's funeral, but there was at least one melancholy note: Fred had not lived long enough to prove his talent to the general public. "That was the genius and the tragedy of Fred Smith," said Freddie Brooks. "Most artists want to be ahead of their time just once in their life. Fred was ahead of his time at least three times that we know of. His career ended only because he died."

"It wasn't important to Fred to be a big deal in rock 'n' roll," concluded Wayne Kramer. "He was always looking for truth and value. He cared about his family. No one could write a song like Fred. He was a bad motherfucker." But Kramer did not romanticize Fred's death, reflecting instead on the internal forces that broke his friend down. "I believe Fred drank himself to death, and I also believe Fred never recovered from the loss of the MC5. I know what a big issue surviving the MC5 has been for me, and what I've had to go through to make peace with the loss of my band and to reclaim lost brothers," said Kramer, who had got deeply involved in drugs after the band's 1971 breakup, before getting his life together and returning to music in the eighties. "I know that Fred Smith never went through any of that process. I actually asked him at Rob Tyner's funeral if he'd ever grieved about the loss of the MC5 and he said, 'Oh no, I just got busy with other things.' But the reality is that it doesn't just go away. I believe he carried that anger and bitterness with him. And I think that was his undoing."

"Fred was a private man who could be difficult," Patti admitted. "But he was a really wonderful father and, though he kept to himself, he was extremely kind." In her opinion, their children were lucky to have a father who stayed at home and shared in their upbringing. The family was rarely separated during the children's formative years, so Jackson and Jesse never felt themselves neglected by either parent. Patti was convinced that "they felt protected." Remembering how the knowledge that God existed had helped her to never feel alone as a child, she tried to impart the same idea to her own children. The concept of God or a Creator had always been a part of the Smith household.

Patti took her children home to New Jersey for Thanksgiving, just as she and Fred had done for each of the sixteen years that they were married. Her brother, Todd, tried to console her, and urged her to start performing again. "When I saw my brother, he took me for a drive, and he had the soundtrack to *Natural Born Killers*," Patti remembered. "My song 'Rock n Roll Nigger' is on it, and he put it on really loud, and we drove around. I was just totally desolate, and he said, 'I'm going to get you back on your feet, you're going to get back to work. Working will help you.' He said, 'I'm going to be right there with you.' We talked about it for days, and I felt that with his help I could do it."

Then one month later, utterly without warning, Todd Smith died of a heart attack. He was forty-five.

On December 30, a severely drained Patti turned forty-eight. "I was writing a book of poems and stories and things that pretty much surrounded a lot of people that I had lost," she recalled. "And also people that I admired—I wrote a poem for Nureyev and Genet and Audrey Hepburn, just different people that I really liked that influenced me. But since I lost my husband and brother—I haven't been able to write much, so I've just set it aside for a while. But when I feel stronger I'll get back to it."

the return of patti smith

1995

> "I am an American artist and I have
> no guilt."
>
> *patti smith*

On New Year's Day 1995, Patti made her first public appearance since 1993 at St. Mark's Church in New York City, where she had begun her career in 1971. She read a few poems and sang "Ghost Dance," a song about the Native American uprisings of the late 1800s. "We will live again," ran its spirited refrain.

"The Indians believed the ghosts of their ancestors would follow them into battle and toss the white invaders off their lands," explained Lenny at the time. "It's a song about resurrection.

When we played it was incredibly emotional for the audience, for her and for me. It was a great moment."

During the set, Patti broke down once, for less than a second, but the large, adoring audience hardly noticed. Time and tragedy had endowed her with a messianic aura. She gave a brilliant performance, and she bathed in the raucous applause that followed it.

"Ms. Smith appears to be taking on a new image in the nineties, that of an extremely empathetic and compassionate woman pushed back into the public eye by the hand of death," wrote Neil Strauss in the *New York Times* that month. "I've seen a lot of death lately," Patti told Strauss, explaining her mien. "When we did *Dream of Life*, I had a child, the engineer had a child, and Jimmy Iovine, one of the producers, had a child. Three children were born in the process of making *Dream of Life*. Since then, Richard Sohl, my keyboard player, died, Fred died and Robert Mapplethorpe died, all had key roles in creating that record. Three children were born and three men died: that's the beautiful way of life."

While 1995 would be Patti's comeback year, it did not begin auspiciously. Living alone in the Detroit suburbs, caring for two children and unable to drive, was a difficult life for the young widow. Freddie Brooks sensed this and began to look in on Patti regularly. Brooks and his wife, musician Carolyn Striho, rescued Patti from the edge of despair—as well as got her making music. "I had been out of touch for a long time," said Brooks,

> but after Fred died I went to the funeral home and saw Todd, who I was close to since we'd been on Patti's road crew together in 1978. A month later, Patti called to tell me Todd had passed away. I started going by her house in St. Clair Shores, and we started talking about doing a record of Fred's music. I have tapes of all the Sonic Rendezvous' stuff. I started going by every so often and she was just grieving really badly; I would play a

certain tape and she would just break down. So I started to try to get her out of the house, just take her out for a drive, get coffee someplace, anything, just to get her out of the house. It didn't seem to be healthy for her to just stay home. I had been trying to figure out some way to get her doing some music, and I ended up working up a version of "The Hunter Gets Captured by the Game." I knew she had done that previously, so I put a version together with keyboard player Luis Resto. One day I went over to her house and the tape fell out of my pocket. She said, "What's this?"—I had been trying to think of some way to ask her to do it—and I said, "It's something you might be interested in," and she says, "Well, I can do that." She did a totally great version of it. In the studio, me and the engineer just looked at each other—we couldn't believe how good her voice sounded.

And then, just as she was emerging from her depths, Allen Ginsberg telephoned in February urging Patti to "Let go of the spirit of the departed and continue your life's celebration." To help her make the transition, Allen invited her to accompany him at a benefit reading in Ann Arbor. Patti gratefully accepted, for Ginsberg was not only a world-famous poet of forty years' standing, but also a genuine admirer of Patti's. While many people helped her get back on her feet after her husband's death, Ginsberg provided the first link to an audience that would begin to accept Patti anew for what she was: a good poet, a fine singer, and still a vital performer.

The benefit was to raise funds for the Tibetan Buddhist group Jewel Heart, an organization dedicated to preserving Tibetan Buddhist culture, a subject of particular interest to Patti since the age of twelve, when she did a school assignment on Tibet. Ginsberg had sold out the four-thousand-seat event on his own before Patti accepted his invitation, so his offer was a clear example of his generosity and compassion. He knew of Patti's recent tragedies and perhaps wanted to coax her back into the spotlight as a form of healing—he had always been supportive of fellow poets. Patti appreciated the gesture and acknowledged the compliment it bestowed. "Allen is such a good man," she said before the benefit. "Look at what he did for the Beat movement. He made sure the work of Burroughs and Kerouac wasn't lost in obscenity, or a heap of vomit. He's so unjealous, he wanted all of them to do well. He doesn't want to be a big kingpin writer. He just wants everyone who deserves to, to excel. He's so generous."

Ginsberg opened the show with a brief selection of songs, backed by a trio of musicians. Before the intermission, he announced that the second half of the show would include "an important rock 'n' roll poet who took poetry from lofts, bookshops, and gallery performances to the rock 'n' roll world stage. We're really pleased and happy that Patti Smith is able to join us," he went on, and despite having sold out the show himself, he flattered Patti adding, "I see we have a full house, and I think that's due to her charisma, glamour, and genius."

With her children, Jackson and Jesse, thirteen and eight years old respectively, seated in the front row, Patti began her performance with a poem she had written after reading the Dalai Lama's autobiography, and she ended her set by saying, "As unfortunately I did live to see Tibet taken from the Tibetan people, I do hope that I will live to see it returned."

In between, Patti's performance included selections of poetry and prose culled from her long career and featured moments of humor and warmth as well as pathos. There were no Patti Smith songs, but she did read the poem "Florence," which she had written after the Patti Smith Group's last performance. "I traveled with a rock 'n' roll band in the seventies," she said to introduce the piece. "And the last job we ever played was in Italy in a big soccer arena. I'd like to read this in memory of my brother Todd." Patti's voice broke as she read from the dedication: "Brother, when you were six I rescued you from the enemy and you pledged alle-

giance. Now you are free and I realize that I shall never again experience such selfless devotion and singular care."

Near the end of her set, Patti announced that she would "like to
sing a little song for my husband, who many of you loved as Fred
'Sonic' Smith." Backed by guitar, bass, and viola, she sang a haunting version of the Johnny Mathis song "The Twelfth of Never,"
with its repeated refrain that has the singer comparing her love to
a poet's rhyme, concluding that the twelfth of never is a period of
extreme duration. She closed with a poem from *Woolgathering*
called "Cowboy Truths." "Standing there, squinting in the sun;
everything so damn beautiful, enough to make the throat ache.
He scans the terrain, the palm of his hand and that golden nui-
sance for one small moment."

Allen Ginsberg then came out and read his longest great poem,
"Kaddish," a prayer in memory of his mother, Naomi. As he entered its last long, breathy, bardic stanza, "Caw caw caw crows
shriek in the white sun over gravestones in Long Island," his
voice, trembling with emotion yet powerful and measured, lifted
the entire audience, the way a good rock concert can, for a few
moments, into that place of emotional reality called Art.

Once more Patti appeared to be in the right place at the right
time—perhaps she had yet again found her spot. Not only did the
reading go well, but on that same night she read with Allen Ginsberg she also met Oliver Ray, a young man with the good looks
and charismatic charm of poetic youth. He would play a central
role in her life through the second half of the decade.

Oliver had recently broken up with actress Tatum O'Neal while
she was in a highly vulnerable state. He came to Patti via a mutual
acquaintance. At the outset of their relationship, Patti clearly had
the upper hand, but as time passed, her dependence on Oliver
grew. Away from his famous friends, he may have seemed just another ambitious kid dabbling in photography and poetry, but as
Patti's boyfriend, he wielded credibility and power. Their relationship cast a question into Patti's personal and professional lives,

always so closely linked: By taking up with Oliver and shutting out a number of people who had been instrumental in her original rise—and, perhaps more significant, her comeback—she jeopardized all the bridges she had so painstakingly built in the first half of the nineties. She also disrupted her family dynamic, for her relationship with Oliver must, at least in the beginning, have been somewhat confusing to Jackson, who was only a few years Oliver's junior and an aspiring guitar player like his father. Jackson saw the world around him as completely mad. Having just lost the father he cared for so deeply, he clearly needed the attention and encouragement Patti began lavishing on Oliver Ray.

Patricia Morrisroe's biography of Robert Mapplethorpe was published in March 1995. Patti had given Morrisroe several lengthy interviews for the book, which had been written with Mapplethorpe's cooperation. Entitled *Mapplethorpe*, its portrait of Mapplethorpe's controversial life disturbed many of the people who knew him best, and none more than Patti, who felt that her friend was cheapened in Morrisroe's portrait. "I gave [Morrisroe] what I thought was a good sense of what it was like to be an artist," said Patti.

> I saw Robert go from an extremely shy misfit to an extremely accomplished person. The years in between were represented in the book as one hustle after another. We were all poor and humble. When I think of those times, I think of the joyfulness, the youthful fervor. We weren't plotting and planning to be famous. We just had a million ideas and lots of energy. Innocence prevailed. If Robert was part hustler, or whatever, fine, but he did his work. Taking photographs as an openly gay man was a revolutionary concept when he began. This book has him screwing all the time. But he worked until the day he died.

Patti's remarks are somewhat at odds with Mapplethorpe's own statements about himself: He boasted of having had literally thousands of sexual partners, and though he certainly had a work ethic, it was not quite the one Patti describes. He told this writer in 1977 that his life consisted of going "from being very social to going to leather bars to working. Those are the three things I do. If anything could be my downfall it could be [sex]. I could just let myself get into sex considering it's the most exciting thing in the world to do." Mapplethorpe felt that his work ethic came from self-imposed guilt, but he solved the problem by defining both the "social thing" and the "sexual thing" as work. And by that definition, he was indeed a dedicated worker.

Meanwhile, she still mourned Fred—and kept venturing out and developing her own work. "Some days I'm happy to talk about Fred and I can do it without any problems at all," Patti told friends that spring.

> But there are days when just the mention of his name is almost too much to handle. . . . [W]hen Fred died, I went through a really tough time. I felt completely desolate. . . . I had no idea how I was going to apply myself musically anymore. But with the warmth and camaraderie of Carolyn Striho and her band, with whom I played some warm-up gigs in the Detroit–Ann Arbor area, and her husband, my sometime producer Freddie Brooks, I started doing the best work I've done in fifteen years. The quality of my singing has strengthened. That's my legacy from my husband. I feel some of the best strengths of Robert Mapplethorpe, Richard Sohl, and my brother, Todd, as well have passed into me; I find myself gifted, enhanced, a richer person because I have magnified aspects of them within me."

On April 8, Patti performed at a tribute concert for Fred at the Ark in Ann Arbor, Michigan. Though some people spoke of a tour—which she had not done since 1979—Patti told friends that she was not planning to tour formally again, but would stick to playing special, one-off dates. She also recorded a song for *Ain't*

Nuthin' But a She Thing, a compilation album to benefit organizations working for women's issues. The song she chose was the Nina Simone standard "Don't Smoke in Bed"; Freddie Brooks produced. During these sessions, she began planning a new solo album—her first in seven years—to be recorded in New York.

Fred and Patti had wanted to return to the recording studio and make another album in order to save up for their children's education. Thus, with this new project, Patti was carrying on the plan she and Fred had made, and this gave her a sense of continuity and purpose. Morever, her belief that she had somehow internalized Fred and was singing for both of them helped focus her drive. As for her voice, everybody noticed how it had improved.

On July 5, Patti moved out of the club circuit and back onto the rock 'n' roll stage, playing at the Phoenix Concert Hall in Toronto. Her show was electrifying. From the moment she walked onstage, she totally captivated the audience. After doing a searing solo rendition of "Piss Factory," she read her old Bob Dylan poem, "Dog Dream," in her "Dylan" voice, and then launched into a ferocious version of "Babelfield," ending with the lines "I step up to the microphone/I have no fear."

"I never left," she told the audience. "I was never gone. I was with you always. When I was cleaning my toilet, I thought of you. When I was changing my children's diapers, I thought of you. Do you believe that? You may." Her audience may have felt uncomfortable about the fact that Patti thought of them mainly in such situations, but it may well have been that it was at these gruesome moments that Patti most longed to be on a rock 'n' roll stage.

The shows reminded Patti of her early days giving poetry readings: "What I most like about performing at this stage of my life," she says, "is to be in a place with these people and it's a meeting ground, instead of an arena for rock 'n' roll stars. I like how it's evolving so that we get to spar a little. We communicate."

Joined onstage by her new Motor City protégés Carolyn Striho and various members of Striho's band, the Detroit Energy Asylum, she charged into the music, playing "The Jackson Song" from *Dream of Life* and "Don't Smoke in Bed." Patti did not try to contain her delight at being in front of her fans once again. "I'm sorry if I'm not cool enough to pretend that I'm not loving every minute of this," she said. Her manner at this show would foreshadow the persona that she would develop over the next three years, combining elements of the rebellious punk poet, the grieving widow and sister, the devoted single mother, and the committed activist.

As would be the case in a number of these "comeback" shows, Patti broke down momentarily when a reference to "daddy" came in the "Jackson Song." Such emotional moments fueled the shows and gave them a unique power. In Toronto, the show was lifted to yet another level of wonder when Lenny Kaye and Jay Dee Daugherty joined her on stage to close with "Ghost Dance" and the song that was becoming an anthem, "People Have the Power."

On July 27, Patti played her first New York show since 1993, choosing Central Park as the venue. To open this "family night," as Patti called it, Patti's old friend Janet Hamill gave a reading. After Janet, Patti then read her own poems and sang a few songs, accompanied by Lenny Kaye and her youngest sister, Kimberly. "I've always liked collaborating with friends," she said about the format of the the show. "And I've lost so many of them."

The rest of Patti's summer was spent recording. She was reluctant to talk to the press, but did give interviews to Lisa Robinson, Evelyn McDonnell, and Gerrie Lim. *Horses* had been voted the number-one rock album of all time by Lim's magazine, the *Big O*, the most influential rock publication in China. Patti spoke with Lim at Electric Ladyland, where Patti was now working on her new album. The choice of studio had been Lenny's suggestion—after all, their previous efforts there, *Horses* and "Piss Factory," had been so successful. As Patti told Lim, "It's an inspirational thing. Everybody's been so great here. It's wonderful to walk in because the room we're in has huge murals of Jimi Hendrix and all of Jimi Hendrix's gold records, and it has a really great spirit."

Patti spoke to Gerrie Lim at length about a number of topics. "I don't have fears," Patti said.

> For myself, spiritually, I look at death as a continuing journey. I don't wish to die, especially being a parent. I wouldn't want my children to be left without a parent. And I love life, love being on the planet. But I really think of death as part of a continuation. I think it's more of a Buddhist point of view. That's the way I feel. Sometimes I just feel ecstatic to wake up. I'm so lucky.
>
> I read in a magazine recently that a writer was really surprised because Michael Stipe had said that I was a viable model for him, and they thought it was unusual coming from a guy. I think that in our time, as we move into the future, future generations will be less prejudiced about gender, race, color, and things like that.

Patti seemed content to be in New York City again. "I'm really happy to be here, even in the heat," she said. "My kids love it here, and I'm happy walking in the streets. People say hello to me wherever I go. A guy in a sanitation uniform said, 'Hey Patti, I'm a sanitation worker, but I'm a poet, too,' and he wished me luck. I feel like I'm back home."

And although she looked back on her life in Detroit with fondness, so many years had been wracked with grief that it was clearly time to relocate. She had started looking for a place in New York, though for the time being she also retained the Detroit house, to which Jackson returned with some regularity. (By the summer of 1996 she would be living in the downtown Manhattan landscape that she had come of age in.)

Patti told Lim about the personnel on the new album: "I have a new keyboard player who plays very similar to Richard [Sohl].

He's from Detroit and his name is Luis Resto. And Lenny's playing guitar and a good friend of Lenny's [Tony Shanahan] is playing bass. And we'll have other guitar players on this record—my
old guitar player Ivan Kral, perhaps Tom Verlaine and certain
other people might be guest-playing."

In August, Patti did another show in Central Park. Coincidentally, the Lollapalooza festival, alternative music's grand summer
road show, made its New York stop at Randall's Island. When
Perry Farrell, the festival's director, heard that Patti was doing a
show in Central Park at the same time, he sent her an invitation
via Jay Dee to do a one-off surprise spot on Lollapalooza's second
stage.

Dressed in a sweat-soaked gray T-shirt and blue jeans, Patti
tore into her Lollapalooza set with the energy and flow of the rock
performer she's always been. Scrapping the planned thirty-minute
set, she played nonstop for an hour as all of the bands on the tour
watched in awe. Courtney Love of Hole was so overwhelmed that
she declined an invitation to meet Patti, saying that she was just
too scared and tongue-tied to meet the person she had credited
with saving her life. "There are so few people I feel unworthy
meeting. Patti has eternal beauty, and has never compromised, not
in her heart, and *never* in her art. I was too scared to meet her. I
couldn't."

Patti later returned the compliment graciously: "When I heard
Hole, I was amazed to hear a girl sing like that. Janis Joplin was
her own thing; she was into Big Mama Thornton and Bessie
Smith. But what Courtney Love does, I'd never heard a girl do
that."

Lollapalooza was the first really energetic, rock 'n' roll show of
Patti's reemergence, and it was welcome. According to a reporter
from *Newsday*,

Smith erased the memory of Thursday night's disappointing
acoustic love-in at Central Park Summer Stage by completely

abandoning herself to the music in an electric—and electrifying—performance. Power flowed into her like lifeblood as
Smith relocated her messianic muse in such songs as Bob Dylan's "The Wicked Messenger," the Byrds' "So You Want to Be
a Rock 'n' Roll Star," and [her own] "Ghost Dance." She finished the inspired set with "People Have the Power." Smiling
beatifically, her arms outstretched in both glory and need, she
screamed her late husband's lyrics with desperate faith, ringing
out their message of hope through years of pent-up fury.

By the end of the set, members of the audience were literally in
tears. The following day, a great photo of Patti, her arms spread
wide looking like Jack Kerouac's rail-thin sister, jumped off the
page of the *New York Times*.

Patti really appeared to enjoy herself that day, and she declared
that was going to take her energy from Lollapalooza back into the
studio with her. "The people were all ages," Patti enthused, "and
very surprised. Many people have never seen us perform. All the
bands made us feel welcome and special. It was a great feeling, especially after having this difficult year."

Patti spent the balance of the summer completing the album
that she would call *Gone Again*. In its structure and feel, the album
was influenced by Bob Dylan's lovely 1992 acoustic album, *Good
As I Been to You*, Patti's favorite record that year. She was pleased
that the songs favored to be singles, "Summer Cannibals" and the
title song, had both been penned by Fred.

After a summer in the studio, Patti, filled with the positive energy generated by her New York audiences, flew out west for a series of well-received performances. "The theme of Patti Smith's
first Southern California appearance in sixteen years was death,
but the message was life," wrote Robert Hilburn in the *Los Angeles
Times*, of her show in LA. "Backstage before the performance,
Smith spoke about the way the shows have lifted her spirits:
'Everywhere I go, it's touching that people really want to comfort

me,' she said. 'Sometimes these young kids will come up and you can tell that they don't even know what to say. They look at me and I wind up telling them that things are OK. I can see in their face that they really feel bad.' "

Her LA show was in a bar called the Belly Up Tavern. As Patti clambered on stage looking as thin and slick as a switchblade, cries of "We love you!" floated up from the attentive audience. "Patti was life itself when I was growing up," the bar's talent booker told Hilburn. "I listened to her music every morning through high school. It was a tension release. This music made me feel like there was someone out there feeling a lot of the things you were."

Patti's set, which included covers of the Grateful Dead, Dylan, and Buddy Holly, was sheer joy for the audience and the singer.

The evening's most haunting number was the final one, "Paths That Cross," which has an optimism that comforted Patti, declaring that everything renews itself in time, and that if one path has crossed another, it is bound to cross it again.

"I feel that the older we get, that all of our different ages come back in us," said Patti. "In my thirties, I felt completely different than in my twenties. But now, at this point, at forty-eight, I feel the same type of tension of adolescent rage is still within me."

In October, she played some East Coast dates that included stops at the Lowell Celebrates Kerouac Festival, the Smith Baker Center, and the Old Cambridge Baptist Church, all in Massachusetts. At the end of the month, it was announced that the Velvet Underground were to be inducted into the Rock and Roll Hall of Fame that coming January, and that Patti Smith would introduce them.

In a *New York Times* article, Patti spoke of her view of the future. Commencing her piece with the observation that technology will surely play a vital role in the future, she ties that together with the startling insight that consequently art will then portray machines rather than human beings. Taking refuge with the mythical American folk hero John Henry, she points out that he was a self-reliant steel worker who lost his job because of technological developments, but took the decision poorly and combated it. Consequently, "he symbolised the hand of man." Through her life, she reflected, a man of John Henry's caliber will always survive. She then compared the steelworker to Jesus, Michelangelo, Picasso, Brancusi, Jackson Pollock, Bob Dylan, and Kurt Cobain. And so, she approaches her closing, when things look bad or seem tiresome, remember that somebody will appear to cast a light on the darkness. Remember the power of the individual, she concludes, "as we move into the future of a technological society."

On November 2, All Souls' Day, Patti honored her late husband with a dedication at the Mariners' Church in Detroit. After Fred's death, she had created the Frederick D. Smith Memorial Fund, and chose the Mariners' Church as its beneficiary. The church had a history as a beacon of comfort to weary sea travelers, and was Fred's favorite Detroit site. With the money raised by the fund, Patti arranged to have an eight-by-eight-foot black granite marker depicting the church's logo, the three crosses of Good Friday grounded by an anchor, placed in the bell tower as a permanent memorial to Fred. "Fred loved church bells," she explained. "In fact, he once wrote a song called 'Bells of Berlin.' It was never recorded, but his idea was for the music to be resounding church bells. For something to be in his name on a bell tower is just perfect." The service was designed to be "positive, upbeat, and celebratory" and was open to the public. Oliver Ray, Patti's new friend and assistant, read a psalm at the memorial. Patti sang a song she had written called "Farewell Reel."

Patti constantly spoke of Fred and Todd in her interviews after their deaths. "Fred was a great man," she sighed. "I'm trying to still do work on his behalf. We had a lot of plans to do things. And so I had to go and do them myself. But also I find the most positive way for me to restructure my life is to work. It also involves me with other people—reinvolves me with my friends—and that's comforting. A lot of it's the camaraderie." Her shows at the Theater of the Living Arts in Philadelphia later that week would have a special poignancy because she had performed there the previous year when Todd was still alive.

Nobody could have written a better ending to the last month of Patti's second annus mirabilis than Bob Dylan did. She had been pulled out of her doldrums at the beginning of the year by Allen Ginsberg, and now, as Christmas approached, with all its inherent focus on Patti's now-incomplete family, Bob Dylan summoned her to open for him on eight dates in December during the East Coast leg of his current tour.

Given her roots and reputation, Patti could not have dreamed of a more powerful and perfect reintroduction to the stage than the ones provided by Allen Ginsberg and Bob Dylan. "The atmosphere was happy at our first show," she said of opening night with Bob Dylan. "I thought the audience was basically Bob's people, but they seemed real happy to see us because they know that I'm one of Bob's people, too."

"This was a joyful period for me," said Patti. "Of comradeship; of shaking off the performance dust." One of the high points of the tour for Patti and this audience was when Dylan invited her onstage to sing a duet with him on his song "Dark Eyes." "Singing with the one who had been an inspiration and influence on my work was an experience I shall always cherish," said Patti.

The tour went smoothly. Patti's band included longtime collaborators Lenny Kaye and Jay Dee Daugherty, as well as Tom Verlaine. Michael Stipe of REM accompanied them, not to perform, but to take pictures and lend encouragement. (Stipe would later publish his photographs from the tour in a book entitled *Two Times Intro.*)

Oliver Ray, who over the course of the year had become Patti's constant companion, came along on the dates with Bob Dylan, as well. He played one song with the band each night, and he was the only musician to be introduced by name. Observers described

Patti's relationship to Oliver at this time as that of an artistic bene-factor: she encouraged the twenty-two-year-old in his pursuit of poetry, music, and photography. She even bought him a Gibson guitar of the same year and model as the six-string that Sam Shepard had bought her in the early seventies. Though some on the tour saw Oliver Ray as a groupie only interested in hobnobbing with Stipe and Verlaine and ignoring the less-stellar members of the entourage, Patti seemed devoted to him. At some point, the nature of Patti's relationship with Oliver changed, and they became lovers despite the twenty-six-year age gap.

Patti was enthusiastic about the tour. "I'm working with some of the same people that I worked with in the seventies," she said.

> There are new ones, too, and I feel that we'll do well. Things between us that are spoken and unspoken are very evolved. Tom Verlaine and I have worked back and forth since 1974. There's also new energy from Oliver Ray, who's twenty-three and in touch with a whole other area of knowledge. Oliver and I wrote the pivotal piece on the new record together. It's a ten-minutes-long track called "Fireflies," and even though Oliver and I wrote it, the most important interpreter of it is Tom. Tom is one of the greatest guitar players we have. I don't know how long we'll work together, but I think we have a good thing.

Dylan, who had invited Patti on the tour to reintroduce her to the heart of his audience, got paid back in spades. Her charismatic sincerity and high aim inspired Dylan to do some of his best shows in years. Patti, for her part, gave her finest performance on the final night, the last of a three-night stand at the Electric Factory in Philadelphia.

The Electric Factory had been in existence in one form or another for almost thirty years, and consists of one rectangular space resembling a small airplane hangar. There, Patti stepped onstage wearing an oversized Unabomber jacket, her head engulfed by the hood—the only way anyone could tell that it was her was from the sound of her voice and her unique use of language. She read the crowd perfectly from the moment she took the stage. "I've been taking a look at your city," she began, in measured tones with just the right edge of terror in them. "Went over to the museum and saw the Brancusi show," she continued slowly, settling the crowd down and setting it up perfectly, describing the exhibition in great detail. Then she sailed across the Schuylkill River, taking the crowd to nearby Camden, where, she reminded them, they could pay their respects to Walt Whitman, whose house has been restored. At this point, some joker yelled out, "It ain't safe in Camden!"

"Then move there," Patti countered, "and make it safe." With that, she yanked off the hood, slammed her face into the microphone, and crashed into "Horses," KOing the audience. With that one tremendous, sweeping move from which she extrapolated and extrapolated, she went on to enrapture the audience with a heavy dose of rock 'n' roll iconography.

Patti showed that she still had a lot going for her as a rock 'n' roll star. She had clawed her way back to the mountaintop, and was able to stand with her hero and mentor Bob Dylan. Their final encore, a duet of "Knockin' on Heaven's Door," a song Patti had sung twenty years earlier at CBGB's, was one of the great musical moments of the nineties. Patti found herself once again at a pivotal moment in American cultural history. What she has, perhaps more than any other female singer, is the combination of an instantly recognizable voice and an equally recognizable face, which she uses along with her religious voice to mirror the mood of the crowd. In juxtaposition to the iconographic microphone itself, her perfectly sculpted Mount Rushmore face flashes anger, flashes destiny, flashes famine, flashes despair, flashes beauty, flashes pain, flashes contempt, flashes attitude. In hearts. Once she hit the boards, she never let up—it was relentless, freezing cold, and skin-crawlingly hot, sweaty and funky, muted and searingly intense. She took on the Liberty Bell and won hands down.

Patti gave a great show that night in Philadelphia. And by holding on to the music and following her through the swan dives, the Stuka bomber raids, and the crashing assembly of great hooks, the crowd was reunited as beautiful individuals struggling under the weight of the burden of life itself. Drunk and exhausted, they momentarily regained their dignity, their sense of humor, and the self-respect that is the prize that a ticket to a rock 'n' roll show holds out, but does not always deliver.

It was in Philadelphia that this beautiful poet with her almost Russian sense of suffering rose from the ashes of her own haunted life, danced in Buddhist celebration on the buried bones of the men who had shaped her fate, and sang in the sweet, wild, high mercury breath of ecstasy. She came back under the wing of the people's poet, the great spiritual captain of generations, Bob Dylan, but by the time she left Philadelphia, she had taken flight on her own wings.

gone again

1996–1998

> "The guardians of history are soon
> rewarded with the attention of history."
>
> *motto of the patti smith group*

After the high of the shows with Bob Dylan in December 1995, 1996 could not have started on a more positive note for Patti. In its first issue of the new year, *Rolling Stone* magazine's reader's poll voted Patti Smith's the comeback of the year. Then, on January 16 at a ceremony in the Waldorf-Astoria Hotel in Manhattan, she gave a speech inducting the Velvet Underground into the Rock and Roll Hall of Fame. "They opened wounds worth opening, with a brutal innocence, without apology, cutting across the grain, gritty, urbanic," she said of them in her trademark stream-of-consciousness cadences. "And in their search for the kingdom, for laughter, for salvation, they explored the darkest areas of the psyche." She followed this with a keening rendition of the Velvets' "Pale Blue Eyes," accompanied on acoustic guitar by Lenny Kaye. Backstage, Lou Reed was brought to the edge of tears.

The Velvets performed "Last Night I Said Goodbye to My Friend," a song they had written for the occasion in memory of their guitarist Sterling Morrison, who had died six months earlier. After the ceremony, Lenny went looking for Patti to take her to a postawards party in music business executive Allen Klein's suite. She was nowhere to be found, however, and he had to explain to Klein's astonished guests that Patti still got jittery at such emotional public appearances, as it was at those times that she felt the absence of Fred most intensely. In such situations, she felt that he should have been there by her side. So, as the Velvet Underground celebrated induction into the Hall, Patti was on a plane flying back to Detroit, in the process blowing off the following morning's date with John Cale to record on his new album.

Cale was sanguine about the matter, and since that time has grown closer to Patti. "I met up with her again when I did my piano part on 'Southern Cross,' a song on her new album," recalled Cale.

> I wanted her to come and read on a record I was doing with the Nouvelle Polyphonic Corsican Choir and I invited her over. It was the dead of winter, and she came and had dinner one night with her family. She seemed a much sadder person. It was obviously a time when she was unraveling certain things in her mind. I felt I had to reassure her, make her feel at home, because there was a certain nervousness about how much of the past was really present.
>
> Now we have a lot of fun. My daughter Eden, who's eleven, has spent time with Patti's daughter. Patti and I have a shared passion for doing things and not thinking about them. The

pure instinct of just doing. She was a poet who wanted to be a rock 'n' roller, and I helped her in both fields. I'm glad she's back on the road now, showing her strength. From here, it can only expand.

That spring, the Patti Smith Group played some scattered East Coast dates, gearing up for the release of *Gone Again* and for a summer tour of Europe. While she was working with old friends, people she could rely on, she also introduced a new musician into the band—guitarist Oliver Ray, her companion. He had accompanied them and sat in for a song or two on the Dylan tour; now he was a full-fledged member.

She felt positive about her return to the studio, touring, and her musical future: "Everytime I walk out onstage these days, I feel like a lotus in a junkyard," she said. "It's like this huge flower just opens slowly through the night."

The media interest surrounding Patti and *Gone Again* brought her to the attention of a younger audience, much of which was hearing of her for the first time. This would lead a new generation to the earlier works—*Horses, Radio Ethiopia, Easter,* and *Wave.*

Up to this point, many of Patti's comeback appearances had focused more on poetry and writing than on rock 'n' roll. And though with the album coming out she had to shift her emphasis back toward playing rock, she still made a point of fitting in literary events as well. On June 1, for instance, Patti made a quick trip to London to give a reading in the ICA's Incarcerated with Artaud and Genet series. At the time, her just-published book, *The Coral Sea,* was receiving mixed reviews. Critic Robert Yates, who had attended the ICA performance, drew a sharp distinction between Patti onstage and on the page. Writing about the book in the Manchester *Guardian,* Yates praised Patti's skills as a songwriter and performer, but said that "many of her words, naked on the page, have the gauche insistence of a fourth-former discovering self-expression."

In early July, Patti paid London another visit, to read at Michael Horowitz's gallant recreation of the famous 1965 Albert Hall reading, which had starred, among others, Allen Ginsberg. It was riveting to see what a difference seventeen years had made. P.O.W. (Poetry Olympics Weekend) was an inspired event boasting English stalwarts Roger McGrough, Adrian Mitchell, and Horowitz himself, as well as pop lyricists Ray Davies, Patti, and Damon Albarn of Blur. It attracted the largest audience for a poetry reading in Britain since its precursor and received widespread press coverage. According to Glyn Brown in the *Independant*, Patti came across as flaky and shaky, but finally emerged as "a stoic if ragged queen."

Gone Again was released internationally on June 15. On its cover was a black-and-white Annie Leibovitz photograph capturing a pensive Patti; inside, *Gone Again* cast Patti in the role of the courageous widow. The album echoed some of the themes present on Lou Reed's 1992 *Magic and Loss*, and while both albums received an inordinate amount of press, they may not have received much airplay due to their grim subject matter. Some critics would charge the two artists with capitalizing on their personal losses to further their careers (or, in Patti's case, gain sympathy as well), but in fact, as rock 'n' roll matured, its subject matter was changing: many artists needed to write about their lives, and death was increasingly a part of that.

Gone Again received predominantly positive reviews. *Rolling Stone* described the album as "the most focused and direct work Patti Smith has ever done," and *Newsweek* called it the best rock album of the year. *Interview*'s editor, Ingrid Sischy, wrote, "Listening to *Gone Again* was an experience I'll never forget." *Spin* bucked this trend and was diplomatically noncommital: "*Gone Again* is a forceful modern record that brings one of our most important voices back to center stage."

The album's two best tracks were "Gone Again" and "Summer Cannibals," both originally written by Fred Smith and completed by Patti and the band. According to Wayne Kramer "Summer Cannibals" went way back—"Fred brought it in for the Ascensions, the band we started after the MC5 in 1972." "Gone Again" was originally not going to be on the album. Fred and Patti had worked on the song the summer before his death, but the tape had been lost. Fate, however, intervened. "Patti was feeling agitated one day, walking around the house kind of restless," recalled Lenny. "She opened up a drawer and there was the 'Gone Again' tape as if by magic. We recorded it quickly, and all of a sudden it seemed to be the glue around which everything could find its place." Of "Gone Again," Patti noted, "If there's anything negative on the album, it's that song. But it's got a sense of humor, in the way I sing it, because I survived it all. It didn't have an unhappy ending for me. It's a survival song."

With the exception of the cover of Dylan's "Wicked Messenger," the rest of the album was weaker. Patti did not tour the U.S. in support of the album, but she gave a series of interviews on the radio and to a wide variety of magazines. She had not expressed herself so fully or effectively since the release of *Horses* in 1975— though Patti had given a number of interviews on the release of *Dream of Life*, those were limited in scope because of Fred, who didn't like her to talk about certain subjects, mainly sex and the other men in her life. Now that constraint was removed, and Patti was the subject of at least fifteen long interviews, which were read by far more people than bought her records or saw her perform. In the interviews, Patti deftly played the widow and survivor.

" 'Gone Again' was Fred's title," Patti told Mim Udovich. "It's what Fred wanted our record to be called. The last song we were working on together was called 'Gone Again.' "

It's a very straightforward American rock song, and originally he wanted it to be a woman coming down from a mountain to reassure her tribe that though things were not going well, the rain would return and children would be born and they would keep going. It has changed somewhat, because in Fred's passing I wound up really writing it in memory of him, so it's more now that the woman comes down from the mountain and tells about the passing of a warrior. So it's a little rock song for Fred. By Fred and for Fred.

"I'm definitely on another plane now, but I don't know how much of that can be attributed to mysticism, or even intelligence," she told another journalist. "A lot of it's to do with grief. So part of my elevation, if it is an elevation, is to do with that. I think of my new songs as gifts from Fred—his last gifts to me. When he died, my abilities magnified through him. At this point in my life, I'm trying to rediscover who I might be. I've been a wife for fifteen years, and my husband and I were very entwined: a lot of who I perceived myself to be was an extension of him."

In an interview with Terry Gross on National Public Radio, Patti discussed the inspiration that she had gained from her brother:

My brother was the same age as Fred, they were both forty-five; my brother was very very supportive, a high-spirited, youthful man. And he loved to see me work, he was in the last month of his life, trying to help me get back on my feet. Encouraging me to get back to work, and get back to performing and songwriting. He said that he would help me. And he did encourage me and fill me with a certain amount of energy. So when my brother passed away, all of the energy that he put into me, all of that encouragement, all of that love, I didn't want it to go in vain. And so I picked myself up and began to work really hard after my brother passed away.

Patti explained to Gerrie Lim how she managed the rock 'n' roll pace at her age:

I've never really indulged much in drugs and things like that or anything negative. Most of my anger or, as they call it, angst or frustration, I've put into my work and not into a drug or into something negative. I've had a lot of anarchistic feelings and a lot of that kind of energy, and I've always put it into work. And even though I've tried a couple of drugs in my life and I liked to smoke pot when I was younger, I never got involved in it. I think that's really important. If one must visit a drug or want to see what a drug can do or use it as a tool for work, you have to be very careful. You have to respect drugs, 'cause drugs won't respect you. They won't respect you so if you don't respect them, you're gonna be in trouble. I'm just happy to be alive and I want to stay that way, and I don't flirt with a lot of stuff that will take my life away.

Some of Patti's statements in these interviews piqued old acquaintances. "They're brilliant interviews," said Wayne Kramer. "They're reinventing and casting her in this Mother Superior role, humble: 'I never really meant to do that much.' Well, if you never really meant to do that much, then why did you have your picture taken with every motherfucker that came through CBGB's?! She's brilliant. When we're doing interviews, we all want to come across as real human beings, with a real good understanding of our humanity and how we fit into the world, but she is really genius at it."

The week after the release of *Gone Again*, Patti, backed by the band that would tour Europe with her, played two sold-out dates at New York's Irving Plaza. She opened the two-hour show with "Piss Factory" and closed with "Farewell Reel," the song about her recovery from her husband's death as she prepared to reenter the world. Neil Strauss, who reviewed the concert for the *New York Times*, noted the changes in Patti's subjects. "Between these autobiographical sketches, an entire life unfurls," he wrote. "She sang lyrics of deterioration and recovery, skepticism and faith, bohemianism and motherhood." Reinforcing Strauss's assessment was the concert's family aura: thirteen-year-old Jackson was brought on to play "Smoke on the Water," and Patti's sister Kimberly came on to sing a song called "I Don't Need."

Patti, too, implicitly endorsed Strauss's observation. "As you get older, you have to go through a certain humiliation of physical deterioration," she pointed out. "But on the other hand, the mental and spiritual process is always shifting. If one can just let go of one's sorrows about how we change physically, one is in for a very interesting journey. I am pretty resilient and I also haven't relied on my looks or physical being, so it's not as hard on me as for some people," she continued. "But I am observing that it's not something you just ignore, it's not something that with the grace of God will get you through every day. Each generation suffers different pain: the one thing young people seem to suffer now is lack of comprehension at how beautiful life is. I've experienced a lot of personal sorrow, but I still feel constant amazement at how beautiful life is."

At the end of June, with an entourage that included her children, Oliver Ray, Michael Stipe, Tom Verlaine and the new band, Patti Smith took off to conquer Europe. The tour blanketed the continent, with shows in France, Denmark, Italy, Spain, Belgium, Germany, Switzerland, the Netherlands, England, Scotland, the Czech Republic, and Sweden. They opened at the Olympia Theater in Paris, and, according to Sam Taylor, "the sheer combustive brilliance of this show was entirely unexpected."

The band, which had found its ground in New York in the shows with Dylan, now hit its stride. Patti's voice was stronger and richer, and as she segued from song to song, she stirred the band up with a voodoo power. Expressions of pain, ecstasy, and fear crossed her face as she focused intently on the songs. Her sets ended with an encore of "People Have the Power," with Patti yelling out the chorus, still promoting it as a new anthem of protest for peace everywhere.

By the time the Patti Smith tour hit Glasgow in early August it was, according to John Mulvey, who witnessed the Royal Concert Hall performance, "Not a tour for reveling in tragedy."

In other words, Patti Smith isn't exactly forgetting her troubles, but she is remembering how to have fun, too. This impeccably ruffled fifty-year old pulls her silver boots off and wafts her white sports socks in the air like an imperious stripper for "Dancing Barefoot," a preternaturally well-preserved hippie mother decked out in crumpled outlaw hand-me-downs (much like her clothes on the *Horses* sleeve) while her, frankly, stellar band rock out. All of them, that is, except for laughing Tom Verlaine, slouched on a chair at the back, picking out fragile guitar lines with the vigor of a grouchy pensioner dozing on his porch.

Asked by every journalist who interviewed her at every stop how it felt to be touring Europe again, Patti consistently replied with statements like, this one, from *Interview:*

It's actually much nicer, although it was always interesting. I've always had the best people with me. Lenny Kaye is my oldest friend who's still amongst us. Tom Verlaine and I have known each other for twenty years. Strange as it might sound, it's a great family unit and it's very good for my kids, who still miss their father. Lenny and Jay were close to my husband and all the men in the band are great role models.

I feel pretty strong now. But there are times when I remember that the whole thing was Fred's idea—he would have loved it. At those times, it's heartbreaking.

After Fred's death, Patti had approached Freddie Brooks about compiling Sonic Rendezvous material for a CD. Brooks, receptive to the idea, reviewed tapes and finally chose a performance that had been recorded on April 4, 1978. Fred had been about to depart for Europe, where he would both open for and back up Iggy Pop. There was a definite air of uncertainty surrounding the band's future, but Fred relished entering uncharted territory—it was one of his essential qualities. Brooks found it in this show and immortalized it on Sonic Rendezvous's *Sweet Nothing*, released in 1998. It is a memorable piece of work, capturing Fred's band at its best.

For all the good it brought, Patti's 1997 was another year well visited by death. In April, Allen Ginsberg died at his home in New York. Among the twenty mourners who sat with him during his final twenty-four hours, Patti was a fixture by his bed, stroking his brow and making numerous drawings of his skull. Oliver, who now accompanied Patti everywhere, grieved by her side. Four months later, William Burroughs died, and Patti and Oliver flew to St. Louis to attend the burial. Taking a limousine from the airport to the graveyard, Patti was late in arriving and held up the burial service by insisting on walking from the graveyard's gate to the burial plot. Once there, she knelt down and was seen to slip a small white envelope into the grave.

Patti was becoming the poet laureate of her generation, and she increasingly felt the need to comment on topical subjects in her songs. In the spring of 1997, for instance, two-thirds of the way through recording an album to be called *Peace and Noise*, she decided to take a short vacation with her two children and Oliver to Provincetown, Massachusetts. However, on hearing of the mass suicides of the Heaven's Gate cult members, she spent the rest of her vacation in an insulated room with curtains over the windows, working around the clock with Oliver on a song titled "Last Call." Later, they recorded it in two takes, and it fit perfectly into the album.

Peace and Noise was released at the end of September. The song that garnered the most attention was "Blue Poles," which took its name from Jackson Pollack's most famous painting. The rest of the album carried on in much the same key as *Gone Again*, which meant that "the monochromatic *Peace and Noise*"—as the *New York Times*'s Ben Ratcliff described the album—was unlikely to win Patti any new fans.

It didn't really matter, however, because Patti Smith had reached a stage at which her life was more important, perhaps, than her work. Such had been the case, too, for her mentors Andy Warhol, William Burroughs, and Allen Ginsberg: in the second half of their careers, all of them had continued to create, but their personae outshone their work.

She could still surprise, though, when the notion struck her. In October Patti went to London to receive *Q* magazine's Inspiration award. The British press was highly amused by her behavior that night. "Looking more like the wicked witch of the east's funky younger sister," Andrew Smith reported in the *Guardian*, "she proceeded to regale a stunned, back-slapping crowd of musicians, journalists and industry officials with an acceptance speech that would have had Marlon Brando weeping with envy."

Patti had taken the opportunity of receiving the award to lecture the press with a harangue that harkened back to her "freeing the wheat" speech to Harry Chapin on WNEW. "I just have one thing to say," she told the crowd.

We must remember that artists are not here to serve the media. Nor is the media here to serve artists. If artists and media serve anybody, it's the people, and what have we been doing to serve them? I find all of this really pathetic. And I'm not saying this in a mean way or to be funny or anything. We're moving toward a new century and *Q* magazine and all these other magazines and all of the cameras and people on the TV, this is a great thing we have. Media is potentially a great thing—let's do something better than this.

After telling a few more jokes, Patti accepted the award with her charming variation of a B. Traven line: "I don't need no fucking award, but thank you for giving it to me." Most of the audience wondered why she had bothered to show up at all.

Patti's act, in fact, was beginning to get on some people's nerves. James Wolcott, writing in *The New Yorker* at the height of the media campaign for *Gone Again*, asked the question on the minds and in the conversations of downtown New York's inhabitants all year: Why was Patti getting away with building a completely mythological account of her married life in Detroit?

" 'Fred is dead,' the album says, but 'She Hath Risen,' " Wolcott wrote. "At the risk of being offensive, I think she's overdoing her widowhood . . . When she sings 'Our love comes from/ above,' I want to say, 'Stop romanticizing!' " One of Patti's talents had always been telling the Outrageous Lie, however, and by 1996 she had ceased being a mere entertainer and had entered that place Richard Hell signaled in his 1974 essay on "celebrity as an art form." Patti was now a full-fledged icon, a living piece of cultural history, not unlike Mick Jagger or Norman Mailer or Muhammad Ali. She was no longer just a rock singer; she was something even stronger, a sort of wandering folk philosopher, like Will Rogers and Woody Guthrie, or the mythical Johnny Appleseed. And Patti understood the power of myth as well as anyone. She had repeatedly compared herself to Paul Revere, and then had used the military rhetoric of the "Field Marshal of Rock 'n' Roll." The press in the 1990s called her the godmother of punk, but Patti saw herself in a bigger field than the tiny sphere of punk.

When *Rolling Stone* polled celebrities about the fate of President Clinton after his sex scandal, Patti's comments were right alongside those of Tom Wolfe and Jack Nicholson. Patti took the opportunity to frame Clinton's plight as part of a larger picture: "When I look at the crucifixion of Clinton, I look at the crucifixion of my generation," she said. "They are finally nailing us for introducing new ideas about sexual mores, sexual freedom, personal freedom."

On March 9, 1998 Patti performed in a benefit concert for Tibet House at Carnegie Hall. She read parts of Allen Ginsberg's "Howl," sang her song about the Tibetan troubles of 1959, and closed the show with "People Have the Power."

When Patti started her run in the early seventies, New York was the cultural capital of the world and had a flourishing underground. Since that time, many of the most important cultural figures in New York were gone, including Andy Warhol, Allen Ginsberg, and William Burroughs. When Patti moved back to New York in 1996, New York was a different place. Bereft of leadership, its formerly vital underground had crumbled, the remnants scattered. The city that had been Patti's muse now perhaps needed her more than ever—as a symbol, as a leader of its underground. It is a role she could hold for the rest of her life.

Patti Smith succeeded in the difficult task of creating a genuinely original musical persona, one that spoke to disaffected audiences everywhere. Then, after disappearing for over a decade, she returned in another guise and attracted an even broader audience. Who would have imagined in 1974 that the punk poet Patti Smith would be featured in *Time* magazine's "Women at 50" cover story alongside Hillary Rodham Clinton? That she would be immortalized by the world's greatest photographers and that her face would grace the covers of magazines all over the world? That a top international clothing designer, Ann Demeulemeester, would name Patti as her muse, the inspiration for her highly successful fashion collections?

Patti will undoubtedly be an important character in the two feature films currently in production about Robert Mapplethorpe's controversial life. She is also now, after the passing of Allen Ginsberg, one of those carrying the torch for the cause of Tibetan Buddhists. The song she wrote with her husband, Fred "Sonic" Smith, "People Have the Power," has become an anthem sung by people at benefits around the world. Only Patti Lee knew these things would come to pass, as she lay awake, dreaming her dreams, alone in her room in her parents' house outside Philadelphia, somehow knowing that it was just a matter of time.

Patti Smith metamorphosed from painter-poet to rocker in the seventies. In the nineties, she's simply an artist—she expresses herself in music, art, poetry, and prose, and devotes herself to her family as well as charitable, political, and artistic causes. As always, she is masterful at using the press to further her agenda, which James Wolcott pointed out in 1996 when he stated that long before Camille Paglia, Patti "perfected the art of the interview as intellectual spiel." From the beginning, journalists were in her thrall, and though some eventually fell out of love with her, in time the praise and acclaim outweighed the backlash. Her fans were always there.

In walking away from fame in 1979 and spending the eighties out of the spotlight, Patti achieved something uncanny: "She managed to be a rock 'n' roll death without having to die," as James Grauerholz put it in *Please Kill Me*. Moreover, the Detroit years gave her time to contemplate and orchestrate her return.

Was Fred's death the event that set Patti free, and her brother Todd's the catalyst that spurred her return, as the death of William Burroughs's wife had freed him to write? The motifs of death, grief, mourning, and loss made up not only the content but the packaging and promotion of *Gone Again* and, to a lesser extent, *Peace and Noise*. Like Yoko Ono, who used a photograph of John Lennon's broken and bloodied glasses on the cover of an album released soon after his murder, Patti is an artist who uses pieces of her life in her art, no matter how painful. As the nineties come to a close, though, it seems that her period of professional mourning is at an end.

By all accounts, Patti seems quite happy these days, back in her beloved New York, living in a comfortable house in Greenwich Village with her two children and her lover, Oliver Ray. "Today, a really great day involves Oliver and me going to Matt Umanov's to check out guitars," she told *Time Out* magazine. "I just can't believe how great life is. Sometimes, when I'm feeling a little dark, I'll come downstairs to see my children, Jesse and Jackson, laughing over some silly thing. And their laughter resounds in the room. I look at them and shake my head, then I go back upstairs and ask myself, 'How much better can life get?' "

VICTOR BOCKRIS: Would you consider yourself to be the greatest poet in New York City?

PATTI SMITH: Um, the greatest poet in New York City? Um . . . shit, I can't think of what to say. I don't think I'm a great poet at all. I don't even think I'm a good poet. I just think I write neat stuff.

VB: Why does it sell well?

PS: 'Cause I sell. 'Cause, you know, I got a good personality and people really like me. When people buy my book, you know, they're really buying a piece of Patti Smith. That book is autobiographical. It sheds the light of my heroes on it. No good poet thinks they're good. Blaise Cendrars said he was a bad poet.

VB: How does it work in relation to people who don't know you? People in Omaha?

PS: Because I think I'm a good writer. I'm a good writer in the same way Mickey Spillane or Raymond Chandler or James M. Cain is a good writer. There's a lot of American rhythms. I mean I can seduce people. I got good punch lines, you know. I got all the stuff that Americans like. Some of it's dirty. There's a lot of good jokes. I mean, I write to entertain. I write to make people laugh. I write to give a double take. I write to seduce a chick. I wrote "Girl Trouble" about Anita Pallenberg. Anita Pallenberg would read it and think twice and maybe she'd invite me over to the south of France and have a little nookie or something. Everything I write has a motive behind it. I write to have somebody. I write the same way I perform. I mean, you only perform because you want people to fall in love with you. You want them to react to you.

VB: John Wieners said to me yesterday that he figured he'd only just become a poet. He's thirty-eight, and he figured this latest book of his [*Selected Poems*] was his first book. And it took him seventeen years to get there. What do you feel about that?

PS: The other day, I reread my book and figured I had written my last book. I don't think that has anything to do with anything. Rimbaud wrote his last book when he was twenty-two, and sometimes I figure I did my best work as an artist from postadolescent energy.

VB: Do you think you're a genius?

PS: I'm not very intelligent.

VB: But genius is something else. So you agree, right?

PS: Yeah, yeah. It's like when I was a little kid, I always knew that I had some special kind of thing inside me. I mean, I wasn't very attractive. I wasn't very verbal. I wasn't very smart in school. I wasn't anything that showed physically to the world that I was something special, but I had this tremendous hope all the time, you know, I had this tremendous spirit that kept me going no matter how fucked up I was. Just had this kind of light inside me that kept spurring me on.

VB: Why don't you take us back there to New Jersey in those days when you were a teenager beginning the great trail out? I mean, tell us when you first started to write and everything. How it happened.

PS: Well, I always wrote. After I was seven, when I read *Little Women*, I wanted to be like Louisa May Alcott. The whole thing to me was in *Little Women*. Jo was the big move. It seems silly, but Jo in *Little Women* with all those fairy tales and plays introduced me to the writer as performer. She would write those plays and perform them and get her sisters laughing even in the face of death, so I wanted to be a chick like her, you know, who wrote and performed what I wrote, and so I used to write these dumb little plays, and then I wrote these banal little short stories, but I wasn't good. I showed no promise, and then when I went to high school, I used to write these really dramatic poems just like any other kid writes. About everything I didn't know about: I was a virgin. I had never faced death. I had never faced war and pestilence and, of course, I read about sex, pestilence, disease, malaria, I read about everything but I never . . .

VB: What year is this?

PS: Sixty-two, sixty-three. Then, in '64, you know, I started really getting involved in the lives of people. You know, it was like around '63 and '64 I got seduced by people's lifestyles, like Modigliani, Soutine, Rimbaud.

VB: How did you get in touch with Rimbaud?

PS: Well, I was working in a factory and I was inspecting baby-buggy bumper beepers and it was my lunch break and there was this genius sausage sandwich that the guy in the little cart would bring, and I really wanted one. They were, like, $1.45 but the thing is, the guy only brought two a day and the two ladies who ruled the factory, named Stella Dragon and Dotty Hook, took these sausage sandwiches. They were really a wreck, they had no teeth and everything.

So there was nothing else I wanted. You get obsessed with certain tastes. My mouth was really dying for this hot sausage sandwich, so I was real depressed. I went across the railroad tracks to this little bookstore. I was roaming around there, and I was looking for something to read and I saw *Illuminations*, you know, the cheap paperback of *Illuminations*. I mean, every kid has had it. Rimbaud looks so genius. There's that grainy picture of Rimbaud, and I thought he was so neat-looking and I instantly, snatched it up and I didn't even know what it was about, I just thought Rimbaud was a neat name—I probably called him "Rimbald"—and I thought he was so cool. So I went back to the factory. And I was reading it. It was in French on one side and English on the other, and this almost cost me my job, 'cause Dotty Hook saw that I was reading something that had foreign language and she said, "What are you reading that foreign stuff for?" and I said "It's not foreign," and she said, "It's foreign—it's communist—anything foreign is communist." So then she said it so loud that everybody thought I was reading *The Communist Manifesto* or something, and they all ran up and, of course, complete chaos, and I just left the factory in a big huff and I went home. So, of course, I attached a lot of importance to that book before I had even read it, and I just really fell in love with it. It was gracious son of Pan that I fell in love with it, 'cause it was so sexy.

VB: At what point in this stage did you figure out and begin to understand what you were doing?

PS: Not until a few months ago.

VB: Why then?

PS: Well, see, what happened is I didn't really fall in love with writing as writing, I fell in love with writers' lifestyles; Rimbaud's lifestyle—I was in love with Rimbaud for being a mad angel and all that shit. And then I became friends with Janet [Hamill] and she was a writer, there was all these writers in New Jersey. There was just like this little scene. I was secretly writing. I was doing a lot of art. People knew me as an artist and so, like, I was secretly ashamed of my writing, because all my best friends were great writers. So I didn't have no confidence in myself. I used to write stuff mostly about girls getting rid of their virginity and I used to write like Lorca. I wrote this one thing about this brother raping his cold sister under the white moon. It was called "The Almond Tree." While his father raped the young stepmother and she died and he was . . . He looked at her cadaver and he said, "You are cold in death even colder to me than you were in life."

VB: What do you find are the major problems you have as a writer at this point?

PS: When I was a kid? Well, I had no understanding of language. I was so romantic, and I thought all you had to do is expel the romance. I had no idea that the romance of language was a whole thing in itself. I had no idea of what to do with language. I mean, all I had was I used to record my dreams. I had no conception of style of words.

VB: Tell me how *Seventh Heaven* got put together. It's a forty-eight-page book. That's a lot of work.

PS: Right before I met Telegraph Books, I started in the last two years reorganizing my style. I started feeling confidence in my writing. I just realized what language was. You know, I started seeing language as magic. Two things happened that really liberated me. The major thing was reading Mickey Spillane. Because I wanted to move out of . . . I was starting to get successful in writing these long, almost rock 'n' roll poems. And I liked to perform them, but I suddenly realized that though they were great performed, they weren't such hot shit written down. I'm not saying I didn't stand behind them, but here's a certain kind of poetry that's performance poetry. It's like the American Indians weren't writing conscious poetry, they were making chants. They were making ritual language and the language of ritual is the language of the moment. But as far as being frozen on a piece of paper is concerned, they weren't inspiring. You can do anything when you perform, you can say anything you want as long as you're a great performer, you know you can repeat a word over and over and over as long as you're a fantastic performer. You know, you never understand what Mick Jagger is saying except "Let it boogie" or "Jumpin' Jack Flash," but it's always so powerful 'cause he's such a fantastic performer.

VB: Well, how do you deal with that problem? That's a central problem in your work, Tony Glover says in his review of *Seventh Heaven*. He talks about the poetry of performance. I feel that's a central thing we're dealing with at the moment. How to get it down so you can have a book that people can read, but that you can also perform.

PS: That book, to me, represents me on the tightrope between writing and performing. I was writing stuff like "Mary Jane" or the Joan of Arc stuff, which is total performance poetry but, you know, I think they were worthy of being printed because their content is important. The Joan of Arc poem is almost total rhythm masturbation, but it puts Joan of Arc in a new light, it puts her forth as a virgin with a hot pussy who realizes that she's gonna get knocked off before she gets a chance to come. So there is a concept there that made the rhythm worthy of being frozen. But, like I said, I was reading Mickey Spillane. I couldn't get into prose, 'cause I don't talk that well. I'm not good in grammar. I can't spell. I have lousy sentence structure. I don't know how to use commas, so I just get very intimidated when I write something that isn't completely vertical. So I started reading Mickey Spillane, you know, and Mike Hammer, his hammer language: "I ran, I ran fast down the alley. And back again." I mean, he wrote like that. Three-word sentences, and they're like a chill, and they're real effective and I got real seduced by his speed. At the same time I started reading Céline. Well, I've never been able to go through a whole book by Céline, 'cause it's just too intellectual, but the idea that he could freeze one word and put a period. He dared put one word—yellow—and follow it by forty other words like forty movements, also like some kind of concerto or something. He's not as seducing to me as Mickey Spillane, but I juggled the two.

And then the third thing, I was reading Michaux. He's so funny. He wrote this thing called *The Adventure of Phene*, and it's about this guy who's totally paranoid. He's so paranoid he goes to Rome and wants to see the Coliseum and the travel guide says, "Stay away from the Coliseum, it's in bad enough shape already without a guy like you poking around it." And Phene says, "Oh, I'm so sorry. Well, could I at least have a postcard?" and he says, "Don't be ridiculous." And he says, "Oh, I never really meant to have a postcard. I don't even know why I came to this country." And he leaves.

So I, mean, I got three things. I got speed, humor, the holiness of the single word. So I just mixed them all up.

VB: Mostly European influences—Rimbaud, Cendrars, Céline, Michaux.

PS: Well, it used to be totally European. I had no interest in American writing at all.

VB: Why?

PS: It's because of biographies. I was mostly attracted to lifestyles, and there just wasn't any great biographies of genius American lifestyles except the cowboys. And I'm a girl and I was interested in the feminineness of men.

VB: What you're trying to do in your writing is create a lifestyle. *Seventh Heaven* is a lifestyle.

PS: If I didn't think so much of myself, I'd think I was a name dropper, but there's a difference. You can read my book and who do you get out of it? Edie Sedgwick, Marianne Faithfull, Joan of Arc, Frank Sinatra . . . all people I really like. But I'm not doing it to drop names, I'm doing it to say this is another piece of who I am. You know, I am an American. It's ironic I should be so involved with the French because I'm absolutely an American. I'm shrouded in the lives of my heroes.

VB: Would you find anybody in America now who you think influences you a lot?

PS: It's mostly dead people.

VB: Anybody alive?

PS: Dylan. You can't reject Dylan. But Dylan seduced me when he had a fantastic lifestyle. I'll always love Dylan all my life, but Dylan was a big thing to me when he was BOB DYLAN. Now he's whatever he is, but when he was there and had America in the grip of his fist, then I got so excited about him. As far as anybody living.

VB: I find the position of a writer is a fairly isolated one. It's a fairly lonely task. Do you find that?

PS: No, 'cause I don't have the balls to say I'm a writer. I don't think I'm good enough. See, I love my works. I think I've written some really good things. I think "Judith" is just as good as anything ever written, but I couldn't sit down and do it all the time. Oh, Sam Shepard. I admire him.

VB: Do you find you learn from him?

PS: Sure, I learn from Sam because Sam is one of the most magic people I've ever met. Sam is really the most true American man I've ever met, inasfar as he's also hero-oriented. He has a completely western romance mind. He loves gangsters, he loves cowboys, he's totally physical. He loves bigness. You know Americans love bigness. In his plays, there's always a huge Cadillac or a huge breast or a huge monster. His whole life moves on rhythms. He's a drummer. I mean, everything about Sam is so beautiful and has to do with rhythm. That's why Sam and I successfully collaborated because he didn't know that he was . . . intuitively he worked with the rhythm. I do it conceptually. I work with being a thematic writer. He just does it because he's got rhythm in his blood. I do it intellectually. He does it from the heart. And so we were able to establish a really deep communion that way.

VB: You're not working with him at the moment, are you?

PS: No.

VB: You don't associate with many writers?

PS: Well, my best friends are writers. I never collaborate.

VB: I wasn't thinking so much of collaboration. People who I feel more comfortable with tend to be writers nowadays because they tend to recognize me and I tend to recognize them.

PS: No, I don't think I have the modern writer's lifestyle.

VB: You don't take yourself seriously?

PS: Ultimately, I don't take anything serious—yet I can take everything seriously. I'm too much of a cynic to take anything serious. If I'm in a good, pure, relaxed state, I can look at certain of my works and like them. But most of the time I look at my stuff and say, Ah, this is a load of shit. Mick Jagger listens to his albums and says they're shit. Bob Dylan listens to his albums and says they're shit. It hurts me to read an interview where Bob Dylan says he hates *Nashville Skyline*. But I know how I feel. The best work to me is the work in progress. Which is why I produce . . . I almost hate to see my work go out. I'm more guilty of not being published than any publisher because I'm always in progress. I didn't like to finish my drawings. Yeats was like that. How many versions of "Leda and the Swan" did he do? It's so difficult 'cause it means it's dead. De Kooning did twenty-eight dead women under *Woman 1* because, you know, he couldn't stand to say that she was done. It's like you know when a woman has a baby, she created it, it's just begun. But when an artist does a piece of work, as soon as he does the last brushstroke or the last period, it's finished.

VB: How did you feel when *Seventh Heaven* came out?

PS: I carried it around with me for weeks.

VB: Did it catalyze anything in your head about writing?

PS: I stopped writing for a while. I was like a kid at first, I didn't understand it. I saw it. It was in front of me. I liked to carry it on buses and hope people would recognize it was me on the cover. I stopped seeing the poetry as soon as it was printed. I'll stand behind that book, I think it's a damn good book, but the only two poems I like the best are the two last ones, which are the most recent ones. I think "Judith" is the best thing I ever wrote.

VB: Would you say anything about the difference between being a man and a woman in relation to writing?

PS: I don't feel it that much.

VB: You write about it a lot.

PS: Being a writer?

VB: No, you're a woman. You used the image a few minutes ago of giving birth to a child. It rang a bell in my mind . . .

PS: I don't consider myself a female poet. It's only lately that I've been able to consider myself as a female at all. But I don't consider myself a female artist.

I don't think I hold any sex. I think I have both masculine and feminine rhythms in my work. In the same sense I don't think Mick Jagger is just a masculine performer.

VB: You're bisexual.

PS: Completely heterosexual.

VB: You talk as if you were bisexual.

PS: Most of my poems are written to women because women are most inspiring. Who are most artists? Men. Who do they get inspired by? Women. The masculinity in me gets inspired by female. I get, you know, I fall in love with men and they take me over. I ain't no women's-lib chick. So I can't write about a man because I'm under his thumb, but a woman I can be male with. I can use her as my muse. I tried to make it with a chick once and I thought it was a drag. She was too soft. I like hardness. I like to feel a male chest. I like bone. I like muscle. I don't like all that soft breast.

VB: You find women inspiring from a distance. Anita Pallenberg, Joan of Arc, Marianne Faithfull, Edie Sedgwick, you knew . . .

PS: No, I don't know any of the girls I wrote about. I wrote about Judy, one of my best friends, but I could only write about her when she was away from me for a year. Then, all of a sudden, she became a muse. I don't like women close up because they're attainable. It's like I met Edie Sedgwick a few times, and she had nothing to do with me. Who was I? But I thought she was swell, she was one of my first heroines. Vali's a perfect example. Vali's one of the only chicks I've ever attained, and she didn't go in my nook. Vali has been a heroine of mine since I was fourteen years old. She was my original heroine. And when I met her, she tattooed my knee. We kissed and all that. She suddenly vanished as one of my great muses. I didn't put her in the book and she's the one chick who deserved it because we touched.

VB: Tell me about the writing of a poem for you.

PS: Let me get the book out. I'll take "Judith." Most of my poems I write two ways. I write them from first writing a letter to someone who will never receive the letter, or I write recording a dream. "Skunk Dog" was a complete dream.

Judy was a girl I was in love with in the brain. I'm in love with her because we have similar brain energy. We can travel through time. We have this fantastic way of communicating. But she doesn't let me touch her. She's one girl that maybe I would have like to have done something to. At one point, I was really obsessed with her and she wouldn't let me, and at one point, she went away to Nepal and right before she left she grabbed me and kissed me and I was so shocked I pushed her away and she said, "You blew it," just 'cause I was too chickenshit. As long as she acted real tough . . . but as soon as she reached out for me I got scared. I'm a phony.

So, anyway, Judy was away, and I loved her so much that I couldn't stand it. I started dreaming of her. So I was trying to write her a letter, but when you really love someone it's almost impossible to write them. It's people you love the most who you can't communicate with verbally. I had such a strong mental contact with this girl that I couldn't talk to her. So I was at the typewriter. It's made writing a much more physical thing. I write with the same fervor as Jackson Pollock used to paint. And all the things that we had, like, we loved the movie *Judex*, I started writing down in a line, just words but, you know, words that were perfect, words like "kodak," "radiant," "jellybitch," and I just tried writing these words.

VB: You built the rest of the poem around the central words?

PS: Yeah, I had these words. I was trying to write her a letter, but I had no idea where she was, so obviously it was a piece of narcissism. I was just trying to write this thing. Sort of jacking off. I was trying to project with words and language a photograph of Judy. So, anyway, I had all these words and they laid around for a couple of days and I looked at them and they were almost a perfect square and that's just how it is. I stretched them, put a few full stops in.

VB: How long did it take you to write that poem?

PS: About two and a half days. I think it's perfect. Another reason I like this poem is it explains our relationship through words like "jewel," "angelfood," "avocado," it illustrates our personal aesthetic, then it illustrates our problem because it says she would not let me touch her. The other thing is it has my love for punch line. My favorite thing in it is "ah spansule." That's another thing. I love words. I heard some guy say "spansule" as I was writing this. I said, "That's a neat word, what does it mean?" He said, "Spansule, gelatine, a hollow pill." I love definitions. I wrote that down and I liked it so much and I wanted to put it in this poem, but what was my motive for putting it in this poem? So I said, "Ah spansule a hollow pill what's in it for me." That's joke enough, but I kept carrying it, for love of Judy Judy Judy punch punch punch which . . . I think that's funny.

VB: Well, why do you find most other writers in America boring?

PS: I think I'm a timeless writer.

VB: You're a writer in the middle of a literary scene and you're totally ignoring the literary scene around you. How long can you keep going on your own?

PS: I can keep going because I'm constantly stimulated by earth's glitter. I'm constantly stimulated. I'm not at any loss for material.

VB: Are you satisfied with holding on to the same style?

PS: No, I write totally differently.

VB: What are you writing now?

PS: Back to Rimbaud again. "Judith" is really a left-handed part of *Illuminations*, and I'm writing more like that now. I'm allowing myself to get more obscure. I've always been against that. I like people to say what they mean. But what I'm moving into now is sort of the style of the *Illuminations*, but more describing situations that have not happened. Like that thing I told you called "Paprade." I like to talk casually about things like I say "regard I've popped out my eye, there it lies on the ground like some sick kodak. I pick it up and throw it in the face of an unsuspecting grandma, a pedestrian." I like writing like a news reporter about more obscure events. In other words, my writing is much more didactic. Documentaries of fantasies. That gives me a chance to get really obscure in terms of actions, but it gives the reader a chance because it's written so rigidly they don't know something really bizarre is happening.

VB: Do you know what you're doing or is it hit and miss?

PS: I know what I'm doing. I was never an egomaniac . . .

VB: You're not?

PS: . . . until lately because I know what I'm doing.

VB: When did that moment come?

PS: It came when I started writing things like "Judith." I know that's a good poem. I know it'll be a good poem in ten years from now. To me, when I am both inspired and have light emitting from me and feel real natural and intuitive but also at the same time clearly walk into my brain and look around.

VB: Before we get on to talking about things in the present, let's clear up a few things in the past. Tell me about Cendrars and his influence on you and how that came about.

PS: I was working at Scribner's. I discovered Blaise Cendrars because of packaging. I should have discovered him years ago, but people are so jealous and want Apollinaire to be the big spirit of the twenties and Blaise has really been sucked in the mud, you know. So I was working at Scribner's and Doubleday published *Moravagine*. It was beautifully packaged, had a drawing on it very similar to how I draw, which immediately seduced me. I saw the drawing on the cover, it looked just like one of my drawings, I looked on the back and it said something about insanity and a collective unconsciousness . . .

VB: Do you write when you're traveling?

PS: Right now I've been in this room in this city for so long, I don't see it anymore and I'm not being stimulated. Lately, I've just been doing a lot of cleaning inside my brain. My eyes are not seeing anything around me. So I've been dreaming a lot, recording dreams and trying to look within, but I'm not worried about it. I'm just waiting for the moment when I'll get to take a train or plane someplace and I know I'll spurt out because I've just got to see new things. I think Rimbaud said he needs new scenery and a new noise and I need that.

VB: Does the fact that you don't find any younger writers you learn from depress you?

PS: Their lifestyles don't attract me. I think I'm ballsier, a better performer. I think they can learn from me.

VB: So you feel the people you can learn from are the rock 'n' roll scene?

PS: Yeah, in the sixties it was Jim Morrison, Bob Dylan; now it's still the Rolling Stones. There was Smokey Robinson. I can still get excited about

Humphrey Bogart. I like people who are bigger than me. I'm not interested in meeting poets or a bunch of writers who I don't think are bigger than life. I'm a hero worshipper—I'm not a fame fucker, but I am a hero worshipper. I've always been in love with heroes; that's what seduced me into art. You know, Modigliani, Jackson Pollock, de Kooning, people that were hot shit, you know. I want to know heroes, not eighth-class writers.

VB: Let's get into the poetry of performance. I've just finished an essay called "The Poet Is a Performer." So that seems to me to be where it's at. What does it mean to you?

PS: Poets have been, I think—part of it because of Victorian England or something or how they crucified Oscar Wilde or something—but poets have become simps. There's this new thing: the poet is a simp, the sensitive young man always away in the attic, but it wasn't always like that. It used to be that the poet was a performer and I think the energy of Frank O'Hara started to reinspire that. In the sixties there was all that happening stuff. Then Frank O'Hara died and it sort of petered out and then Dylan and Allen Ginsberg revitalized it, but then it got all fucked up again, because instead of people learning from Dylan and Allen Ginsberg and realizing that a poet was a performer, they thought that a poet was a social protester. So it got fucked up. I ain't into social protesting.

VB: You obviously have a real belief in the possibility of poetry becoming a big public art again, which I really dig. But exactly how do you think that can happen?

PS: I've found it has more to do with the physical presence. Physical presentation in performing is more important than what you're saying. Quality comes through, of course, but if your quality of intellect is high and your love of the audience is evident and you have a strong physical presence, you can get away with anything. I mean, Billy Graham is a great performer even though he is a hunk of shit. Adolf Hitler was a fantastic performer. He was a black magician. And I learned from that. You can seduce people into mass consciousness.

VB: Don't you think you're directly competing with the Rolling Stones and how can you possibly win?

PS: It's not that I want to win. It's just that I think the Rolling Stones aren't always around, you know. I think Mick Jagger is one of the greatest living performers. The other thing that gave me hope for the future of poetry is the Rolling Stones concert at Madison Square Garden, because Jagger was real tired and fucked up. It was Tuesday, he had done two concerts, he was just really on the brink of collapse, but the kind of collapse that transcends into magic. He was so tired that he needed the energy of the audience. And he was not a rock 'n' roll singer Tuesday night—he was closer to a poet than he ever has been. Because he was tired, he could hardly sing. I love the music of the Rolling Stones, but what was foremost was not the music but the performance, the naked performance. And it was like his naked performance, his rhythm, his movement, his talk. He was so tired, he was saying things like "very warm here warm warm warm it's very hot here hot hot New York New York New York bang bang bang." I mean, none of that stuff is genius, but it was his presence and his power to hold the audience in his palm. There was electricity. If the Rolling Stones had walked off that night and left Mick Jagger alone, he was as great as any great poet that night. He could've spoken some of his best lyrics and had the audience just as magnetized. Maybe just with Charlie's drum, Charlie's drums and Mick (I'm not renouncing the others, I love Keith Richards to death). Just the drum-beat rhythm and Mick's words or refrains that are always magic could have been very powerful and could have I believe held the audience. And that excited me so much I almost blew apart because I saw almost a complete future of poetry. I really saw it, I really felt it. I got so excited I could hardly stand being in my skin and, like, I believe in that. That's given me faith to keep going.

VB: Inasmuch as there is the possibility of poets becoming public figures, what is the public function of the poet?

PS: All I try to do is entertain. Another thing I do is give people breathing room. In other words . . . I don't mean any of the stuff I say. When I say that bad stuff about God or Christ, I don't mean that stuff. I don't know what I mean; it's just it gives somebody a new view, a new way to look at something. I like to look at things from ten or fifteen different angles, you know. So it gives people a chance to be blasphemous through me. The other thing is that through performance I reach such states in which my brain feels so open, so full of light, it feels huge. It feels as big as the Empire State Building, and if I can develop a communication with an audience, a bunch of people, when my brain is that big and very receptive, imagine the energy and the intelligence and all the things I can steal from them.

VB: Would you give up writing tomorrow if you could continue performing in some other way?

PS: No, I can't give it up, I have no choice.

VB: Is that really true?

PS: I wanted to be an artist, I worked to be an artist for maybe six years, and so as soon as I became a good artist, all of a sudden I couldn't draw because in 1969 it began that I put my piece of paper and my canvas in front of me and I could see the finished product before I even touched the paper and it was frightening to me.

I like to work. I like that anguish you go through when you're writing something. I like to battle with language. When I started being able to see the finished product before I got a chance to work it out, it had no interest for me. I'm not interested in the finished product; I'm interested in creating the moment. I mean, the finished product is for the people who buy the stuff, you know. And I'm not interested in doing stuff so other people can get their rocks off only. I gave up art just like that in one day after putting seven years into it. And I was fucking good and then I wrote and now what happens is I became so good at writing those vertical poems, those performing poems, they're no longer a challenge.

VB: So what did you do?

PS: I stopped.

VB: Are you in a transition phase?

PS: Yeah. Transition phases are very hard for me. They usually come in the summer and last about three months, and they're usually the worst three months of my life. This one wasn't, 'cause I happened to be in love. They usually come when I'm most fucked up. My brain is hungrier than it ever has been in my whole life but my pussy is being fed so I can ... So I'm not as fucked up as I could be. Last year when this happened, I just wanted to kill myself. I thought I wasn't learning, I wasn't developing.

VB: Are you self-critical?

PS: Extremely self-critical. So much as I love my work, I hate it.

VB: If I was to offer you a reading tour with three other poets, who would you choose as the three other poets?

PS: Jim Carroll, Bernadette Mayer, Muhammad Ali.

VB: Why?

PS: Because they're all good performers. Ali's a good performer. He's got great rhythms. He's a good writer in a certain frame of reference. He's entertaining. Bernadette Mayer because I like what she does conceptually. She's a real speed-driven poet. Sometimes I don't like her because she's overly political and too influenced by St Mark's, but she's also a good performer. Jim Carroll, because I think he's one of the best poets in America. At least he was when he was writing; I don't know if he still writes. Jim Carroll is one of America's true poets. I mean, he is a true poet. It kills me he's twenty-three, he wrote all his best poems the same year of his life as Rimbaud did. He had the same intellectual quality and bravado as Rimbaud. He's a junkie. He's bisexual. He's been fucked by every male and female genius in America. He's been fucked over by all those people. He lives all over.

He lives a disgusting life. Sometimes you have to pull him out of a gutter. He's been in prison. He's a total fuck-up. But what great poet wasn't?

I think the St. Mark's poets are so namby-pamby they're frauds. They write about "Today at 9:15 I shot speed with Brigid, sitting in the such and such." They're real cute about putting it in a poem, but if Jim Carroll comes into the church and throws up, that's not a poem to them, that's not cool. If you could play with it in your poetry that's OK, but if you're really with it, that's something else. They don't want to face it.

I think he's got all the characteristics of a great poet. He was St. Mark's chance to have something real among them. And they blackballed him because he fucked up. I mean, he didn't come to his poetry reading. He was in jail. Good for him. "Oh, well, we can't ask him to do poetry readings anymore." That's ridiculous.

VB: Are you at all interested in writing a long poem?

PS: I'd get bored. Blaise does that successfully 'cause it's like riding a railroad train. When you're riding a neat railroad train the whole ride is great, from the moment you get in till the moment it ends. And Blaise is able to sustain himself and seduce you page after page, but most people don't have power. I get bored.

VB: Do you read Pound or Olson?

PS: I like some of Pound. I'd rather read Eliot. I like pieces of Pound. I like Jules Laforgue better than either of them. I like Pound when he uses ditties same as Eliot, but I don't understand much of what they're saying. My intelligence is really dubious. I memorized "Prufrock" when I was a teenager. I thought it was beautiful. It had a lot to do with instilling in me a love of flowing rhythms, but I don't know what that poem's about.

VB: Do you find you learn a lot from Warhol?

PS: I used to think he was real cool in the sixties 'cause I liked his lifestyle, I liked the people he surrounded himself with, and there was a lot of energy in the Factory. It paralleled with Bob Dylan, but I think his whole family has gotten a lot tackier. But every time I want to say something about Andy Warhol, I don't trust him. Socially, you know, I've met him a lot of times, and he's always very nice. I don't know how to take him . . . Let me just say one nice thing about Andy Warhol: He gave Stevie Wonder a camera, which was really cool, which is also what a good hustler he is. He has the ability to zoom in on the heart of things. Such an action reveals the two moods of Andy.

VB: Are you interested in interviewing people?

PS: I'd like to talk with Mick Jagger, mostly because I'd like to talk about performing. I'd like to talk to Dylan if he was in a certain mood, but that's why I stopped doing rock writing. I started interviewing people like Rod Stewart, who I admire, but because of my ego and my faith in my own work I don't like meeting people on unequal terms, so I figured I'd stop doing that and would wait until they discovered me and we can meet on equal grounds. I couldn't wait to meet Rod Stewart, and then, when I met him, I didn't want to ask him anything, I wanted to tell him stuff. I didn't want to ask Rod Stewart about his work, I wanted to show him mine. That's because right now I'm into performing. I'm into extending myself rather than putting other people into me. I've spent half to three-quarters of my life sucking from other people, and now I'd like to give some.

VB: Do you think you're really a phony?

PS: When I say that, I mean it totally endearingly, I say it with love, you know. I just think I get a kick out of myself. I act tough. I act like a bitch, a motherfucker. It's like when I'm doing this interview—I act real tough, and then my boyfriend comes in and I apologize to him and say, "I'll be finished

quick, baby." I'm like a chameleon, I'm not a phony, I'm like a chameleon. I can fall into the rhythm of almost any situation as it calls for me. If I'm supposed to be a motherfucker, I can be a motherfucker, if I'm supposed to be a sissy or a pansy, I'll be that too. I'll be a sexpot, I'll be a waif. It doesn't mean I'm phony, it just means I'm flexible. I can marry the moment.

discography

a l b u m s

Horses Patti Smith (Arista, 1975)
Producer: John Cale
"Gloria/in excelsis deo" (P. Smith), "Gloria" (Van Morrison), "Redondo Beach" (P. Smith/R. Sohl/L. Kaye), "Birdland" (P. Smith/R. Sohl/L. Kaye/I. Kral), "Free Money" (P. Smith/L. Kaye), "Kimberly" (P. Smith/A. Lanier/I. Kral), "Break It Up" (P. Smith/T. Verlaine), "Land: Horses" (P. Smith), "Land of a Thousand Dances" (C. Kenner), "La Mer(de)" (P. Smith), "Elegie" (P. Smith/A. Lanier).

Radio Ethiopia Patti Smith Group (Arista, 1976)
Producer: Jack Douglas
"Ask the Angels" (P. Smith/I. Kral), "Ain't It Strange" (P. Smith/I. Kral), "Poppies" (P. Smith/R. Sohl), "Pissing in a River" (P. Smith/I. Kral), "Pumping (My Heart)" (P. Smith/I. Kral/J. D. Daugherty), "Distant Fingers" (P. Smith/A. Lanier), "Radio Ethiopia" (P. Smith/L. Kaye), "Abyssinia" (P. Smith/L. Kaye/R. Sohl)

Easter Patti Smith Group (Arista, 1978)
Producer: Jimmy Iovine
"Till Victory" (P. Smith/L. Kaye), "Space Monkey" (P. Smith/I. Kral/T. Verlaine), "Because the Night" (P. Smith/B. Springsteen), "Ghost Dance" (P. Smith/L. Kaye), "Babelogue" (P. Smith), "Rock n Roll Nigger" (P. Smith/L. Kaye), "Privilege (Set Me Free)" (M. London/M. Leander with 23rd Psalm), "We Three" (P. Smith), "25th Floor" (P. Smith/I. Kral), "High on Rebellion" (P. Smith), "Easter" (P. Smith/J. D. Daugherty)

Wave **Patti Smith Group (Arista, 1979)**
Producer: Todd Rundgren

"Frederick" (P. Smith), "Dancing Barefoot" (P. Smith/I. Kral), "Citizen Ship" (P. Smith/I. Kral), "Hymn" (P. Smith/L. Kaye), "Revenge" (P. Smith/I. Kral), "So You Want to Be a Rock 'n' Roll Star" (McGuinn/Hillman), "Seven Ways of Going" (P. Smith Group), "Broken Flag" (P. Smith/L. Kaye), "Wave" (P. Smith)

Dream of Life **Patti Smith (Arista, 1988)**
Producers: Fred Smith and Jimmy Iovine

"People Have the Power" (F. Smith/P. Smith), "Going Under" (F. Smith/P. Smith), "Up There Down There" (F. Smith/P. Smith), "Paths That Cross" (F. Smith/P. Smith), "Dream of Life" (F. Smith/P. Smith), "Where Duty Calls" (F. Smith/P. Smith), "Looking for You (I Was)" (F. Smith/P. Smith), "The Jackson Song" (F. Smith/P. Smith)

Gone Again **Patti Smith (Arista, 1996)**
Producers: Lenny Kaye and Malcolm Burn

"Gone Again" (F. Smith/P. Smith), "Beneath the Southern Cross" (P. Smith/L. Kaye), "About a Boy" (P. Smith), "My Madrigal" (P. Smith/L. Resto), "Summer Cannibals" (F. Smith/P. Smith), "Dead to the World" (P. Smith), "Wing" (P. Smith), "Ravens" (P. Smith), "The Wicked Messenger" (B. Dylan), "Fireflies" (P. Smith/O. Ray), "Farewell Reel" (P. Smith)

Peace and Noise **Patti Smith (Arista, 1997)**
Producer: Roy Cicala

"Waiting Underground" (P. Smith/O. Ray), "Whirl Again" (P. Smith/L. Kaye/O. Ray), "1959" (P. Smith/Shanahan), "Spell" (Footnote to "Howl," A. Ginsberg/O. Ray), "Don't Say Nothing" (P. Smith/J. D. Daugherty), "Dead City" (P. Smith/O. Ray), "Blue Poles" (P. Smith/O. Ray), "Death Singin' " (P. Smith), "Momento Mori" (P. Smith/L. Kaye/O. Ray), "Last Call" (P. Smith/O. Ray).

The Patti Smith Masters **(Arista, 1996)**
Boxed set of the first five albums. Unreleased tracks are included at the end of each album:

Horses, "My Generation" (P. Townshend) (Live in Cleveland, Ohio, 1976); *Radio Ethiopia*, "Chiklets" (P. Smith Group); *Easter*, "Godspeed" (P. Smith/I. Kral); *Wave*, "5-4-3-2-1"/"Wave" (Jones-Hugg-Mann/P. Smith), "Fire of Unknown Origin" (P. Smith/L. Kaye); *Dream of Life*, "As the Night Goes By" (F. Smith/P. Smith), "Wild Leaves" (F. Smith/P. Smith)

U S s i n g l e s

"Hey Joe (Version)" (P. Smith), "Hey Joe" (J. Hendrix) / "Piss Factory" (P. Smith) (Mer Records, 1974)

"Gloria" (V. Morrison), "In Excelsis Deo" (P. Smith) / "My Generation" (P. Townshend) (Live, Cleveland, Ohio, Jan. 26, 1976) (Arista, 1976)

"Hey Joe (Version)" / "Piss Factory" (Sire, 1977)

"Because the Night" (P. Smith/B. Springsteen) / "Godspeed" (P. Smith/I. Kral) (Arista, 1978)

"So You Want to Be a Rock 'n' Roll Star/"5-4-3-2-1"/"A Fire of Unknown Origin" (Arista, 1979)

"Frederick" (P. Smith) / "Frederick" (P. Smith) (live) (Arista, 1979)

"People Have the Power" (F. Smith/P. Smith) / "Wild Leaves" (F. Smith/P. Smith) (Arista, 1988)

"People Have the Power"/"Wild Leaves"/"Where Duty Calls" (F. Smith/P. Smith) (Arista, 1988)

"Looking for You (I Was)" (F. Smith/P. Smith) / "Up There Down There" (F. Smith/P. Smith) (Arista, 1988)

U K s i n g l e s

"Gloria" / "My Generation" (live) (Arista 12" 45 rpm, 1976)

"Because the Night"/"Godspeed" (Arista, 1978)

Set Free (EP): "Privilege (Set Me Free)" (M. London/M. Leander), 23rd Psalm / "Ask the Angels" (P. Smith/I. Kral) / "25th Floor" (live version) (P. Smith/I. Kral)

"Babelfield" (P. Smith) (Arista, 1978)

"Frederick" / "Fire of Unknown Origin" (Arista, 1979)

"Dancing Barefoot" / "5-4-3-2-1-Wave" (Arista, 1979)

"People Have the Power" / "Wild Leaves" (Arista, 1988)

CD #1 "Summer Cannibals" / "Come Back Little Sheba" (L. Kaye/P. Smith) / "Gone Again" / "People Have the Power" (LP version) (Arista, 1996)

CD #2 "Summer Cannibals" / "People Have the Power" / "Beneath the Southern Cross" / "Come On in My Kitchen" (R. Johnson) (Arista, 1996)

c o m p i l a t i o n s f e a t u r i n g p a t t i s m i t h

New Wave (Vertigo/Phonogram, 1977) Features "Piss Factory."

The Sire Machine Turns You Up (Sire, 1978) Features "Hey Joe."

Times Square (1979) Features "Pissing in a River."

That Summer! (1979) Features "Because the Night."

Rock at the Edge (Arista, 1986) Features "Gloria" and "My Generation" (live).

Until the End of the World (Warner Bros, 1991) Features "It Takes Time."

Just Say Yesterday Vol. 6 (Sire, 1992) Features "Piss Factory."

No Alternative (Arista, 1993) Features "Memorial Song" (live) from NYC SummerStage, 1993.

Natural Born Killers (Nothing/Interscope, 1994) Features a remix of "Rock n Roll Nigger" by producer Flood.

Ain't Nuthin' But a She Thing (London, 1995) Features Patti's version of Nina Simone's "Don't Smoke in Bed."

Dead Man Walking (Columbia, 1995) Features "Walkin' Blind."

b o o t l e g s

Teenage Perversity and Ships in the Night (January 30, 1976)
Live recording of a show at the Roxy Theater in Los Angeles, California

Tracks: "Real Good Time Together," "Set Me Free," "Ain't It Strange," "Kimberly," "Redondo Beach," "Pale Blue Eyes," "Louie Louie," "Pumping (My Heart)," "Birdland," "Gloria," "My Generation"

Hard Nipples (1976)
Live tracks: "Real Good Time Together," "G. Verdi," "I Keep a Close Watch," "Ain't It Strange," "Free Money," "Pale Blue Eyes," "Louie Louie," "Birdland," "Gloria," "My Generation"

I Never Talked to Bob Dylan (October 3, 1976)
Live recording of a show in Stockholm

Tracks: "Real Good Time Together," "Redondo Beach," "Free Money," "Pale Blue Eyes," "Ain't It Strange," "Time Is on My Side," "Radio Ethiopia," "Gloria," "Land"

Live in London (May 16, 1976)
Live recording of a show at the Roundhouse, Chalk Farm

Tracks: "Real Good Time Together," "Kimberly," "Ain't It Strange," "Set Me Free," "Pumping (My Heart)," "Free Money," "Pissing in a River," "Gloria," "Time Is on My Side"

Live in Paris (1978)
Live tracks: "Ask the Angels," "25th Floor," "Rock n Roll Nigger," "Till Victory," "Set Me Free," "Because the Night," "Gloria," "Free Money," "I

Was Working Real Hard," "Keith Richards Blues," "I Was Working Real Hard (Reprise)"

Superbunny (1975)
Live tracks: "Real Good Time Together," "Privilege (Set Me Free)," "Ain't It Strange," "Kimberly," "Free Money," "Redondo Beach," "Pale Blue Eyes," "Louie Louie," "Hunter Gets Captured," "Birdland"

Live May 1975 WBAI Radio, New York City
"We're Gonna Have a Real Good Time Together," "The Hunter Gets Captured by the Game," "Birdland," "Redondo Beach," "Son of Space Monkey," "Snowball," "Distant Fingers," "Break It Up," "Gloria," "Scheherazade," "Aisle of Love," "Piss Factory," "Land"

Live in Detroit (December 1976)
Live tracks: "Real Good Time Together," "Kimberly," "Redondo Beach," "Poppies," "Ask the Angels," "Pissing in the River," "Pumping (My Heart)," "Ain't It Strange," "Band of Gold," "Radio Ethiopia," "Rock n Roll Nigger," "Gloria," "My Generation"

works by other artists featuring contributions by patti smith

Rick Derringer, *All American Boy* (Blue Sky Records, 1973) Patti wrote the lyrics for the track "Hold."

Ray Manzarek, *The Whole Thing Started with Rock & Roll, Now It's Out of Control* (Mercury, 1974) Patti appears on "I Wake Up Screaming."

Blue Oyster Cult, *Agents of Fortune* (Columbia, 1976) Patti contributed lyrics to and sang on "The Revenge of Vera Gemini"

Bob Neuwirth, *Look Up* (Watermelon Records, 1996) Patti cowrote and sang on "Just Like You."

Ivan Kral, *Nostalgia* (BMG/Ariola, 1996) Patti appears with John Cale on "Perfect Moon." A poem written by Patti appears on the CD's liner notes.

Les Nouvelles Polyphonies, *Corses in Paradisu* (Mercury/Phillips, 1996) Patti introduces the track "Dies Irae" with a poem.

patti smith bibliography

Seventh Heaven. Boston: Telegraph Books, 1972.

A Useless Death (chapbook). New York: Gotham Book Mart, 1972.

Kodak. Philadelphia: Middle Earth Press, 1972.

Witt. New York: Gotham Book Mart, 1973; Paris: Michel Esteban Editeur, 1977; Zurich: eco-verlag, 1979.

Ha! Ha! Houdini! (chapbook). New York: Gotham Book Mart, 1977.

Patti Smith-Gallerie Veith Turske. Cologne: Gallerie Veith Turske, 1977.

Babel. New York: G. P. Putnam's Sons, 1974.

Woolgathering. New York: Hanuman Books, 1992. 80 pp.

Early Work, 1970–1979. New York: W. W. Norton, 1994.

The Coral Sea. New York: W. W. Norton, 1996.

The primary source for *Patti Smith* is the information that Patti Smith herself has provided about her life in the many interviews she has given throughout her career. The author did an interview with the subject in 1972, on the occasion of the publication of her first book, *Seventh Heaven*. This interview provides a paradigm for all the Patti Smith interviews that were to come, illustrating how she has always been able to take the most mundane question and weave her answer into a piece of spoken poetry. Along with Bob Dylan and Keith Richards, Patti Smith remains among the best interview subjects in rock. Interviews and articles drawn on for this book were done by: Dan Acquilante, A. D. Amorisa, Carl Arrington, Robb Baker, Kate Ballen, Adele Bertei, Michael Bowen, Michael Bracewell, Chris Brazier, Julie Burchill, William Burroughs, Jim Carroll, Chris Charlesworth, Robert Christgau, Diana Clapton, Scott Cohen, Caroline Coon, Jonathan Cott, Sue Cummings, Michael Davis, Stephen Davis, Stephen Demorest, Ben Edmonds, Danny Fields, Stephen Frehr, Craig Gholson, Fiachra Gibbons, Tony Glover, J. Gosciak, Gary Graff, Amy Gross, Penny Green, Mary Harron, Cynthia Heimel, Douglas Heller, Kristin Hersh, Clinton Heylin, Robert Hilburn, Tony Hiss, Cliff Jahr, Richard Johnson, Allen Jones, Jon Kaye, Nick Kent, Pattie Klenke, Stephen Lake, Gerrie Lim, Richard Lingeman, Shelley Lustig, Gillian McCain, Bob McCarthy, Evelyn McDonnell, Daisann McLaine, David McLelland, Legs McNeil, Greil Marcus, Brett Milano, Thurston Moore, Suzan Moore, Paul Morley, Charles Shaar Murray, Lucy O'Brien, Jon Pareles, Tony Parsons, Ian Penman, Ramsey Pennybacker, Joy Presi, Paul Rambali, Dave Ramsden, Simon Reynolds, Dusty Roach, Lisa Robinson, John Rockwell, Shaar Murray, Andy Schwartz, Steve Shapiro, Susan Shapiro, Sam Shepard, Steve Simels, Ingrid Sischy, Wilson Smith, Matt Snow, Neil Strauss, Jane Suck, Adam Sweeting, Nick Tosches, Jim Sullivan, Mim Udovitch, Lee Underwood, Jann Uhelski, John

Walker, Andy Warhol, Paul Williams, James Wolcott, and Charles M. Young.

Their pieces were published in: Andy Warhol's *Interview* magazine, the *Boston Globe*, *Big O* (Singapore), *Crawdaddy*, *Creem*, *Circus*, *Elle*, the *Guardian* (London), *High Times*, *Hit Parader*, *Life*, *Music Gig*, *New York Times*, *New York Times Magazine*, *New York Daily News*, *New York Post*, *Music Paper*, *New Times*, *Mademoiselle*, *Music News of the World*, *Los Angeles Times*, *New York Observer*, *Option*, *Pulse!*, *Punk*, *Penthouse*, *Rolling Stone*, *Stereo Review*, *Philadelphia Inquirer*, *Philadelphia Weekly*, *Rock Scene*, *Trouser Press*, *The New Yorker*, *New York Press*, *New York Rocker*, *New York Times Book Review*, *Spin*, *Oxford Literary Review*, *Village Voice*, *Philadelphia City Paper*, *Stereo Review*, *Zigzag*, *White Stuff*, *P.H.T.P.*, *New Musical Express*, *Sounds*, *Melody Maker*, *Mojo*, and broadcast on WNEW Radio.

The author conducted interviews for this book with: Gerard Malanga, Terry Ork, Miles, John Cale, William Burroughs, Allen Ginsberg, Clinton Heylin, Bebe Buell, Glenn O'Brien, Robert Mapplethorpe, James Grauerholz, Damita Richter, Legs McNeil, Christian Hoffman, Roberta Bayley, Lance Loud, Wayne Kramer, and Andrew Wylie.

Secondary in importance to the interviews, but indispensable to any writer, are the numerous books about Patti Smith or that include information about her. They are:

Angry Women in Rock, vol. 1. New York: Re/Search Publications, Juno Books, 1996.

Bangs, Lester. *Psychotic Reactions and Carburetor Dung*. New York: Vintage, 1986.

Bauldie, John, ed. *Wanted Man: In Search of Bob Dylan*. New York: Citadel Press, 1991.

Book of Punk Legends, The. London: Q magazine, 1996.

Burchill, Julie, and Tony Parsons. *The Boy Looked at Johnny*. Winchester, Mass.: Faber & Faber, 1978.

Carroll, Jim. *Forced Entries: The Downtown Diaries*. New York: Penguin, 1987.

Christgau, Robert. *Rock Albums of the Seventies*. New York: Da Capo, 1981.

Cohen, Scott. *Yakety Yak*. New York: Simon & Schuster, 1994.

Garr, Gillian. *She's a Rebel*. Seal Press, 1992.

Goldsmith, Lynn. *Photo Diary*. New York: Rizzoli, 1995.

Hackett, Pat, ed. *The Andy Warhol Diaries*. New York: Simon & Schuster, 1989.

Henry, Trician. *Break All the Rules: Punk Rock and the Making of a Style*. Ann Arbor, Mich.: UMI Research Press, 1989.

Heylin, Clinton. *From the Velvets to the Voidoids.* New York: Penguin, 1993.
————. *The Great White Wonders.* New York: Viking, 1994.
Heylin, Clinton. ed. *The Penguin Book of Rock 'n' Roll Writing.* New York: Viking, 1992.
Johnstone, Nick. *Patti Smith: A Biography.* London: Omnibus Press, 1996.
McDonnell, E. Evelyn. *Rock She Wrote.* New York: Delta/Dell, 1995.
Maloy, Merritt, ed. *The Great Rock 'n' Roll Quote Book.* New York: St. Martin's Press, 1995.
Morrisroe, Patricia. *Mapplethorpe: A Biography.* New York: Random House, 1995.
Muir, John. *Patti Smith—High on Rebellion.* Babylon Books.
Murray, Charles Shaar. *Shots from the Hip.* New York: Penguin, 1991.
O'Brien, Lucy. *She Bop.* Penguin: 1995.
O'Dair, Barbara, ed. *Trouble Girls: The Rolling Stone Book of Women in Rock.* New York: Random House, 1997.
Oumano, Ellen. *Sam Shepard.* New York: St. Martin's Press, 1986.
Pavletich, Aida. *Sirens of Song.* New York: Da Capo, 1980.
Punk, the Original. New York: Trans High Publishing, 1996.
Reynolds, Simon, and Joy Presi. *The Sex Revolts.* Cambridge, Mass.: Harvard University Press, 1995.
Roach, Dusty. *Patti Smith: Rock 'n' Roll Madonna.* South Bend, Ind.: and books, 1979.
Saroyan, Aram. *Friends in the World: The Education of a Writer.* Minneapolis: Coffeehouse Press, 1992.
Savage, Jon. *England's Dreaming.* New York: St. Martin's Press, 1991.
Stambler, Irwin. *The Encyclopedia of Rock and Soul.* New York: St. Martin's Press, 1989.
Verbal Abuse no. 2, ed. Chi Chi Valenti, 1993
Witts, Richard. *Nico: The Life and Lies of an Icon.* London: Virgin Books, 1993.
Woliver, Robbie. *Bringing It All Back Home.* New York: Pantheon, 1986.

acknowledgments

Victor Bockris

I want to primarily thank Roberta Bayley for the enormous amount of help she gave me in completing this book, and my editor Leo Hollis at Fourth Estate and Ingrid von Essen. My editor at Simon & Schuster, Dominick Anfuso and his assistants Ana DeBevoise and Catherine Hurst were particularly helpful in bringing this edition of the book to its present state. And I give special thanks to Legs McNeil and Gilliam McCain for their help and support.

I also want to thank for their support: Andrew Wylie, Bridget Love, and Zoe Pagnaménta at the Wylie Agency; Christopher Whent, Glenn O'Brien, Bobbie Bristol, Lisa Krug, Miles, Stellan Holm, John Lindsay, John Cale, Paul Katz, Gerard Malanga, Sharon Hird, Bunty Crawford, Anna Bockris, Steve Mass, Helen Mitsios, Chantal Rosset, Stewart and Jenny Meyer, Joe Gross, James Grauerholz, John Giorno, Ira Silverberg, William Burroughs, Allen Ginsberg, Chris Charlesworth, Andrew King, Bridget Behrens, Ed Friedman, Legs McNeil, Gillian McCain, Clinton Heylin, Chris McGuire, Gerrie Lim, Diana Rickard, Jim Condon, Eddie Berrigan, Marianne Erdos, Stewart and Jenny Meyer, John Giorno, Michael Dorr, Debbie Harry, Romy Ashby, Chris Stein, David Cronenberg, Rise Cale, John Cale, James Marsh, Rosemary Bayley, Arthur and Kym Garfunkel, and Ingrid von Essen, again without whom nothing I have written would exist. Thank you, thank you very much.

The following parties have granted permission to use extended quotations from copyrighted works:

From William Burroughs's interview with Patti Smith. Copyright 1986 by William Burroughs. Reprinted by permission William Burroughs estate/Andrew Wylie Agency.

From Charles M. Young's *Rolling Stone* cover story, "Visions of Patti."

Copyright 1978 by Straight Arrow Publications. Reprinted by permission of Straight Arrow Publications.

From Gerrie Lim's interview with Patti Smith. Copyright 1995 by Gerrie Lim. Reprinted by permission of Gerrie Lim.

From *Please Kill Me*'s interviews regarding Patti Smith. Reprinted by permission of Legs McNeil and Gillian McCain.

From *Yakety Yak*'s interview with Patti Smith. Reprinted with permission of Scott Cohen.

From Nick Tosches's interview with Patti Smith in *Penthouse*. Reprinted by permission of Nick Tosches.

Roberta Bayley

I would like to thank the following people for their generous help and support during the writing of this book: Nick Tosches, Glenn O'Brien, Richard Hell, David and Eileen Godlis, Jeff Tompkins, Miles, Mim Udovitch, and Helen and Preston Bayley.

index